THE
EVERYTHING®
Singing Book

Dear Reader,

Singing well is one of the most powerful and satisfying accomplishments a person can ever have. It can also be frustrating when you aren't getting the sound you want. You can hear it in your head, but it just doesn't come out the right way. That was my experience as well. I was trained as a musician and have been singing since I was a child, but still felt that my voice was weak. I couldn't get the full vocal power to really express what I felt in the music. The most common advice I heard was that if I felt the music more deeply or just "let go," my full voice would magically appear. All that happened was that I pushed and ultimately hurt my voice in the process. I got by as a professional singer for many years, all the while knowing that something was wrong and that I could do better.

I found that learning and practicing solid vocal technique saved my voice and my career. Once I figured out that the voice is an instrument to be trained and I learned the proper exercises, I was finally able to achieve a strong and healthy voice. I now love teaching because it allows me to share what I've learned and see the same exciting results in my students. I wish I could hear each one of you personally, but in the meanwhile, I truly hope that you find improvement and success from following the exercises in this book, and most of all, that you have great fun in the process of learning to sing.

Bettina Sheppard

Welcome to the EVERYTHING Series!

These handy, accessible books give you all you need to tackle a difficult project, gain a new hobby, comprehend a fascinating topic, prepare for an exam, or even brush up on something you learned back in school but have since forgotten.

You can choose to read an *Everything*® book from cover to cover or just pick out the information you want from our four useful boxes: e-questions, e-facts, e-alerts, and e-ssentials. We give you everything you need to know on the subject, but throw in a lot of fun stuff along the way, too.

We now have more than 400 *Everything*® books in print, spanning such wide-ranging categories as weddings, pregnancy, cooking, music instruction, foreign language, crafts, pets, New Age, and so much more. When you're done reading them all, you can finally say you know *Everything*®!

QUESTIONS?
Answers to
common questions

FACTS
Important snippets
of information

ALERTS!
Urgent
warnings

Quick
handy tips

PUBLISHER Karen Cooper

DIRECTOR OF ACQUISITIONS AND INNOVATION Paula Munier

MANAGING EDITOR, EVERYTHING SERIES Lisa Laing

COPY CHIEF Casey Ebert

ACQUISITIONS EDITOR Lisa Laing

SENIOR DEVELOPMENT EDITOR Brett Palana-Shanhan

EDITORIAL ASSISTANT Hillary Thompson

MODELS Danilo Barbieri, AC Jermyn, Shelly Ley

ILLUSTRATIONS Patrick Neitz of Bits & Bytes Creative Design

Visit the entire Everything® series at *www.everything.com*

THE EVERYTHING SINGING BOOK

WITH CD

From mastering breathing techniques to
performing live—all you need to hit the right notes

Bettina Sheppard, M.A.

Aadamsmedia

Avon, Massachusetts

For Vashek Pazdera, whose life, teachings, and passion
for music are forever a lesson in grace and integrity.

An Everything® Series Book.
Everything® and everything.com® are registered trademarks of F+W Publications, Inc.

Published by Adams Media, an F+W Publications Company
57 Littlefield Street, Avon, MA 02322 U.S.A.
www.adamsmedia.com

ISBN 10: 1-59869-539-8
ISBN 13: 978-1-59869-539-7

Printed in the United States of America.

J   I   H   G   F   E   D   C   B   A

Library of Congress Cataloging-in-Publication Data
is available from the publisher.

This publication is designed to provide accurate and authoritative information with regard to the subject matter covered. It is sold with the understanding that the publisher is not engaged in rendering legal, accounting, or other professional advice. If legal advice or other expert assistance is required, the services of a competent professional person should be sought.

—From a *Declaration of Principles* jointly adopted by a Committee of the American Bar Association and a Committee of Publishers and Associations

Many of the designations used by manufacturers and sellers to distinguish their products are claimed as trademarks. Where those designations appear in this book and Adams Media was aware of a trademark claim, the designations have been printed with initial capital letters.

This book is available at quantity discounts for bulk purchases.
For information, please call 1-800-289-0963.

Contents

Acknowledgments

My thanks to editor, Lisa Laing, and friend, Ernie Jackson. And special thanks to my teacher, Vashek Pazdera; my husband, John Blaylock; and wonderful friends, Patrick Neitz and Steve Gordon, who all gave me invaluable hours of their time, patience, and expertise in graphics and proofreading; Shelly Ley; Brenda Montagna; my supportive family; and most of all, my amazing and courageous students who have taught me more than they'll ever know.

Top Ten Things You Should Know about Singing

1. Your voice is a musical instrument.

2. Everyone can learn to sing.

3. Learning to sing properly can give you the freedom to express yourself.

4. Singing is fun.

5. Learning to sing builds self-confidence.

6. Singing promotes good health, both physically and emotionally.

7. Singing relieves stress.

8. Singing is a heightened form of communication.

9. Singing creates opportunities to meet a new group of friends.

10. Most people have a secret (or not so secret) desire to sing.

Introduction

▶ The human voice is the original musical instrument. People have been singing, we assume, since long before recorded history. Songs have expressed every emotion and rite of passage throughout time, and have both united people and divided them. Music has remained one of the most powerful tools of communication that exists. It has the power to heal you and to elevate your mood as well as the ability to connect you with people from other places and times. Imagine that someone could write and sing a song hundreds of years ago, and that it can still be just as effective today. No wonder everyone loves to sing and wants to sing well!

Some people are fortunate enough to sing well without any training or guidance. They may be skilled at mimicking what they've heard and liked, or they may have been raised in a musical family and grown up singing. Even these lucky few need to learn what they're doing right if they want to keep a great voice and pursue a demanding music career. In some ways the new singer who approaches this instrument as a beginner is even more fortunate. A beginner has the chance to learn good habits right away, before spending too much time drilling in the bad habits. Your body will respond to whatever action is repeated, so exercises really can work to develop a healthy and strong voice. Singing *can* be learned.

Reading this book will give you the information you need to understand how your voice works. But the important part is in the doing. You'll need to sing along with the exercises and keep trying out your voice to see what works and feels comfortable. If anything ever feels uncomfortable, just stop, rest, and try again. Reread the directions for each exercise and listen to the CD. If you want to practice your exercises and warm up your voice, you can use the vocal lesson in Chapter 9 every day for more rapid results. Hopefully this practice will lead you to singing lessons, in which someone is there to listen to your voice, guide you, and give you feedback.

Keep in mind that learning to sing can be hard work as well as fun. Too many people give up when they don't immediately get the results they want. The best artists are able to achieve both a sense of •dedication and real enjoyment in studying and learning. The process is often more rewarding than the end result. Great singing is a combination of good vocal health and technique, the ability to connect emotionally to your song, and experience. Nobody achieves those goals overnight. It takes time and effort, but every singer will tell you it's worth it. Singing is challenging, but it has the capacity to change people's lives. It can be a delicate balancing act between extreme focus and total abandon. Letting go of inhibitions is frightening for most people, and singing can make you feel both silly and vulnerable if you judge yourself. Many times people feel exposed and humiliated by a bad vocal sound but wouldn't at all mind making the same mistakes in learning piano or guitar. Fortunately, this trepidation is more than matched by the excitement you'll feel when you sing well.

The best starting point for this book is a sense of adventure. Singing is exciting and it takes a large dose of courage to overcome its challenges. It's important that you find ways to keep your lessons enjoyable so that you're encouraged to continue to learn and grow. Let part of your time be spent learning the technical aspects that will allow you to depend on your voice, but also explore the story of each song you sing. If you make that story the most important thing to communicate whenever you sing, you'll have an appreciative audience. And finally, you can copy other singers at times to get the feel of a certain style, but ultimately you should learn to love your own voice with its unique sound and personality. Your individuality is your greatest gift and source of artistic power. Have fun with the exercises in this book, and happy singing!

CHAPTER 1

Getting Started

Everyone can sing. Everyone can also sing better than they do at their present level. No matter what the starting point, everyone has the capacity to improve. There is a common misconception that you can either sing or you can't. But the voice can easily be approached as the instrument it is, and you can train your voice as you would any other instrument. Just as you wouldn't begin piano lessons and then expect to play Beethoven's *Moonlight Sonata* tomorrow, you will have much more fun learning how to sing if you're both patient with yourself and willing to work hard.

The Voice as an Instrument

The human voice is the original musical instrument. It's organic, primal, and basic to our very human nature, but it is also capable of being a whole orchestra of various sounds. The voice can be melodic and lyrical or percussive. It can sound like a flute, violin, trumpet, bass, or drums, all by accessing the sounds in your imagination. Whatever its sound, your musical voice is part of the human spirit, and the desire to sing seems to be an innate part of being human. In fact, animals in general, not just humans, communicate emotion and information through song. Birds sing identifiable melodies that composers have borrowed for centuries.

The vocal instrument is unique in that you are both the instrument and the instrumentalist. Your body is the instrument you are playing and, as such, you will need to learn about its structure, maintenance, and technical requirements for getting the best sound. The more you understand about the instrument, the better able you are to make use of it. Since the voice is a living instrument, it's subject to all the conditions and changes that happen constantly within the body. It is both complex in its structure and familiar because of its everyday use.

The part of you that serves as the instrumentalist, the singer, will need to learn the ways you can use your body to make the sound you want to hear. There are many styles, colors, and variations available to you, but they may seem out of reach without some technical guidance. The exercises provided in this book will give you a healthy starting point as well as a regular warmup routine.

ALERT!

The exercises and information in this book are designed to be an organized reference and explanation for more experienced singers as well as a solid starting point for beginners. There is no substitute, however, for a good teacher who will hear and correct your technique, giving you immediate guidance. For advice about finding the right teacher for you, read Chapter 15.

You can spend some of your study time just listening to other singers. It's helpful to hear how people deal with vocal challenges in different genres of music. How does the jazz singer differ from the classical or rock singer? It's also very beneficial to watch singers in live performance. Can you tell how they form their vocal sound? Listening and observing will give you a lot of information about your instrument.

Why Do You Want to Sing?

People have many different reasons why they want to improve their voice. It may be that you want to sing in a band or in a Broadway musical. Singing in a church or community choir can provide great experience and satisfaction. You may have a special event coming up and would love to be able to sing a dedication, or you may be interested in recording. Many people just enjoy the sensation of singing and would like to sing freely and without strain.

No matter what your goal is, it's helpful to identify a reason for wanting to sing. Keeping your goal in mind can be powerful motivation for sticking to the exercises needed to reach that goal. So many times, people give up their practice when it feels too difficult or discouraging. If you keep your goal in mind and remember why you want to improve your voice, your sense of commitment is much stronger.

You may want to take a moment now to identify your reasons for wanting to sing and your future goals. Setting goals is an ongoing process and may take time to develop. Don't worry if your goals change over time.

Rehearsal time can be not only pleasurable, but also can become a time of transcending your everyday concerns. Strong focus on a particular task requires that you remove other thoughts and give attention to the job at hand. Most people find this sort of concentration much more deeply relaxing and satisfying than passive entertainment.

The Value of Technique

The goal of technique is freedom. Strong singers can be free of worry about upcoming phrases in the song and free of the need to control every moment. Good vocal technique means that muscle memory will take over the job of managing your voice and allow you to concentrate on delivering the meaning in the music. When you've trained your body to know how to respond to the demands placed upon it, you're able to think of other things, namely the music you're singing.

FACT

Studying vocal technique can make singing an enjoyable experience rather than a frustrating one. Too many potentially good singers won't sing because they don't know what to do with the instrument. Learning how to deal with certain technical issues allows you to express yourself and convey the emotional content of the song.

There's a common misconception that studying voice will restrict a natural singing style and will make you sound too classical. But in fact, vocal study will only develop and enhance your capacity to create a natural style with no limitations. It would take years of intensive vocal study to achieve an operatic quality. Most people will not develop an overly classical sound without choosing that particular training and career path. Similarly, much as people are afraid that weight training will develop bulging muscles, it would take a specific regimen over a long period of time to achieve this.

Good vocal technique also will not dampen any natural enthusiasm or musical passion. The emotional connection to your music can be strengthened by the technical adjustments that allow your voice to be free and open. At first you may find that you concentrate only on the physical requirements of a good sound, but remember that the ultimate goal is a healthy, open voice that is able to express the excitement of the music.

So what can good vocal technique do for you? It can:

- Increase your range
- Increase both your power and flexibility

- Develop muscle memory so that the body will learn what to do without having to think about it
- Free you to concentrate on delivering the meaning of the music without the worry of physically managing your voice
- Strengthen your emotional connection to the music

If you're worried about the sound of your voice, you won't sing as well as you will when you have the assurance of having trained your body. Vocal technique is the release, not the cage. The muscles involved in singing will need practice and repetition of specifically designed exercises, but the reward is a newfound confidence. You will replace frustration with trust in yourself and your vocal abilities.

What You Will Need

Since you already have your instrument with you at all times, you will be able to practice with no added expense or equipment. Your practice time will be facilitated, however, with a few considerations.

A Place to Practice

You should have some place to practice where you won't feel the natural inhibitions of the beginning singer. New sounds and exercises can feel awkward and even embarrassing. It's important that you feel comfortable and safe so that you'll be willing to give full attention to your voice. You should be able to develop confidence in your new skills without interruption or unwelcome comments. This could be a place in your home, a rehearsal studio, a community center, school, or even your car.

A Way to Hear Yourself

The voice you hear inside your head does not sound the same as the voice others hear from the outside. Your body conducts sound in a way that reflects a different vocal quality to you than the sound that is projected into the room. You will never know exactly what you sound like from the inside. Just recall the first time you heard your recorded voice. Remember how shocked you were? Almost everyone is surprised at the sound of his or her own voice, but the surprise is potentially a positive one! You may sound better than you think. Or you may hear qualities of your voice you'd like to change.

It's best to have some method of recording yourself so that you can objectively hear what others hear. This could be any of the following:

- A cassette recorder
- A mini disk player
- A recording attachment for the iPod
- Recording software for the computer
- Any other recording device of reasonable quality

Try to be as objective as possible. It's hard to hear yourself at first without feeling overly critical. If you let your own ears be your teacher while you're practicing, you'll learn what's working or not working for you. Keep in mind, however, that, unless you're in a recording studio, the sound quality won't be a perfect mirror or exact representation of live sound.

Helpful Equipment

A piano or electronic keyboard, guitar, or some other musical instrument will be extremely valuable to facilitate vocal study. You'll need to match pitch and find starting notes for songs, or entire melodies. You can also determine single pitches with a tuning fork or a pitch pipe. A pitch pipe is a small, round instrument with holes into which you blow much the same way you would a harmonica. It's very convenient and will give you accurate tone for the twelve pitches of a chromatic scale, but it would be a tedious way to hear an entire melody line.

You should also have a mirror. It's helpful to see yourself when studying the positions in the upcoming exercises. As you feel the sensation of correctly producing an exercise, you can check to see what it looks like as well. Eventually you can feel what's correct, but, while studying, you should see it as well.

Dancers take class in front of a mirror to see themselves, but ultimately they must be able to feel the correct body position without the aid of a mirror. When you work on the vocal exercises, you can do the same thing. Watch yourself in the mirror and compare your image to the pictures in the book. Notice the sensation you feel in the related muscles so that you'll be able to reproduce the shape and sound without the mirror.

Patience

Acquiring any new skill requires patience, time, and dedication to the final goal. Consistent daily practice, even short sessions, will provide steady improvement over time. Musicians need perseverance in developing their craft as well as their careers. It's also helpful to have a sense of humor and a willingness to try out new sounds that might sound silly or unpleasant at first. Singing is much more fun if you realize that you don't have to be perfect.

Using Imagery

A good imagination will help a singer in several ways. In learning a healthy placement of the voice, you'll need to think of images to help certain muscles respond. You aren't able to see or touch much of the body that creates vocal sound; you can't just place a finger on a key or a string, as you would with a piano or violin. Therefore it becomes necessary to use mental pictures to guide proper positioning of the vocal mechanism. You will find examples of imagery included in the vocal exercises.

A singer also needs imagination to understand and interpret the meaning of the music. The ability to hear the musical line in your head is the first route to musical artistry. Imagining the sound you want and the type of delivery will help convey the emotion of the material. Equally important, the lyrics form a story that you will have to tell. All good storytellers are able to imagine the scene they are describing in their minds as they tell the story. A singer is really a storyteller with music, making the story doubly powerful and dramatic.

Your Unique Vocal Quality

A very powerful learning tool is imitation. If you can hear another's sound in your mind and reproduce it, you can feel the quality of that sound. By just imagining it, you can mimic a person, animal, horn, flute, machine, and a limitless collection of sounds. Ultimately you'll want to find and respect your own unique vocal quality, but spending some of your practice time in imitation can provide a fun and quick route to understanding placement and new techniques.

Finding your own voice is a way to let your personality enhance the music. Your goal is to sound like you, not someone else. In fact, *your* vocal sound is completely unique. When you realize that no two people will ever sound exactly alike, you'll lessen the inclination to compete on any level with other voices.

FACT

Because each person's voice is unique, some police departments now use voice printing as well as fingerprinting as a means of identification. Voice biometrics looks at a characteristic sound pattern in the human voice that can establish identity. Voice recognition is becoming increasingly important in developing security systems because of the distinctive quality of each person's voice.

Try listing some of the various qualities you have in your personality. What would others say are your strongest characteristics? What do you like best about yourself, that you would enjoy sharing with the world? What makes you uniquely you? These are the qualities that your audience will want to hear in your singing voice. Ideally your voice will be a reflection of your individuality.

Have Fun

Singing can be one of the most exhilarating experiences you ever have. When your voice is open and free, you're able to express emotion and intention that go beyond language. The most important factor in studying voice is to keep a fun and joyful attitude. If you get too discouraged or judgmental, you'll create physical tension that will inhibit the production of sound.

Students, as well as professional singers, often report feeling an uplifting sense of well-being after singing even a few exercises. By singing in a healthy manner, you'll have more oxygen throughout your system and you will experience sound vibrations in your body that can be both energizing and healing. So enjoy the journey. The path can be as rewarding as the goal.

CHAPTER 2

Voice as an Instrument

Learning to sing is like learning to play an instrument. It's helpful to understand how the instrument is formed in order to better utilize all of its capabilities. Singers have to project sound in a way that is more demanding than everyday speech, so careful training to access your vocal power and control in a way that won't do damage is important and can be a great benefit. Your vocal exercises and songs will be much easier to achieve if you first recognize some basic principles of sound transmission and the anatomy of the instrument. This chapter will explain some of these basics and give you exercises to warm up the body.

Principles of Acoustics

Sound is created when vibrations are transmitted through air, or another medium such as water, and reach the ears of the listener. Musical sound has regular, continuous vibrations, distinguishing it from noise, which has irregular vibrations. A musical tone is considered to have a certain pitch and resonance, which will be discussed later. These musical sound transmissions travel in waveforms that are repetitive to maintain a specific tone. Sound waves have four basic elements: frequency, amplitude, duration, and form.

Musical pitch is also called *frequency* and refers to the number of vibrations per second. This frequency must repeat steadily in order to hold a musical tone. Any change in the frequency of vibrations is a change in the pitch you perceive as a listener. The faster the frequency of vibrations, the higher the pitch. Conversely, slower vibrations have a lower frequency rate and a lower pitch. Imagine the sound of a machine or a wheel when the rotations become faster. You can hear a higher pitch when the wheel turns more quickly. The same is true of any method of producing sound vibrations.

FIGURE 2-1.

Sound wave

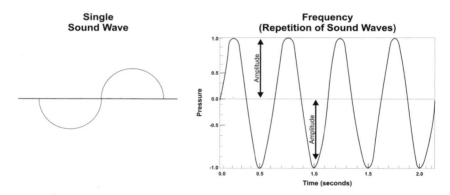

The height of a sound wave, its *amplitude*, determines the volume and intensity of the sound. When you sing louder, the amplitude will be greater, and can even be seen by the sound engineer when you record your voice. Sound waves can also be reflected backward when hitting against a rigid wall, or absorbed through material that allows the sound waves to pass through it.

Later on we will look at examples of conditions in the body that will either reflect or absorb sound, but for now you can think of the acoustical differences in various room environments. Try talking or singing in the bathroom, where tile walls will reflect the sound. Now try the same thing in a room with rugs and curtains. The soft fabrics will absorb the sound. The same principle holds true for the body. Hard surfaces will reflect sound and soft surfaces will absorb it.

Voice as a Wind Instrument

The voice is considered to be a type of wind instrument, which means that air is needed to create the vibrations. All wind instruments have three basic elements needed to create tone: an actuator, vibrator, and resonator. In the voice, air is the actuator and source of the power. As you exhale, the air causes the vocal folds in the larynx to vibrate, and they become the vibrator of the instrument. Finally, the resulting air column continues to vibrate in the pharynx (throat) and mouth and may increase the intensity of the vibration, altering its quality and volume. In doing so, the throat and mouth become the resonator.

FIGURE 2-2.
Sound production
in the voice

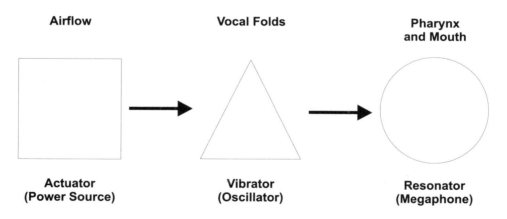

Airflow	Vocal Folds	Pharynx and Mouth
Actuator (Power Source)	Vibrator (Oscillator)	Resonator (Megaphone)

Because these three elements make up the vocal instrument, each will be explored in more depth in the next three chapters. Your breath will need to function with control but remain free of tension. The way you approach the onset of sound in the vibration of the vocal folds will determine the capacity for a pleasing tone. And the shape and texture of the throat, mouth, and tongue can drastically change the resonance and quality of the tone.

Overtones

Musical instruments have an acoustical character wherein other pitches, called *overtones*, are produced in conjunction with the original note. This is a natural function of sound when given the right preparation. The initial tone sounded is called the *fundamental*. When the fundamental is sounded, an infinite series of resulting tones sound in conjunction with the fundamental. The resulting tones are in certain arithmetic proportions to the fundamental tone and are called *partials, harmonics*, or *overtones*. These additional overtones above the fundamental pitch you sing are responsible for the quality of your voice.

FACT

The terms *partials, harmonics*, and *overtones* are used interchangeably by most musicians, even though there are qualifying differences in physics. For singers' purposes, you may hear any one or all of these terms to describe the resulting pitches of the initial note sounded.

The fundamental is always the lowest note and the resulting partials sound above that pitch, or higher in tone. The first overtone is the octave above the fundamental, the next highest is a fifth above that, then a fourth above the previous note. The division of partials above the fundamental is called the *harmonic series* and continues infinitely.

FIGURE 2-3. The first notes of the overtone series

You can train your ear to hear the first one or two overtones, but most people have difficulty distinguishing specific pitch beyond that. The entire series is vibrating simultaneously and blends into the sound of one note. The note has a particular ringing quality when the overtones are present in the tone. You can create this ringing quality in your voice with overtones by changing the length and shape of the throat, tongue, and mouth, and also by proper onset of vibration in the vocal folds. The overtone series is fascinating to study. If you're interested, you could search the Internet for more information in the fields of acoustics, overtones, or harmonic series. Although a bit technical, one excellent reference is *Fundamentals of Musical Acoustics* by Arthur H. Benade. At the very least, you should know that the ringing quality you can achieve in your voice comes from accessing the overtones by the various shapes you create in the vocal tract.

The Relationship Between Singing and Speaking

It's clear that the same basic instrument manages both your speaking voice and your singing voice. The acoustical principles are the same for each action. But it's also true that there are vast differences in the requirements of singing when compared to the needs of basic speech. The musical demands of your singing voice change the parameters of the acoustical space in your throat. The duration of sound, the pitch, and the intensity all contribute to the differences.

As a singer, you'll need to hold a tone in your voice longer than you would in speech in order to achieve the rhythm of the song. Holding that tone requires that you physically hold the space in your throat that makes that sound and, just as when you hold any position in your body, certain strength and understanding of the position is necessary. And as a wind instrument, steady breath control keeps the continuity and movement of the sound waves. Most people don't need to worry about breath control while speaking because the words are spoken quickly and not held out for any period of time as they are in music. The rhythmic patterns of music require a method of holding tone without wavering, which is not necessary in speech.

In singing, you'll also use different, primarily higher, pitches than you would need in everyday speech, which is limited to a much narrower range most of the time. Your voice has different registers, or regions of sound, each requiring a different position in the vocal tract. Most speaking voices utilize only one of those registers. This is your comfort zone and what you're accustomed to feeling, but as soon as you make a sound higher or lower than this limited range, you'll experience a different sensation in your voice.

Vocal technique helps you to retrain your concept of how to create sound when reaching outside of your comfort zone. Again, there are positions of the throat required for high pitches that aren't needed for the lower pitches of your speaking voice. You can read more about this in Chapters 5 and 6.

Finally, you'll need to have control over changes in volume that need more subtlety and fine-tuning than most speech, in order to make tasteful choices in the dynamics of the music.

You may hear people say that singing is just like speaking or thinking words on pitch, but there really are significant differences. What they may mean is that your singing voice should sound natural. While the capacity of your voice to sing long, high phrases is natural, in that your body is fully capable of achieving it, the execution isn't always within the reach of a singer with no training. Adjustments must be made within the body of the instrument to accomplish the singing of demanding material. Approaching the singing of high notes by merely thinking words on pitch may cause your body to respond in a way that will close your throat rather than open it, ultimately causing vocal difficulty, or even damage, at some point in your singing career. Singing is a natural process, but should have the same careful guidance you would give to any art form or demanding physical exercise.

Some Basic Anatomy

Unlike other wind instruments, your entire body is your instrument. If you were first studying violin as an instrument, you'd learn the anatomy of the violin and the bow. In the same way, you should have some basic knowledge of how your body creates sound. Then you can function as both the player and the instrument. When other instruments are manufactured, their capacity to create tone, amplify sound, and access overtones is built in. A singer has to create the instrument with every breath, constantly resetting its shape for the best tone. In addition, you are inside the instrument and hear it differently than you would on the outside. If you remember that you are learning to play the most complex musical instrument, it might be easier to remain patient with the process.

Your skeletal structure creates the framework of your entire body and is important to understand for alignment and support. When the skeleton isn't balanced properly, every other system in the body has to compensate for it in some way. This basic structure is made up of bone, which is the densest substance in the body, and cartilage, which is also firm but elastic. The bones and cartilages are held together by various forms of connective tissue that are somewhat elastic. Ligaments connect bones to other bones to form joints and provide joint stability. Tendons attach muscle to bone. Both ligaments and tendons stabilize but also limit certain kinds of movement. You'll need to respect your body's natural range of movement and alignment in order to stay free of undue tension. Tension in the body shows up directly in the voice.

FIGURE 2-4.
The skeletal and musculoskeletal systems

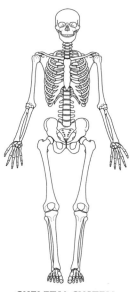

SKELETAL SYSTEM

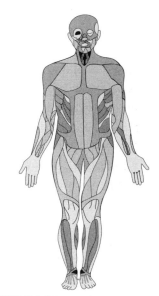

MUSCULOSKELETAL SYSTEM

Many groups of muscles work together to form the vocal mechanism. The act of breathing provides the instrument with the air required to produce sound, among other functions necessary to maintain life. The most important muscles involved in breathing are the abdominals and the intercostal muscles between each set of ribs. Details about the breathing mechanism follow in Chapter 3. During exhalation, air passes across the vocal folds, also known as *vocal cords*, which are housed in the larynx and serve as the vibrator of the instrument. The larynx has a framework of cartilage, allowing for certain elasticity. The air continues its path of exhalation through the pharynx (throat), which also has a skeletal structure composed of moveable cartilage. The throat can change in size, shape, and length. This mobility, along with movement of the tongue, allows for changes in tuning and tone quality, and it is the body's resonator. Finally the tone is emitted through the mouth after it's further shaped by the articulators, namely the tongue, teeth, lips, and jaw. Each step of this process is discussed in more depth in Chapters 4 through 7.

Posture

A good place to begin your vocal study is with an examination of your posture. Even when your posture is continually changing during performance, it's vital that you give proper support to the vocal instrument. Back to the analogy of the violin, you would first learn how to hold the violin and the bow before you could begin to play. The same would be true of a clarinet, saxophone, or guitar. All require a different body position to play, but that position allows for the greatest freedom and expression of the instrument. The vocal instrument is held toward the same goal, which is ease of movement. When your body is properly aligned, the vocal mechanism is free to do its job. Body alignment is important to keep the path of the air unrestricted. The throat needs to remain open to get enough air during inhalation and to create the sound and pitch you want during the exhalation.

Alignment is easiest to master if you imagine hanging like a puppet from strings. Attach these imaginary strings to the top of your head and the top of the breastbone, and really let yourself hang from these two points. You'll probably feel the spine lengthen, especially through the vertebrae of the neck and the lumbar region, and the pelvis will tip into a balanced position. Usually this sense of hanging the skeletal frame is all you need to correct problematic posture. When the spine is aligned in this way, you relieve tension in your neck, throat, and jaw. Any tension in one part of the body causes a reaction somewhere else as your body attempts to compensate for the muscles that should be working. The area of your body that usually suffers most for this compensation is the neck and head, creating a blocked throat and airway.

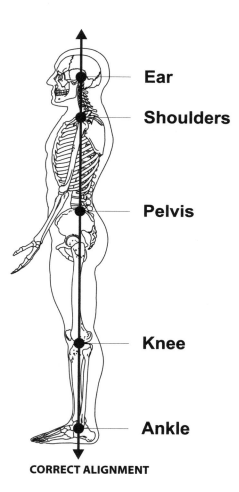

FIGURE 2-5. The skeletal structure in correct alignment

Ear

Shoulders

Pelvis

Knee

Ankle

CORRECT ALIGNMENT

Look at the diagram of the skeleton and notice how the spine relates to the straight line. Imagine this line in your body and check yourself in the mirror. There are five points of alignment you should aim to achieve. Let the top of the line be that puppet string that lifts you, and look at the line passing through these points:

- Ear
- Shoulder
- Top of the pelvis
- Knee
- Arch of the foot

Check for unnecessary tension and try to release it by visualizing the strings from your head and top of the sternum. Hang loosely but in this straight line. You definitely don't want to look or feel stiff in this posture. It should look relaxed and natural, even if you're not used to the feeling of some of these adjustments yet. Now turn away from the mirror and feel the sensation of this posture. You won't have that mirror while singing, so spend some time getting the sense of this placement in your body. Awareness of your body position and posture may take time, but is necessary for healthy singing.

FACT

There are several techniques that specialize in training body awareness and alignment. The Alexander Technique, developed by the singer/ actor F. M. Alexander, is now famous as an excellent discipline for singers. Classes and private sessions are available in most schools and communities and are well worth the time and investment. Other excellent sources for singers include the Feldenkrais Method and many of the martial arts.

Creating a natural body alignment requires that the proper muscles do their job. If one muscle compensates for another, a chain reaction of tension will develop. Corrections in posture have the added benefit of improving your overall health. Both breathing and movement are much easier as channels of energy are opened throughout the body. You may be required to move in many different body positions while performing. No matter what you may have to do onstage, learning to keep good alignment will protect and enhance the freedom of your sound.

FIGURE 2-6.
Corrected alignment

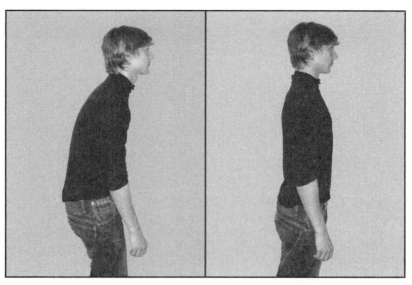

INCORRECT ALIGNMENT   **CORRECT ALIGNMENT**

Alignment and Warmup Exercises

Try these exercises in the given order. The first few are designed for your awareness of alignment and won't be necessary to continue on a regular basis, except to check yourself now and then. The later exercises are a good general physical warmup for the beginning of your vocal exercises. You'll see them again in Chapter 9, which is a basic voice class.

Alignment Exercises

EXERCISE 2-1

1. Lie on your back on the floor and place your feet flat on the floor, so that your knees are bent. Feel your spine against the floor and notice where there's a natural curve in your neck and lower back.
2. Now extend your legs to a straight position, trying to maintain the contact with the floor. Again, allow for the natural curve of the spine.
3. Lengthen your spine by placing your arms over your head and stretching up through your fingertips and down through your feet.
4. Release your arms to your side but keep the feeling of length in your spine.

EXERCISE 2-2

1. Stand with your back against a flat wall and check to feel the same connection against the wall that you felt on the floor.
2. Stretch your spine by pulling up through the top of your head and down through your feet.
3. Now slide your back down the wall into a sitting position. Feel the contact of your back on the wall.
4. Slide back up to a standing position. Be sure that your head touches the wall as it did on the floor. It's easy to let your head drift forward and lose the alignment in your neck.

EXERCISE 2-3

1. Stand away from the wall in the same posture you felt in Exercise 2-2.
2. While pulling up with your head and sternum, bend your knees until you're in a sitting position. Pretend you're about to sit down in a chair that's right underneath you. This is a type of plié, which is a dance exercise used for stretch and warmup. Notice the abdominal muscles working to keep your back in alignment. (See Figure 2-7.)
3. Straighten your legs to a standing position again and continue to feel the length of your spine and the strength of your abdominals.

FIGURE 2-7.
Sitting in plié
position

Physical Warmup

1. Stand with your feet comfortably apart and lean over to touch your toes. Stretch over your right leg, then over your left leg, and back to the center. Slowly roll up to a standing position.
2. Pull your shoulders up toward your ears, hold for three seconds, then release your shoulders down and relax. Repeat twice.
3. Slowly circle your head clockwise. Reverse the circle to counterclockwise. Center your head, lifting it up away from your shoulders.
4. Open your mouth as wide as possible, and then place the tip of your tongue behind your bottom front teeth. Press the middle of your tongue out in an arch shape while keeping the front of your tongue behind your teeth. Retract your tongue and close your mouth. Repeat twice. Gently move your jaw from side to side. (See Figure 2-8.)

FIGURE 2-8.
Arched tongue

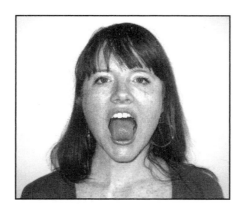

Basic stretches are helpful before you begin to sing in order to warm up your body and release any tension. Stop and repeat these stretches anytime you begin to feel the least strain or tightness while singing. You can even manage subtle adjustments in your spine while performing. The main idea is to support your body during the demanding physical requirements of singing and performance, and to keep yourself as free of tension as possible.

The maintenance of overall good health is a fairly obvious necessity for any musician, but especially for singers who use the body as an instrument.

Special health concerns for the voice are addressed in Chapter 10, but you can begin now to observe your daily routine of nutrition and exercise. You can't really expect to get the best sound from an instrument you mistreat. It's important to develop an awareness of your body and how your health affects your voice. Whether or not you already participate in any sports or regular workouts at the gym, you might want to investigate classes in yoga and Pilates. Both of these practices are excellent lifetime programs for good health, muscular strength, and relaxation. A primary concentration of yoga is the use of breath as a means to sustain life force and energy. The benefits of learning this breath control have direct correlation to breath management while singing. Meditation is also useful for singers, as it is for everyone, to focus on a calm and mindful breathing pattern. And remember that overall good health is the best way to take care of the instrument you play, your voice.

CHAPTER 3

Breathing

You might wonder why you need to focus on breathing when it's such a natural function. You've been able to breathe since birth, continue to breathe constantly, and never had to be taught. It becomes necessary to focus on the breath, however, when you place demands on your body that go beyond sustaining life. As a wind instrument, the voice needs to use air for much more strenuous activity. The inability to sustain musical phrases on one breath is often a source of confusion and frustration for singers. This chapter will describe the mechanism of breathing and how to best utilize it for singing.

Basic Anatomy of Breathing

The act of breathing is one that can be a subconscious reflex or a matter of conscious control. In order to use the air efficiently for singing, it's helpful to understand how it works. There's a great deal of confusion and disagreement concerning how to best utilize the breath for singing. It might be helpful to discard all your previous ideas of what you think you should be doing and just look at the events involved in a breath cycle.

Notice the path of your breath as you're falling asleep. Place your hands on your belly and feel the natural pattern of breath as it slows and deepens. The body's reflex action at rest is the most instructive movement to bring to your awareness. If you can remember, notice it again in the morning as you wake up. It should also be free of tension.

The reflex action of breathing is called *respiration*. Respiration involves a continuous cycle of inhalation, or breathing in, and exhalation, or breathing out. This requires a steady interaction between certain muscles, organs, tissue, and skeletal structure. Air enters the body through the nose and mouth. It then travels through the pharynx (the upper part of the throat) and the larynx into the trachea, or windpipe. The trachea divides into two main tubes called *bronchi*, with one bronchus extending into each lung. The bronchi then further subdivide into many branches throughout the lungs. Think of an upside-down tree and imagine the trachea as the tree trunk and the bronchi as the branches. This system of the trachea and bronchial branches is called *the bronchial* or *respiratory tree*. When you exhale, the path is reversed: breath leaves the lungs, flows through the trachea, larynx, pharynx, and out of the mouth and nose.

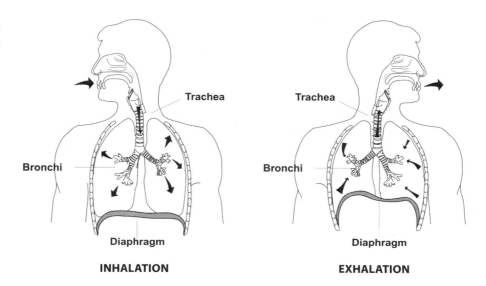

FIGURE 3-1. Upper respiratory tract

Trachea

Bronchi

Diaphragm

INHALATION

Trachea

Bronchi

Diaphragm

EXHALATION

Lungs

The right and left bronchi open into the right and left lungs respectively. The lungs are encased in double layers of protective elastic tissue called *pleurae*. Within the lungs there is an exchange of oxygen coming into the body and carbon dioxide leaving the body. The lungs fill with air and expand but remain protected by the pleurae and the rib cage. Your lungs operate like a bellows, drawing air in by suction as they expand, and releasing air through a single tube after pressing in to collapse the volume of space to their original position.

Diaphragm

Breathing is governed by the body's need for oxygen to live. The brain coordinates the response to this requirement by sending regular and rhythmic signals to a muscle called the *diaphragm*. The diaphragm is a large muscle that lies below the lungs and above the abdomen. It is inside the cavity created by the rib cage and is curved downward like an upside-down pan. It's attached to the lung cavity above it, to the lowest ribs in the back, and the breastbone in the front.

FIGURE 3-2.
Diaphragm
positions

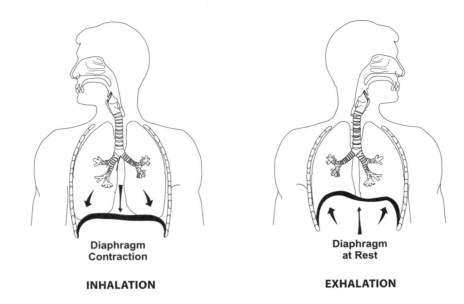

Diaphragm
Contraction

INHALATION

Diaphragm
at Rest

EXHALATION

When the body needs oxygen, the brain sends a message to the diaphragm, which then contracts and lowers into a wider and flatter position, although it does still maintain some of its dome shape. This contraction and downward movement of the diaphragm displaces the abdomen below it, causing it to lower as well. The entire chest cavity expands, especially the movable bottom ribs, to make room for the diaphragm as it presses downward, pulling with it the elastic tissue of the lungs and pleurae. This creates a vacuum that pulls air into the lungs from the outside. After air enters the lungs, an exchange of gases occurs in small sacs called *alveoli*. The diaphragm relaxes its contraction and it returns to its original position, while carbon dioxide is released from the body in the exhalation.

Ribs

The skeletal framework of the chest includes twelve pairs of ribs, or twenty-four ribs in total. All the ribs are attached in the back to the thoracic vertebrae of the spine. The first (uppermost) seven pairs are attached in the front to the sternum, or breastbone. The next lower three pairs, ribs eight through ten, are not attached directly to the sternum, but are connected by a length of cartilage in the front. Because they are not directly attached in the front, they have more mobility. The last two pairs of ribs are called *floating ribs* and are not attached at all to the front of the chest cavity. The point of attachment in the back is lower than in the front for all twelve pairs.

FIGURE 3-3. Ribs

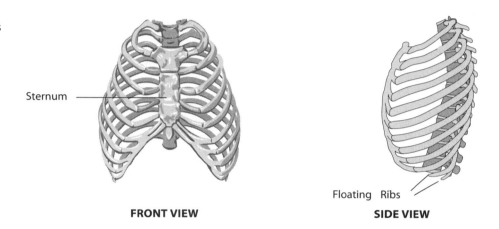

Sternum

Floating Ribs

FRONT VIEW   **SIDE VIEW**

You can see from looking at this structure that there's a greater capacity for movement in the lower ribs than in the relatively stationary upper ribs. If you place your hands on your sides, you can feel the lower ribs expand as you breathe in. Now place your hand on your chest and feel the difference in the motion of your inhalation. The upper chest may move up and down a bit, but isn't able to widen and expand in the same way as the lower ribs.

The ribs have muscles around and between the bones to aid in respiration and stabilization. The most basic of these are two sets of muscles, the internal and external intercostal muscles. Previously, the external intercostals have been considered to be of prime importance for inhalation and expansion of the ribs, while the internal intercostal muscles function more during exhalation. Ongoing new research, however, has shown that the primary function of both sets of muscles is to stabilize the position of the ribs and chest wall during the respiration cycle, which can help to regulate the amount of air pressure needed for singing.

Inhalation

It's important for a singer to be able to inhale quietly, quickly, and inconspicuously. The space in the chest cavity will need to expand as air comes in and the greatest area of movement is in the lower ribs. The upper ribs should stay lifted and fairly stable, since their activity is limited to movement up and down and not significant outward expansion. Tension in the lower back or abdominal muscles will limit the movement of the lower ribs, which do need to expand with each breath. Therefore you'll need to keep the natural posture discussed in Chapter 2. Practice with a lifted chest and straight spine until you're comfortable enough to alter your posture if needed. There may be situations in performance in which you're unable to maintain this posture, but if you've practiced the ideal body posture, muscle memory will help get you through more difficult positions.

Exercises for inhalation are really about focusing on what already happens naturally. Once you've been able to identify the natural process of inhalation, you're better able to check yourself for tension and stiffness. A natural and useful breath has a sense of movement and shouldn't feel rigid or inflexible.

While singing, you'll most often need to breathe in through your mouth for a quick and silent inhalation. You should breathe through your nose, however, if you're singing in cold air or a polluted environment, such as a smoke-filled room. Inhale with the sensation of the beginning of a yawn, the beginning of a sneeze, or imagine inhaling the scent of something pleasant, like roses.

EXERCISE 3-1

1. Stand with your feet comfortably apart and place your hands on your sides.
2. With your chest lifted and your spine straight, breathe in and feel your ribs expand to the side. Release and repeat.

EXERCISE 3-2

1. Sit in a chair and lean forward until your chest rests on your thighs.
2. Breathe in slowly and feel the ribs in your back expand. Release the breath.
3. Sit up and place your hands on your back at the lower ribs.

FIGURE 3-4.
Exercise 3-2

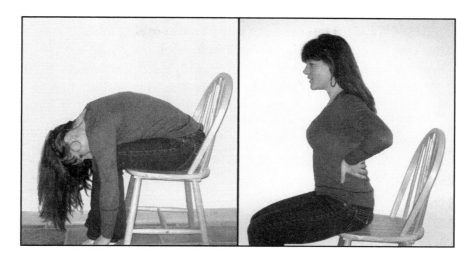

4. Inhale again and try to feel the expansion you felt while leaning forward. Release.
5. Now try standing up and see if you can still feel your back expand with the inhalation. Release.

EXERCISE 3-3

1. Lie on your back on the floor and place your hands on your belly and waist.
2. Breathe in and feel your belly expand. Relax and don't try to hold it in. Release the breath.
3. Repeat this exercise sitting up straight in a chair, and then again while standing.

ALERT!

Although your chest should remain in a high position as you inhale, be sure that you aren't raising your shoulders for the inhalation and dropping them for the release of breath. Your shoulders and chest shouldn't move up significantly. If you feel you're doing this, try to relax your abdomen and lower back and concentrate on the movement of your lower ribs against your hands. Check yourself in the mirror if needed.

One of the biggest mistakes singers make during inhalation is overfilling the lungs. In anticipation of possibly running out of air, the psychological impulse is to gulp in as much air as they can. This is actually detrimental rather than helpful because it causes tension in the entire respiratory process. If you have air left over after a phrase and haven't rid your body of it in exhalation, you won't have freed the space to take in the next breath. Most people really do take in enough air. The problem is more likely a too-rapid exhale on the first syllable of the phrase.

Exhalation

A stream of moving air is required to make sound. Since air is the initial source of singing, causing the vocal cords to vibrate, learning how to control and use your breath is definitely of primary importance. Breathing is something we all do constantly without thinking about it. It's a natural process and you can trust your body to take care of the job most of the time. Singing demands that you alter this natural cycle, however, by controlling the exhalation to get through a long or difficult phrase of music without running out of breath. The music changes this natural cycle because of its rhythmic demands. Since certain words or phrases will be held for a longer time than in speech, you'll need to guide the air in exhalation to provide a steady release. If the air stops at any point, the sound will also be stopped.

During exhalation, the abdominal muscles are doing most of the work by contracting and thereby exerting pressure on the abdomen to return to its upward position at rest. At the same time, the diaphragm moves up into its passive part of the cycle. The abdominal muscles are providing the support for the exhalation process, while the ribs and diaphragm release. Thus the singer will need to focus energy in the contraction of the abdominal muscles, but without creating tension or rigidity. There should be a sensation of steady movement and flow.

EXERCISE 3-4

1. While sitting or standing with a straight spine, cross your arms over the top of your head and breathe in and then out.
2. Continue to exhale until you feel you have fully emptied your lungs of air.

3. Concentrate on the lower abdominal muscles pressing in toward your lower back. Don't push or actively contract the muscles, just identify the feeling of their natural movement.

EXERCISE 3-5

1. Breathe in, then exhale with the sound of a snake hiss. Say "hiss" and extend the *s* as long as you can.
2. Try to make a very steady stream of sound without variation and pushing.

EXERCISE 3-6

1. Breathe in, then exhale through a straw with a steady stream of air.
2. Try to keep the movement even and stop when you feel any tension or desire to push the air.

EXERCISE 3-7

1. Breathe in, then blow air through a flute or recorder. You can buy inexpensive children's instruments for practice.
2. Try to keep the sound steady as you exhale. Feel the movement of your abdominal muscles.

EXERCISE 3-8

1. Breathe in for four counts and out for eight counts.
2. Repeat the inhale for five counts and exhale for ten counts.
3. Continue to increase the length of the inhalation and double the number of counts for the exhalation.

Exercise 3-8 is based on breath concepts in yoga and meditation. Both of these practices are excellent for learning breath control and awareness. Try a class in yoga, meditation, or both, and concentrate on the path of the breath during the class.

1. While keeping your spine straight, bend your knees as if you were getting ready to sit in a chair.
2. Circle your arms forward at shoulder height as if holding a large column. Try to maintain the high chest position at the same time.
3. Breathe in and out slowly and identify which muscles you're able to feel working. You might find that the abdominal and pectoral muscles are more fully engaged in this position.

FIGURE 3-5.
Exercise 3-9

Appoggio

Appoggio is a technique of breath management that many singers claim to be the only reliable method of controlling your breath while singing. The term comes from the Italian *appoggiare*, which means "to lean" or "lean on." The technique involves the sensation of leaning the air against the sternum in the exhalation, rather than thinking of the air immediately coming out of the mouth. The sternum lifts for inhalation and normally collapses slightly for exhalation. If you leave the sternum lifted and imagine the air and the lungs pressing against it, you can maintain a much greater feeling of control and security in the exhalation.

FIGURE 3-6.
Appoggio
illustration

One exercise you can try in order to increase the feeling of appoggio is to hold an elastic exercise band, or even a dishtowel, in front of you in a vertical line. Pull up and down at the same time so that you feel the tension in opposite directions. Make sure your chest is lifted and then breathe in while pulling on the band.

This use of appoggio is probably the single most important element of good breath control. If you feel the gentle push of air against your chest, you can avoid the problem of sending too much air pressure against the vocal cords. Tension in the throat will both sound strained and feel uncomfortable, as well as damage delicate tissue of the cords.

Voiced Breathing Exercises

It's important to practice breathing for the increased demands of singing. Both the rhythmic demands of long notes or phrases and the use of a wider range of pitch contribute to the fact that you need more breath control for singing than you do for speech or for basic life sustenance. It's far too cumbersome to think constantly about how you're breathing while you're singing, but it will become an automatic response if you practice. Your body will retain the new information in muscle memory if you make it a part of your daily life. That way you won't have to think about it while you're performing.

FACT

You can practice breathing exercises as often as you like. You won't need the same degree of guidance that you need in the beginning of vocal training since it would be difficult to hurt yourself while practicing breath control. Any time you think of it, add in breathing exercises to your daily life. Some exercises can be done while carrying on other activities such as walking or waiting in line.

EXERCISE 3-10

TRACK 1

1. Place your lips together so that they are loosely touching.
2. Blow air through your lips to make them flutter.
3. When the air is moving your lips evenly, add a hum tone to create a lip trill. This is like a propeller sound.
4. Slide up and down in pitch on the lip trill, keeping the air as steady as possible. If you have trouble with this, place your hands gently on the sides of your mouth to keep your lips relaxed.

This exercise feels silly, so have fun. Try repeating the exercise using a rolled *r* sound.

EXERCISE 3-11

1. Open your mouth to a comfortable position and then inhale through the mouth, as if you didn't want someone to see you yawning. Concentrate on the sensation and the cooler temperature of the air across the soft palate.
2. After the inhalation, hold this open placement and exhale through your nose without lowering the yawn position.
3. Repeat the yawn inhalation, exhale through your nose while maintaining the lifted soft palate and, after you feel the air through your nose, sigh out on "ha."

EXERCISE 3-12

1. Breathe in comfortably. Don't overfill your lungs.
2. As you exhale, count numbers on a steady pitch as far as you can. Remember to lean the air against your sternum and stop when you feel tension.
3. Repeat and try to increase the length of your counting.

You can also use the alphabet for this exercise. Place your hands on your lower abdominal muscles while you are counting and try to get rid of all of your air.

EXERCISE 3-13

TRACK 2

1. Using the vowel "ee", sing the five-note scale three times on one breath.
2. Repeat the same scale six times, then nine, then twelve. If you run out of air, just stop and rest rather than trying to finish the exercise.

Your focus should be on getting rid of all of your air, not guarding it in a way that will cause tension.

EXERCISE 3-14

TRACK 3

1. Sing the following exercise using one breath. As in the previous exercises, stop if you feel tension. Keep the air moving and try not to stop or hold your breath at any point.

Four score and seven years ago our fathers brought forth on this continent a new nation, conceived in liberty, and dedicated to the proposition that all men are created equal.

FIGURE 3-7. Exercise 3-14

You can increase the sensation of support in these exercises by placing your hands on a flat wall or the back of a chair and leaning forward in a pushup position. Keep your elbows bent and your chest high and forward, as if you were leaning your chest against the wall. Be sure to keep your body completely straight and don't bend at the waist. Now try the set of exercises in this position.

Common Problems

Remember that most people take in plenty of air but let it escape too quickly on the first word or syllable. You do need to think of getting rid of the air as you sing; however, it should be expelled as a gradual, steady stream. Let your body be your guide in deciding if your breathing feels relaxed and comfortable while slightly energized. Your ear can tell you if the sound is steady and secure. If a sustained note wobbles or trembles, you'll need to spend some time on these breathing exercises. Here are some of the most common mistakes made by singers:

- Trying to inhale too much air
- Forcing out all the air on the first syllable
- Controlling the breath too rigidly, causing tension
- Sending too much air pressure to the throat rather than leaning the air against the chest

When singing a song, you need to increase the length of time appropriated for the exhalation. Words and phrases are elongated in a way that is unnatural to our regular breathing pattern or even to speech. More muscular control is required to augment the amount of air needed for the more demanding activity. This control needs to remain gentle and sustained without causing tension in the body. Try out a few phrases of a song you're working on and check to see if the words are steady. Practice gently and consistently and you'll find the length of the musical phrase will increase.

CHAPTER 4

Phonation

It's easy enough to make sound with your voice and never think about how it happens. If you want to develop that sound to manage something more difficult than everyday speech, however, it's useful to understand how it works. Most musicians understand the mechanics of their instrument and certainly wouldn't settle for damage or poor quality. Singers learn to feel the same way about their bodies, especially the parts of the vocal tract responsible for initiating sound. Read through this chapter to understand the way you produce sound, and then concentrate on the exercises that will help you develop a healthy and beautiful tone.

Anatomy of the Larynx

Phonation is the process of making sound at its first source, namely the vibration of the vocal cords. Vocal sound is initiated in the larynx, commonly called the *voice box*, which houses the vocal cords. Remember from Chapter 2 that your voice is a wind instrument and needs air to begin the process of creating sound. Now you can examine what happens when you intend to speak or sing. With this message from the brain, air passes across the vocals cords during exhalation, causing them to vibrate.

The larynx is an attached extension and upper part of the trachea (windpipe). Behind the trachea is the esophagus, which leads to the stomach. The primary function of the larynx is to operate as a valve that can close off the trachea if anything, such as food, drink, or dust, tries to enter it, and also to hold in the breath during physical exertion. Everyone has had the experience of swallowing something "down the wrong way" and this literally is the case if the larynx doesn't function properly. Its secondary function is to produce sound. The dual functions of serving as a protective valve and producing sound are the reason you're told not to eat and talk at the same time.

The larynx is composed of rings of cartilage attached at the top to one bone, the U-shaped hyoid bone. The hyoid bone is also attached to the base of the tongue, so any movement of the tongue will affect the larynx. There are four different cartilages, listed here from bottom to top:

- The cricoid cartilage, which is attached to the top of the trachea
- The thyroid cartilage, which is shaped like a shield and protects the vocal cords
- Two arytenoid cartilages, which are attached to the vocal cords and the muscles that open and close the cords
- The epiglottis, which closes over the opening of the larynx when swallowing

The front of the thyroid cartilage is known as the *Adam's apple*. It's more visible in men and often not apparent at all in women. Some research has shown that the more prominent the Adam's apple is, the lower the range of the man's voice.

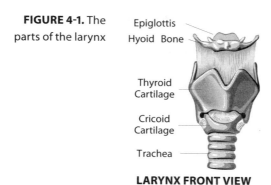

FIGURE 4-1. The parts of the larynx

Epiglottis
Hyoid Bone
Thyroid Cartilage
Cricoid Cartilage
Trachea

LARYNX FRONT VIEW

Muscles in the Larynx

There are two sets of laryngeal muscles: extrinsic and intrinsic. The extrinsic muscles attach to the larynx on one end and to a structure outside the larynx on the other end. These various muscles are responsible for raising, lowering, and stabilizing the larynx. The intrinsic muscles are entirely contained within the laryngeal walls and are responsible for the movement of the vocal cords. They can open (abduct) and close (adduct) the cords to form the vibratory action, and they can shorten or elongate the cords as needed to change pitch and vocal register.

FIGURE 4-2.
Vocal folds

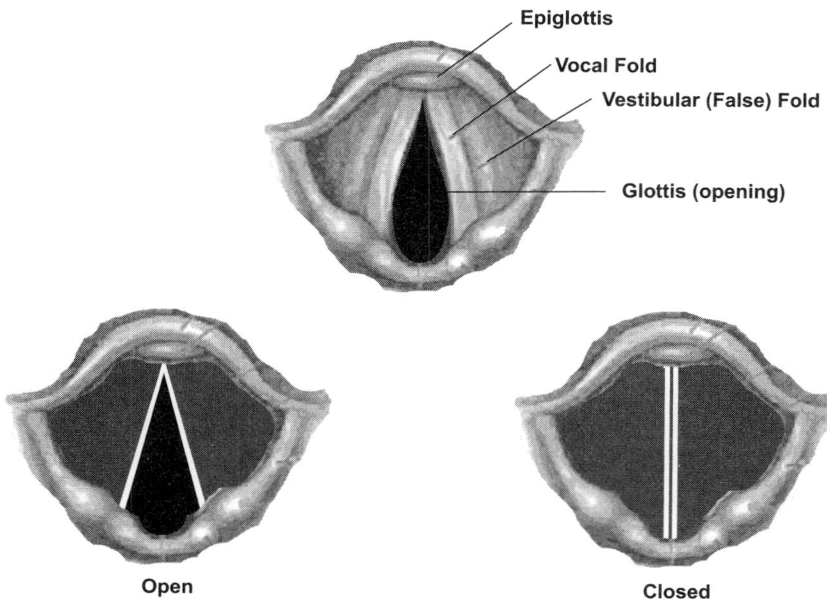

Epiglottis
Vocal Fold
Vestibular (False) Fold
Glottis (opening)

Open

Closed

The length of the vocal cords is a determining factor of how high or low your voice sounds. Men have longer vocal folds than women, and children's cords are even shorter than both. A baby's cords may be as short as ⅛ inch, but are obviously capable of power and volume!

When you inhale, the vocal folds open to let air into the windpipe. As you exhale with the intent to speak or sing, the vocal folds close and vibrate as the air passes over them. In the length of each vocal fold is the vocalis muscle, which is responsible for shortening and thickening the folds. The cricothyroid muscle lengthens and stretches the vocal cords by contracting and tilting the thyroid cartilage. When you sing a high note, the cords stretch like a rubber band. In your lower range, the vocalis muscle shortens the cords. These muscles need to be interactive and flexible to allow you to navigate through the high and low parts of your vocal range quickly.

Daniel Bernoulli was a Dutch mathematician who formulated the aerodynamic theory referenced in most studies of vocal phonation. The theory as applied to vocal study states that the vocal folds will close together by suction if there is a stream of air flowing in the space between them, the glottis. You can try out this theory by holding two pieces of paper together and blowing air between them. There is debate among vocal pedagogues concerning the validity of this theory relating to the vocal mechanism.

The space between the vocal folds is called the *glottis*. It opens in a triangular shape for breathing and closes into a narrow slit for making sound, with just the edges of the vocal folds touching. How the folds come together (technically called *approximation*) is the most important element in creating the sound you want. There are two main theories of how the folds come together and begin to vibrate. One is a muscular explanation and the other is an aerodynamic explanation called *the Bernoulli Effect*, but there is no real conflict in these theories, as both may be true simultaneously. Ultimately, however, this action can't be controlled directly, but only by the message sent from the brain. Your concept of the sound you want to make is the most important part of initiating that tone.

The Onset of Sound

Your first note actually begins in the brain. The intent to sing a musical tone causes the vocal folds to begin to close. The breath then comes up from the lungs and pushes against the partially closed folds, causing them to vibrate as air escapes through them. The amount of air flowing across the cords is called *subglottic pressure*, meaning the air just below the glottis. The subglottic pressure is enormously important to the onset of the tone, and fortunately it is within the control of a trained singer. The production of the tone can be analyzed in three segments: the beginning, holding the tone, and ending it.

The Attack

The beginning of the note is called *the attack*, an unfortunate name given the need for gentle air pressure. Some teachers now refer to the attack as "the onset of tone." During this phase, the breath should flow gently for a clear sound that's free of tension. The preparation in the mind and body is crucial, and it must be your main focus since the action of the vocal folds happens on a subconscious level. To properly prepare the tone, you should think the pitch before you start to sing, not after. Too many people get nervous about the attack and just begin singing, resulting in scooping and sliding to find the right pitch. You should also prepare your body for the breath with the lifted chest and straight alignment you learned about in Chapter 2.

Try this exercise to practice initiating the sound with air.

EXERCISE 4-1

TRACK 4

1. Open your mouth to a comfortable position and then inhale as if you didn't want someone to see you yawning. The jaw should drop slightly and feel very loose. Concentrate on the sensation and the feeling of the cooler temperature of the air across the soft palate.

2. After the inhalation, hold this open placement and exhale through both your nose and the mouth without lowering the yawn position. It's particularly important to feel the air flowing through your nostrils.

3. Repeat the yawn inhalation, exhale through your nose and mouth while maintaining the lifted soft palate, and, after you feel the air through your nostrils, sigh out gently on a "hum." Make sure that this is one continuous action.

4. On the next exhalation, repeat these steps but sigh on "ha." Try to feel the same humming sensation in "ha." This is called a yawn-sigh onset of sound, and it's very important to master this exercise. Some singers refer to this action as "singing on the air."

There are two common problems associated with the attack. The first is called a *glottal attack, glottal stop,* or *hard attack.* It happens when there is tension in the larynx and the cords close completely before the sound is initiated. If they are totally closed together, the buildup of too much air pressure bursts through the vocal cords all at once, creating a clicking sound before the tone. The combination of muscular tension and force between the cords will ultimately result in damage to the cords. The glottal stop is occasionally needed to clearly voice an important word beginning with a vowel, but should be approached with care. The glottal attack at its most forceful is the action of coughing or clearing your throat, something to be avoided if possible because of the friction and irritation of the vocal folds.

FACT

Manuel Garcia, a famous tenor and vocal instructor, invented the first laryngoscope in 1854. It consisted of a small mirror attached to a handle, much like a dental mirror, which could be held at the top of the throat and reflect the image of the vocal folds by reflecting light from a second mirror outside of the mouth. Garcia was the first to observe the movement of the vocal folds during phonation.

The other extreme is too much breathiness in the voice. An airy sound occurs when the vocal cords don't come together closely enough during the attack and allow too much air to escape through the opening. This could be caused by too much air pressure or lack of body support. Sometimes a beginning singer will hold back and be timid about producing tone, for fear it will sound bad. Use the posture exercises to ensure that you are supporting the tone. The most sensation you should feel while singing is in your body, particularly the chest and abdominal muscles, and the vibratory sensations in your head. You shouldn't feel anything in your throat. If you do, you're probably either using too much force or guarding the sound too carefully.

EXERCISE 4-2

TRACK 5

1. Put a comb in a small plastic bag and hum across it as if it were a harmonica. Place your lips lightly around the teeth of the comb.
2. Hum or sing "oo" until you hear and feel a buzz in the sound. Use this sound to hum the five-note scale.

Sustaining the Tone

Holding a musical tone once you've begun it is a matter of keeping a steady flow of air moving across the vocal folds to keep them vibrating. There shouldn't be spurts of air or a waver in the tone. How long you need to sustain the note will depend on the note's duration in the music. The best way to keep the air steady is to practice the appoggio technique explained in Chapter 3. You can control the flow of air pressure by feeling the sensation of the air in your lungs gently pressing against the inner walls of your chest and sternum. Your chest should be lifted while maintaining a feeling of expansion around the torso. Also, remember your posture and be sure to keep your spine aligned by imagining that your body is hanging from puppet strings attached to your head and chest.

Musical tone should always have the sense of continuous movement even when sustaining the same pitch. It seems paradoxical, but imagine that the air is moving steadily up from the lungs and that it doesn't leave your body. This can help control the amount of air that actually escapes during phonation. Picture a paddle wheel inside your mouth, touching the roof of your mouth, and then visualize the air turning that wheel. The air just keeps cycling but doesn't escape through the lips. You can add the image of inhaling the air rather than exhaling it in order to keep your throat open and relaxed. While sustaining the tone, there's no need to move or adjust any of the articulators. Keep your tongue, lips, and jaw steady. Sometimes the hardest thing you have to do is relax and stay out of your own way.

Ending the Tone

The tone should be released distinctly and clearly. So many singers fade off at the end of the note or cut off the air in their throat. Cutting off the air will produce audible strain in the sound, and fading out the note only results in making the word unclear or unintelligible. This problem often stems from not knowing when to end the note properly. If you're unsure of the number of beats the note should receive, it's easy to "fake it" and hope the audience won't notice. If you learn how to count the beats, you'll be more secure in the release of the tone. The release shouldn't be anticipated and elongated, but rather accomplished at the last moment of the beat. Anticipating the end might close your throat, stop the airflow, or allow you to relax the support in your body.

Once you've determined the exact end of the beat, be sure to use the articulators to end the tone. If you're singing the word "love," you would sustain the tone on the *uh* vowel and then cleanly and quickly place your top teeth at your bottom lip to pronounce the *v* at the very end of the beat.

EXERCISE 4-3

TRACK 6

1. Practice singing these syllables and words. Be sure to get a clear mental image of the sound and pitch before you begin the initial attack.
2. Sustain the tone by imagining the moving air cycling in the mouth.
3. Release the tone with clear articulation of the ending consonant or vowel at the last possible moment of the beat.

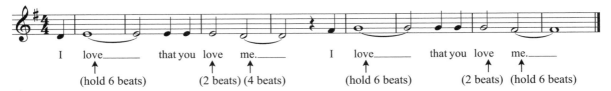

FIGURE 4-3. Exercise 4-3

Pitch

The mental intent to sing a certain pitch will automatically adjust the length and thickness of the vocal folds. Your concept of pitch also determines the number of times the vocal folds will vibrate per second. If you sing the note A above middle C, for example, your vocal folds will open and close 440 times per second. As the pitch gets higher, so does the frequency of vibrations. Eventually the vibrations are so fast that there isn't time for the entire length of the folds to meet, so they remain partially closed, allowing only a small section to vibrate. The cricothyroid muscle contracts and tilts the thyroid cartilage forward, which thins and stretches the cords. Imagine a rubber band in various degrees of stretch. Singers need to be especially careful to sustain the movement of air when singing in the upper range. This is best accomplished by appoggio and proper body support. If you are timid about making this sound, the cords will not meet in the manner necessary for each pitch level. But if you approach the attack of a high note too strongly or harshly, you'll risk disturbing this delicate balance. You'll probably need a period of trial and error to discover the proper balance and right amount of air pressure needed for each note. As you practice with the exercises in Chapter 9, remember that you should continue only as far as you feel comfortable and free of tension in the throat.

Vibrato

Vibrato is a natural fluctuation of pitch that adds a rich and flexible quality to the musical tone. The rate of the vibrato may be from five to seven times per second and may vary the pitch by a half step up and down. It may also have pulsations of intensity (volume) and of tone quality. Vibrato is considered to be a natural function of artistic expression and desirable in most of your music. There are times you may need to straighten the tone and sing without vibrato for certain effects and to blend vocally in some choral settings. The straight tone, however, is physically exhausting to the singer since the muscular action in the larynx is constant. Vibrato allows changes of movement in the larynx that offer alternation of work and rest.

ALERT!

The greatest danger many young singers face is the desire to keep the straight tone, sometimes called *white sound*, in preference over vibrato. They might assume the sound of vibrato is too classical. In rejecting this natural function of healthy singing, however, they may be limiting themselves to very short singing careers.

Developing your vibrato is a function of both breath control and phonation. It's important that you don't try to push vibrato, because it really is a result of a relaxed and open throat and should never be forced. As you continue to work exercises of breathing and flexibility, you'll find that it will develop naturally.

Common Problems of Phonation

Healthy phonation requires a balance of a steady and controlled airflow and muscular coordination of the vocal fold vibration. A singer can't think about any of this while performing, but rather should concentrate on the more artistic elements of the music and lyrics. Use your regular practice routine to address any potential problems of phonation in the following list:

- Harsh glottal attack stemming from too much tension in the larynx

  Correct with Exercise 4-1 and general relaxation exercises for the body and neck. Also sing the word "who" on a single sustained pitch or any line of music.

- Breathiness caused by inadequate closure of the vocal folds

  Correct with Exercise 4-2 and humming in the roof of the mouth. Also use more body support and vocalize on forward vowels (see Chapter 7).

- Straight tone with no vibrato

  Correct with exercises using back vowels and rounded lips. Don't force it.

- Wavering tone during the sustain of a note

  Correct with appoggio, body support, and posture exercises from Chapters 2 and 3.

Just as in any demanding physical activity, the moment of preparation before you begin to sing is key. If you concentrate on the mental image of the pitch and sound of the word you're about to sing, you can usually trust your body to take care of the rest. Tension and worry about the way you might sound will constrict the muscles that need to do their job. Focus on the breath cycle, body support, and the mental sound of the music and lyric just before you sing. This may be all you need to accomplish balanced phonation.

CHAPTER 5

Resonance

The beauty of the voice and its tone quality is determined by its resonance. Your audience can hear the quality of your voice in a way that you can't as the singer, but you can know the difference in how it feels. People rarely argue that the most pleasing tone sounds very open, and this indeed implies that the throat is open and not constricted by tension. The best singers spend a lifetime perfecting the quality of their sound by paying attention to the physical positions and sensations in the vocal tract. This chapter will give you some technical information, but also the basic exercises necessary to create a more beautiful vocal tone quality.

What Is Resonance?

You can better grasp the reasons for certain exercises and vocal positions if you have a basic understanding of the principles of resonance. Resonance is defined as reverberation, the prolongation of sound by reflection, or the amplification of the audible range of speech sounds. In other words, given the right setup, it can make the sound better and stronger. It is created when two vibrating bodies relate to each other at the same frequency. When the right conditions exist, one vibrating object, the vibrator, can cause another to vibrate at the same frequency, or pitch. Once the primary vibrator has been set in motion, the tone may be practically inaudible if there is no way to reflect and enhance it. When sound is transmitted through the air it can be greatly amplified if there is a cavity with walls containing the air. The size and shape of the cavity create certain conditions for resonance. Think of blowing air across the mouth of an empty bottle, which is the resonating cavity. The size and surface matter of the cavity will affect the sound. If you fill the bottle halfway, or get a different size of bottle, the tone will be different.

The mechanics of the voice are similar to those of a double-reed wind instrument. When you sing, the air from the lungs passes over the vocal cords and generates the motion and vibration of the cords, as you learned in Chapters 2 and 4. This causes the air column to vibrate in the throat, which in turn creates secondary vibrations in the surrounding structure. Secondary vibrations, also called *sympathetic vibrations*, are set in motion by the primary vibrator, or the vocal folds in the case of the voice. The concern now is how the sound is amplified in the resonating chamber so others can hear you and how to improve the quality of the sound.

Age and gender also determine the length of the vocal tract, which is shorter in women than in men, and shortest in children. This is important to keep in mind when you consider that the length of the resonating tube is one of the factors affecting vocal quality.

The resonator for the voice is the vocal tract, which consists of the larynx, pharynx (throat), mouth, and sometimes the nose, which would be used only for a more specialized nasal sound. The length of the vocal tract is the distance from the glottis to the lips, and it can be modified to some extent. The primary resonator is the pharynx and it will be helpful to singers if they understand how the changes of size and shape within the throat affect the quality of the sound.

The quality of tone is called *timbre* in musical terms. Timbre refers to the distinctive color of sound. The same singer is able to access a different timbre in various registers of the voice, high or low, or by imitating another person, animal, musical instrument, or even machine. By altering the resonating cavities, you can change the character of your voice. Descriptions of vocal timbre can be quite subjective, and include terms such as *bright, dark, pure, sweet,* and *grating*. Some people may also use colors to describe timbre. One well-known choral conductor asks her choir to use more burgundy color in the tone, and the singers immediately adjust their timbre to a darker and richer sound.

The Pharynx

The throat, or pharynx, is the main resonating cavity for the vibrating air column. It's shaped like a tube and extends from the larynx on the bottom to the soft palate on the top and opens into the nose and mouth. The pharynx is capable of changing size, shape, and texture, adjustments that are all very important to the singer in tuning and determining the quality of tone. This large cavity can be divided into three sections: the nasal pharynx, the oral pharynx, and the laryngeal pharynx.

Nasal Pharynx

The nasal pharynx is the upper section behind the nasal cavity and just above the soft palate. The soft palate closes off this portion when swallowing so that food can't go in the nose. The eustachian tube opens into the nasal pharynx and also leads into the middle and inner ear. The bones of the middle and inner ear can conduct the vibrations from the pharynx, causing you to hear sound differently than your audience. Certain nasal vowels in languages such as French and Portuguese, and certain consonants such as *m, n,* and *ng* are amplified in the nasal pharynx.

Oral Pharynx

The oral pharynx is the middle section of the throat and extends from the soft palate to the epiglottis. This is the largest and most mobile segment, able to change its shape and size by the movement of the soft palate, the larynx, and the tongue. Because of its mobility, it's the most important part of the throat for the singer to understand. Most of the shaping of tone quality occurs in the oral pharynx and, with practice, the singer is able to control the positions responsible for different coloring and timbre.

Laryngeal Pharynx

The laryngeal pharynx is the lowest section of the pharynx, extending from the epiglottis to the cricoid cartilage at the bottom of the larynx. It lies the closest to the primary vibrator and is important as the first area of resonance. When the vibration of the vocal cords creates the fundamental pitch, the entire spectrum of overtones is present, each partial having its own frequency. The uppermost portion of the larynx, often called *the laryngeal collar*, acts as the first resonator of these overtones. The top of this tube can be narrowed by constriction or widened during relaxation and, in changing shape, can either positively or negatively affect the production of overtones responsible for the timbre and ring in the voice. (Overtones are discussed in more detail in Chapter 2.)

FACT

The oral pharynx and laryngeal pharynx together make up the main part of your body used to create resonance and access overtones. These two sections of the throat are often referred to collectively as the *orolaryngeal pharynx*. The nasal pharynx is closed off most of the time and not as immediately crucial to the cylindrical shaping of the cavities.

Orolaryngeal Pharynx

It's important to gain an awareness of the orolaryngeal pharynx since it's of prime importance in creating overtones in the voice. The presence of overtones gives the ringing quality that's most pleasing to hear. Without this ring, the voice sounds flat and dull. The only way to bring overtones into the voice is to keep a long, cylindrical shape to the throat. Have you heard people say you need to keep an open throat? This is the most common correction for singers, but what does it really mean?

An open throat has the shape of a long tube or cylinder. The walls of the cylinder are flexible because they're composed of cartilage, which is elastic in quality. But these walls are also capable of maintaining a rigid texture to reflect the vibrations of the air column. The firm pharyngeal wall is crucial to sustain high notes. This open-throat position also helps the singer feel a sense of anchoring sound in the sternum and a strong body connection throughout the full range of the voice.

EXERCISE 5-1

1. You can widen the space in the back of your mouth by lifting your back top teeth up to create the feeling of a square opening between the upper and lower teeth. When you do this, you're stretching the throat into the position that keeps the pharyngeal walls firm. This opening in the back of the mouth and rigid texture in the pharynx will secure your high notes by providing the proper resonating cavity.

2. You can also create this space by imagining that you're about to bite into a large apple. It's always better to think of opening your mouth by lifting the top jaw rather than lowering the bottom jaw. Lowering the bottom jaw may cause tension, whereas lifting the top jaw releases tension in the lower jaw.

3. Practice opening your mouth by lifting your top back teeth. You might imagine there are strings pulling them up.

Every change of shape in the cylinder changes the sound and tone quality. It's important to keep this area open for the air column to vibrate. After the primary vibration is initiated by the vocal folds, sympathetic vibrations occur if the proper environment is set. The most significant changes in the shape of the orolaryngeal pharynx are created by the tongue position and the raising and lowering of the larynx and the soft palate.

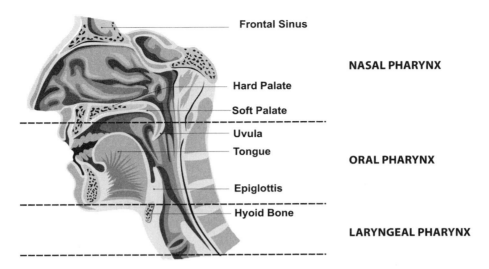

FIGURE 5-1.
The pharynx

Frontal Sinus

NASAL PHARYNX

Hard Palate

Soft Palate

Uvula

Tongue

ORAL PHARYNX

Epiglottis

Hyoid Bone

LARYNGEAL PHARYNX

The Tongue

The tongue is one of the primary articulators and is made up of a group of muscles, which can operate in both a voluntary and involuntary manner. It's extremely strong and capable of changing your resonance for the better or the worse. The tongue is able to move in all directions: forward and back, side to side, up and down, and it can even curl in different positions. Every time it changes shape, the area of your vocal tract changes, which in turn alters the resonance.

The tongue is attached at its base to the hyoid bone, pharynx, jaw, and the soft palate. A third of the tongue lies out of sight in the throat. The root of the tongue is directly associated with the function of the larynx because of its attachment at the base. Look at the diagram and you'll see that this lower third of the tongue is actually forming the front wall of the orolaryngeal pharynx. That means that it's a crucial part of the process of resonation. Remember that the size, shape, and texture of the walls in the resonating cavity determine the quality of the tone. The changing shape of the tongue will affect every syllable you pronounce and create the different vowel sounds.

The movement of the tongue creates different vowel sounds and, in doing so, is also the action that changes the shape of the cylindrical tube in the orolaryngeal pharynx. Tension in the strong muscles of the tongue is one of the most problematic challenges of every singer. The back of the tongue can close off the throat with any signal interpreted as danger, since one of its functions is to protect your air passages. The goal of a relaxed tongue is best achieved by focusing on the shape and position necessary to form each vowel sound distinctly.

FIGURE 5-2.
The tongue forms part of the resonating cavity

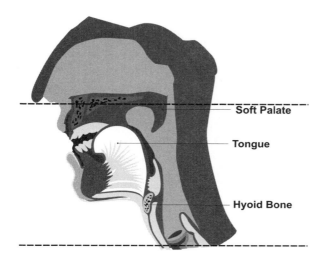

Soft Palate

Tongue

OROLARYNGEAL PHARYNX

Hyoid Bone

Vowel Sounds

The base of the tongue will largely determine the sound and quality of the vowels you speak or sing. The only way you can accurately pronounce a vowel sound is by altering the shape of the tongue, especially at the base. This is not a conscious effort, but comes from the intention to speak a vowel sound clearly. Every time you make a different vowel sound, the tongue changes the shape, size, and texture of the walls of the throat, so the conditions for resonance change as well. Vowel pronunciation and clarity are really within the realm of resonance, since they are the basis of musical tone. You'll see in Chapter 7 the way in which the tongue shapes the various vowel sounds.

The Palate and Larynx

The palate includes the hard palate, which is the roof of the mouth, and the soft palate. The soft palate, technically called the *velum*, lies behind the hard palate at the top of the oral pharynx. The primary function is to close the nasal passages when you swallow so that no food particles can be inhaled. Secondarily the palate acts as a vocal resonator. The soft palate, like the tongue, can move up, down, forward, and back. Because of its mobility, it plays an important role in changing the shape of the cylindrical throat position. At rest, the soft palate hangs in a nearly vertical position, which allows an opening into the nasal passages. When it lifts, the nasal pharynx is closed off, creating more space at the top of the oral pharynx.

The uvula is a small set of muscles that hangs down from the soft palate and is visible in the upper portion of the back of your mouth. You can see the position of the soft palate as it relates to the uvula and determine if the palate is raised or lowered. Eventually you can feel the muscles involved in the soft palate and move them at will.

In addition to creating more length in the throat, the lifted soft palate forms a wall at the entrance to the nasal passage that will prevent a nasal sound. If the soft palate is low, or at rest, the secondary vibrations can go directly into the nasal pharynx, which is what causes the nasal twang. If your voice sounds too nasal, just lift the soft palate. When the soft palate is high, the vibrating air will come into contact with the wall of the raised soft palate rather than travel into the nasal cavities.

EXERCISE 5-2

1. While looking in a mirror, open your mouth wide enough to see the back of your mouth. Can you identify the uvula? Since this is the visible portion attached to the soft palate, you'll be able to tell if the palate is up or down.
2. Breathe in as if beginning a slight yawn. Notice the lift in the palate. You can also try to feel the beginning of a sneeze, or imagine the sensation of breathing in the scent of roses. All of these actions lift the soft palate.
3. Try these methods of inhaling again and see if you can feel the cooler temperature of air across the upper back part of your mouth, which is the soft palate.

The soft palate can work in conjunction with the larynx to lengthen the throat. When the soft palate moves up, the larynx lowers as a result. Keeping the larynx in a low position is desirable for creating the most elongated cylindrical shape in the throat. A common correction for singers is to lower the larynx. The problem is that most people have no familiarity communicating with the muscles of the larynx and are left wondering how to accomplish this task. But almost everyone can identify the feeling of a lifted soft palate after practicing Exercise 5-2. Try placing your hand very lightly on the larynx in the front of your throat. You can identify the larynx by swallowing and feeling the up and down movement. Now yawn slightly and feel it lower. This is a much easier and gentler method of identifying and lowering the larynx.

It's easier to maintain the length in the throat if you also think of narrowing the center of your face. Trace the lines from the outer edges of your nose to the corners of your mouth and notice the triangular shape they form with the mouth. If you try to make these lines parallel, you can feel the elongation of the throat. Notice also that the position of the lips, which form an oval shape, mirror the position of the throat.

FACT

The term *embouchure* refers to the position of the lips a musician uses when playing a wind instrument. The way you hold your lips against a trumpet is different from the position used for a flute. Singers also have an embouchure to achieve the best resonance for each vowel sound and pitch degree. The singer's embouchure is actually helping to set the appropriate vertical length in the throat.

In most cases, you shouldn't open your mouth so wide that it appears unnatural or overly exaggerated. If your mouth is too open, it can actually cause your throat to close. The openness you feel should be in the back of your mouth, not necessarily the front.

Secondary Vibrations

Singers regularly refer to *chest resonance* and *head resonance*. These terms will probably continue to be used for years to come because they do describe a definite sensation of vibration in these two areas. But technically there is no actual resonance in the chest or skull. The sensation is caused by secondary or sympathetic vibrations, which are conducted through bone and tissue. This is also true of the vibrations you may feel in the nose and sinus cavities. The bones can conduct the vibrations, but these are not actual resonating cavities. The "resonance" you feel is actually the result, not the cause, of tone production.

You may have heard someone refer to "placing" the voice in a particular area, especially some part of the face. The most common reference is the mask, meaning the section of the face from the upper lip, across the cheekbones, and up to the eyebrows. Again this is technically inaccurate, as you can't literally place the sound there, but still it's a useful image for a singer. If you can feel the sympathetic vibrations in the mask area, you are experiencing a "forward placement" and the sound will most likely be vibrant to the outside ear. The danger of "placing" sound results from the confusion about how sound is formed and trying to drive the sound muscularly rather than recognize that it's actually a sympathetic vibration. Singers must work with mental imagery to achieve the complex interaction of the vocal mechanism. Much of the muscular function is outside of our conscious control, but responds well to appropriate imagery. This is especially true of resonance.

Mental Imagery

The use of mental imagery is possibly the most important tool available to a singer. Since much of the musculature of the voice isn't visible or under your direct control, the only way to access it is to envision the placement that will encourage the best resonance.

Try out some of these images to maintain the vertical throat position:

- Widen the top molars as in Exercise 5-1. Imagine a square box in the back of your mouth and raise the lid of the box to lift the upper back teeth. Feel the stretch in the throat.
- Imagine that you're biting into an apple to lift the top jaw.

- Imagine the sound is traveling to the top of your ears rather than out of your mouth.
- Picture the sound traveling in the shape of a question mark around the back and top of your head when singing high notes.
- Imagine the shape of a vertical candy cane with the length as your throat and the hook as your soft palate.
- Picture the sound traveling across the roof of your mouth in your middle range.
- Imagine inhaling the scent of roses to lift the soft palate.

Use this picture of the imaginary path of sound to help lift the soft palate to an appropriate height according to pitch.

FIGURE 5-3.
Imaginary path
of sound

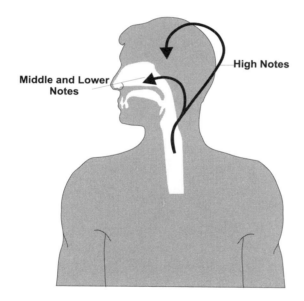

IMAGINE THE PATH
OF SOUND

Be sure to think of positive mental images. It's much easier to imagine lifting the upper back teeth in a slight yawn in order to relax the jaw. If you think in terms of not tensing the jaw, you'll usually just create more tension by focusing on what you shouldn't do. In other words, it's easier to *do* a positive action than to *not do* a negative action.

More Exercises

In these exercises, there are three main areas of resonance in which you can feel the secondary vibrations. You may feel sensation in the mask area of the face, the hard palate, or the open back space of the mouth. Don't forget the vertical positions you've learned. Check in a mirror for the proper mouth position and make sure your jaw is relaxed. Once you've created the form you need, you should leave it alone and not move around too much. Begin each exercise with an exhalation through your nose to practice the concept of secondary vibration in the mask.

ALERT!

When you hear someone tell you to "place the tone" in a particular location, remember that you are setting up the position that allows you to feel the secondary rather than primary vibrations. It's important to identify the feeling of a forward placement in order to project sound, but be careful that you don't use a forceful attempt to drive it forward. This will only cause tension.

EXERCISE 5-3

TRACK 7

1. Sing "yay-ee-oo-ah" on a single pitch. Try to feel the onset of "yay" in the hard palate; "ee" adds on the sensation of the tongue against the back of the bottom teeth and secondary vibrations behind the nose; "oo" lengthens to add secondary vibration in the chest to make the sound feel grounded and to add vertical length to the throat; and finally "ah," which is a cumulative combination of the first three vowels. Try not to lose the sensation of each vowel as you move to the next, but rather add each new placement sensation to the previous one.

EXERCISE 5-4

TRACK 8

1. Put a comb in a small plastic bag and hum across it as if it were a harmonica. Place your lips lightly around the teeth of the comb.

2. Hum or sing "oo" until you hear and feel a buzz in the sound. Use this sound to hum the five-note scale. (You have seen this exercise before in Chapter 4, but now concentrate on the sensation of resonance.)

EXERCISE 5-5

TRACK 9

1. Sing "meow" on the five-note descending scale.

Meow   meow   meow   meow   meow.

FIGURE 5-4. Exercise 5-5

EXERCISE 5-6

TRACK 10

1. Sing "meow" on the five-note descending scale and then continue one long "meow" across the ascending and descending scale.

Meow meow meow meow   meow_____

FIGURE 5-5. Exercise 5-6

EXERCISE 5-7

TRACK 11

1. Maintaining the same forward feeling of meow, sing "had" on the five-note scale. This exercise should sound like a bratty child saying "nya, nya." You may also try this exercise with the tongue between the teeth and gently touching the top lip.

had_____
hah_____

FIGURE 5-6. Exercise 5-7

TRACK 12

1. Repeat the previous exercise, alternating the "ha" sound in "had" with other vowels as you hear them on the CD.
2. Pronounce the vowels as you have in the earlier exercises, but try to keep the forward placement and sense of buzzing behind the nose.

CHAPTER 6

Registers of the Voice

Have you noticed that your voice has a different feel and sound depending on how low or high you sing? Your lower singing voice may feel similar to your speaking voice, but when you sing high or imitate a child or certain animals, it feels lighter and higher in your head. There are sections of the voice, based on pitch, that require an adjustment on the part of the singer in order to sing comfortably and openly in the entire range and to transition smoothly between these different parts of the singing voice.

What Is a Register?

There has been much debate over the definition, and even the existence, of vocal registers. It's most commonly accepted, however, that there are different regions of the voice, called *registers*. A register is a section of the voice determined by pitch range in which the quality and production of sound is similar. The division of these regions and the technical requirements of the larynx and vocal folds within each section are referred to as *registration*. Different vocal registers within the same singer have such a different timbre and tone quality that they're often referred to as different voices (e.g., chest voice and head voice), even though they're all related as part of the same voice. One of the main goals of a singer is to smooth out the transition between these sections in a way that the audience won't hear any changes.

Various studies have analyzed the process of sound production according to the level of pitch frequency, and there is an increasing tendency toward a more scientific investigation. Exciting new research is developing a clearer understanding of the vocal mechanism, which can only help singers to further develop their own awareness.

Most singers refer to the vocal registers not by scientifically accurate terms, but by the sensations created by vibration in the body, hence the terms *chest voice* and *head voice*. The chest voice, or chest register, refers to the lower part of the voice, which feels closer to speech. If you place your hand on your chest while you speak or sing in your lower voice, you can feel the sound vibrations there. Now try singing with your light, high voice and feel the vibrations in your head. These are the sympathetic vibrations you read about in Chapter 5.

Registration and the Larynx

The vocal folds vibrate in different ways according to pitch. In Chapters 2 and 4, you learned that the vocal folds are shorter and thicker when you sing low notes, and stretch to a longer and thinner position when you sing high notes. Lower pitches have a lower frequency of sound waves, which in turn causes a different response in the body than that of a high pitch. This response to pitch information comes from the brain and is then governed by a complex muscular action within the larynx. The vocalis muscle, the centermost part of the thyroarytenoid muscle, is most active in the lower pitch range and speaking voice. The cricothyroid muscle is active in the upper part of your range and stretches the length of the vocal cords so that only the ligament vibrates. The rapid movement of higher frequency doesn't allow for complete glottal closure, whereas the low frequency of your lower range allows full glottal closure and wider amplitude of the vocal folds. Look at the diagrams in Chapter 4 for a picture of the larynx. It can be helpful for the singer to have a very basic understanding of how the sound is produced.

If you were to sing an ascending scale, beginning with your lowest note, you could continue to sing up the scale for several notes and feel the same basic sensation in your voice. But at a certain point, when the notes are higher, you can't sing them anymore in the same way. If you try, your voice will break or crack on the higher notes. That's the point many singers call a "break." When you readjust your voice position and sound to continue up the scale, you're now in a new register, or section of your voice. It feels different in your body and may have secondary vibrations in different places than those of your lower notes.

How Many Registers?

Once again, opinions vary concerning the number of registers. Some teachers claim there is only one register, which in effect means no registers. Overwhelming research and singer testimony agree that there are different registers, so the one-register theory is most likely a description of a voice that is well blended through these sections so that no break, or change, is heard or felt between them. Others claim there are up to five registers. This theory includes two registers that exist in the human voice but are of little practical use in singing. One of these is the growl, called the *vocal fry*, which is used in the lowest part of the voice for special effect. The other is the whistle tone, which is an extremely high part of a woman's or child's voice and also used sparingly for effect.

Even if you are fully aware of different physical sensations in different parts of your voice, you don't want the audience to hear the changes. It's helpful for you to understand what's happening and to identify the feeling, but good vocal technique means you move through these changes so carefully and gradually that your listeners will never know you made any adjustment to get there.

For most practical purposes, the majority of singers and vocal teachers agree that there are three separate vocal registers. Some claim there are only two, with the third being an equal blending of the two primary registers. This blend, in effect, acts as a third register and is important to understand, especially in a woman's voice. The three registers are slightly different for men and for women, so the following description of the three registers are divided by gender.

Vocal Registers in Women

Women have three main vocal registers in the most commonly used pitch range: chest voice, middle or mix voice, and head voice. These are the terms frequently used by singers and refer to the area of the body in which the sound vibrations are felt most strongly. It doesn't mean that the sound is produced in the chest or the head, but only that the physical sensation of secondary vibrations resides there. Another register is the whistle, or flute register, and is too high to be of practical use in most music. An example of whistle register is the highest notes of Mariah Carey's riffs. Notice that she doesn't place words on those notes, but only uses them for effect.

Chest Voice

The lowest part of the woman's voice is referred to as chest voice. It's often the most comfortable part of your voice because it's the register of most women's speaking voice. The feeling may be described as solid, strong, or secure. It has the sensation of being anchored in the body and you can feel vibrations in the chest area, especially throughout the sternum and in the lower part of the neck. Place your hand on your chest as you speak and you'll feel the secondary vibrations there. It's this sensation that gave rise to the popular name of chest voice. Chest voice may also be called *heavy registration*. The timbre, or tone quality, of this part of your voice is darker, heavier, and richer than the upper voice.

The unifying elements of chest registration are determined by vocal production at this frequency, or pitch range. The vocal folds are thicker and vibrate across their entire length, utilizing the vocalis muscle and closing firmly with each vibration. Also the amplitude of the vibration is greater since the vocal folds vibrate at a slower rate for low notes. The higher the pitch goes, the more the muscle has to work. Extra air is needed as well. If the same muscle continues to work harder and more air is forced across the folds, the voice will crack, or break into the next register.

The range of the chest voice is very important but cause for much disagreement. The bottom of the range is easy: it starts from your lowest notes. The top of the range should end at D to F above middle C. It's physically possible to use the chest voice a little higher, but to do so will cause an audible break between registers as you sing higher, and it will also harm your voice over time. Some singers believe they can extend their chest range up through the entire middle register of the voice, but this will place too much tension on the vocalis muscle, causing vocal strain and eventually damage to the vocal cords. There is no way to blend smoothly in your transition out of chest voice if you force this register beyond the point of change in the vocal folds and larynx.

Middle Voice

The middle, or mixed, voice is the next position of the female voice and is a balance between the chest voice and the head voice. The range extends from E or F above middle C for about an octave, up to the next F, depending on the singer. It's the predominant range used in most published music, but it can also be the most difficult vocal register for many women. Since the muscles within the larynx are physically capable of using heavy or light registration within this octave, the singer has to make choices about how to navigate the balance. Too much chest voice will sound pushed and heavy, and will eventually tire and damage the voice. Too much head voice will sound weak and unsupported, with no excitement or ring to the voice.

QUESTIONS

What is the ratio of head to chest voice in my middle register?
The amount of head voice and chest voice you use in your middle register depends on the phrase of music you're singing. If the phrase will be ascending into head voice, use a lighter feeling of mixture so that you don't carry too much chest voice weight up into the head voice. You can use a little more heavy registration in the middle voice if the range of the upcoming phrase stays below the head register.

Adding in a mixture of head voice to the chest voice means a different use of the muscles within the larynx. As the pitch rises, the cricothyroid muscle begins to pull against the vocalis muscle, which causes the vocal cords to stretch into a tighter and thinner position. This stretch increases with higher pitch, or sound wave frequency, which means that the lower part of this octave can maintain more of a chest quality whereas the upper part moves more toward a lighter head voice quality. The strongest, healthiest, and most beautiful middle voice is truly a blend of the color and timbre from each of the other registers.

Head Voice

The highest usable register is the head voice, also called *light registration*. The sensation of the sound is higher in the head and you will no longer feel vibration in the chest. You may now feel the secondary vibrations in some part of your face or skull, hence the name *head voice*. There can be a light, flute-like quality to this register, but it is also clear, strong, and brilliant, with the capacity to carry a greater distance. You may have noticed a singer pull her microphone away when singing a high note; this is because the sound travels most easily and can often be too loud and piercing for amplification.

Most singers make a transition into head voice around the top of the middle voice range, that is E to F♯. At this point the cricothyroid contracts more and stretches the vocal cords to a greater degree, causing them to be thinner and more taut. There is less amplitude in the vibration since it's so rapid. More lift is needed in the soft palate to support the position, as well as more air. This register may feel unfamiliar because it's not used in speech.

ALERT!

It's important when moving into head voice that you feel the sense of an anchor in your sternum, much as you did in your chest voice. Using the technique of appoggio, explained in Chapter 3, you can feel the air in the lungs gently press against the interior walls of the chest and thereby bring more body into the sound. This anchoring enables you to maintain the warmth and richness of tone in your high notes.

The head voice can be extended down through the lower ranges, which creates an overlap of tonal quality. It's dangerous to pull the chest voice up too high, although some of the heavy registration may be added to create color and depth in the middle register. All voices should naturally begin to adjust toward the head voice in the upper half of the middle register with a lengthening of the vertical position of the throat. A slight yawning sensation will lower the larynx and raise the soft palate to achieve this position.

Belt Voice

You may have heard the term *belting*, or using your belt voice. There's a great deal of misunderstanding of this term because of the way it sounds as opposed to the way it feels. Belting has been described as a type of yelling on certain notes, and it's easy to confuse the sound with pure chest voice. It's very strong and powerful and should be reserved for a moment in the song that requires that emotion. Too many women feel they should belt an entire song to show off their vocal skill and power, but that would be the equivalent of yelling at your audience for a whole song. It's tiring to hear when extended too long, but can be very exciting when used for a few choice notes.

The only way to achieve a healthy belting technique is to engage your head voice in the middle range mixture, as previously mentioned in the section about the middle register. Don't try to carry your chest voice up into the higher notes. The palate will be somewhat lowered from the head voice position in order to engage both the vocalis and cricothyroid muscles. You can feel this position by moving the palate in between the two opposite extremes of your highest and lowest notes. The secondary vibrations should be forward in the face, in the area of the mask. There may be a slightly nasal quality to the sound unless you maintain some lift in the soft palate, opening the back of the throat. Even though it sounds like chest voice, you'll need to resist the temptation to make it too heavy in the middle voice. If you try to use too much chest voice, the larynx will rise and cause a scratching or painful sensation in the throat. Remember, it's always incorrect if you feel any pain! The following exercises, which you learned in Chapter 5, can also be used to develop your belt voice. You may want to record these exercises in order to hear how strong your voice sounds. That way you won't be as tempted to push.

EXERCISE 6-1

TRACK 13

1. Sing "meow" on the five-note descending scale.

FIGURE 6-1. Exercise 6-1

EXERCISE 6-2

TRACK 14

1. Sing "meow" on the five-note descending scale and then continue one long "meow" across the ascending and descending scale.

FIGURE 6-2. Exercise 6-2

EXERCISE 6-3

TRACK 15

1. Maintaining the same forward feeling of meow, sing "had" on the five-note scale. This exercise should sound like a bratty child saying "nya, nya."

FIGURE 6-3. Exercise 6-3

TRACK 16

Look at the following chart of register ranges and notice that the gray area of the middle register can borrow from each of the surrounding heavy and light register to form its own unique timbre. The usual belt range is the middle register.

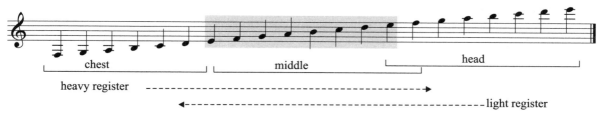

FIGURE 6-4. Register ranges in women

Vocal Registers in Men

Men also have three usable registers with many similarities to the women's registers. The three registers are chest, head, and falsetto, and they function in much the same way as the female registers. The major distinction between the male and female registers is the use of chest voice. Men can use their chest voice through a much wider range than women, and in some cases it may be the only register used.

Chest Voice

A man's chest voice extends from his lowest notes to anywhere from D to F♯ at the top of the range, at which point the head voice begins to blend in or there will be a break in the sound. The speaking voice is usually in chest register. When using chest voice, or heavy registration, the glottis closes completely during almost half of the cycle of vibration, and the full length of the vocal folds meet. The folds are also thicker and have wider amplitude in movement. Chest voice is rich in harmonic overtones and has a deeper and often more natural sound. It's sometimes called *real voice*. As in women's voices, there should be an adjustment toward the head voice starting at about the middle of the chest voice range so that the change into head voice won't be too abrupt.

Head Voice

The man's head voice is somewhat similar to the woman's middle voice, in that it uses a blend of heavy and light registers. The soft palate is more lifted as the cricothyroid activity stretches the ligament of the vocal cord to a more taut position. The male head voice is best suited, however, to what is called a *covered* position. This means that the vocalis muscle remains active but there is a narrowing or closing of vowel sounds with slightly increased airflow. The vowel sounds are modified to a somewhat darker pronunciation and the throat feels like a vertical tube. The man's head voice mixture is more closely related to his chest voice, whereas the woman's middle voice is more closely related to her head voice. The more open and less covered approach will sound very bright and more suited to a Broadway style of voice.

Falsetto

The highest part of the man's range is called *falsetto*. This has a high, light sound similar to a flute. The vocalis muscle is completely relaxed while the cricothyroids are contracted and pulling the ligaments to their most stretched position. Because of the rapid frequency of the high pitch, the cords are unable to fully close with each vibration. Rock and pop singers frequently use falsetto voice, such as artists Frankie Vallee, the Bee Gees, and Prince.

FACT

The term *falsetto* comes from the Italian word *falso*, meaning "imitation" or "fake." Some feel this sound is an imitation of a woman's soprano voice and has been used for singing female roles in theater and opera. Even though it's not considered to be a man's full voice, it is now a legitimate register and used frequently in rock and popular music.

TRACK 17

The approximate ranges of the three registers are shown in the following scale. Remember that exact points of transition will vary from one singer to another.

FIGURE 6-5. Vocal registers in men

Blending Registers

It's important to move freely between registers rather than try to hold the placement of one register into the pitch range of the next register. One of the greatest challenges of good vocal technique is the ability to move through the registers smoothly. This will require adjustments of breath, position of the larynx, and vowel modification. While you're singing, there is no time to think of these things or to carefully maneuver through each transition, or *passaggio*. That's why it becomes essential to regularly practice the exercises designed for this purpose until they become part of your muscle memory. The goal is always one seamless voice in which there's no audible transition between registers.

One vocal register should never suddenly shift to another register. There is always some overlap between any two registers. Imagine the colors of a rainbow blending together and notice that there are no definite lines where the colors change, but rather a subtle merging of two colors until the transition is complete. This same sort of transition is the goal of a unified voice with the smooth blending of registers.

There is a small range of notes that will overlap any two registers. These notes are referred to by various terms such as *passaggio*, or *passageway*, *a bridge*, or *a lift*. All are descriptive of the sensation of moving from one position to another. These points of transition occur at specific pitches because the vibrations increase and become too rapid to handle in the same way as the lower notes in an ascending line. If you don't adjust the position at that point, the voice will sound pushed and strained, and then eventually break or crack. This is usually embarrassing to a singer and sometimes causes people to give up singing altogether. This can be adjusted by using a gentle yawning action, allowing the larynx to move down and the soft palate up, which will create the feeling of a more vertical position in the throat. Conversely, you will also need to make an adjustment to move smoothly from a higher register to a lower one by adding in more of the chest resonance. If this doesn't occur, the sound will be too weak to project. Learning how to blend through this bridge area can take time, but is definitely worth the effort.

Passaggio

The description of methods used to make this adjustment is often subjective and dependent on the individual singer. Most singers describe the feeling of the passaggio as a narrowing, as if going through a short tunnel from one chamber to another. You might also visualize the narrow neck of an hourglass as the bridge between two registers, with each large chamber representing the ease and openness of the arrival into the next register.

This description of narrowing means that you can literally narrow the structure physically. Look in the mirror at the lines from the edge of your nose to the outside corners of your mouth, called the *nasolabial folds*, and notice that they spread out like the sides of a triangle. Now open your mouth and try to make these lines parallel. You might also feel your nose narrowing as you do this. This will alter the position of the larynx as well and help you navigate the passaggio. Male singers can see that the Adam's apple lowers slightly. Keeping your tongue forward, notice that it narrows as well.

The vowel pronunciation will automatically adjust away from a bright vowel to a narrower and more neutral sound if you hold this physical position in the mouth, tongue, and jaw. As you cross the passaggio, the *ee* vowel adjusts to *eu* and the *ah* vowel adjusts to *uh*. Add to this position a slight lowering of the jaw by lifting the soft palate. This can be achieved by imagining yourself yawning gently or inhaling a pleasant aroma, such as flowers. Some singers, and especially choral directors, might refer to this action as *a lift*, or *a lift of the breath*. The air pressure across the vocal cords can be controlled by the use of appoggio (see Chapter 3) and shouldn't be sudden or too strong. Think of the gear changes in a car. If you try to move through them harshly or suddenly, the gears will scrape against each other rather than mesh properly.

Exercises for Blending Registers

While singing these exercises, pay attention to the feeling created by specific positions. If you are moving through the notes comfortably, see if you can come up with your own images to help guide you through passaggio. These exercises are also included in your full lesson and warmup in Chapter 9.

EXERCISE 6-4

TRACK 18

1. Slide through the notes of your comfortable range on "ee." Think of imitating the sound of a siren. Remember to always begin the sound with a silent *h* and keep your lower jaw relaxed by focusing on the air across the roof of the mouth and the soft palate.
2. Listen for any breaks in the siren and try the narrower position through these notes.

EXERCISE 6-5

TRACK 19

1. Beginning on "ee," sing down the five-note scale.
2. As you descend the scale, pull your lips into an *oo* position, while still singing the *ee* vowel.
3. Keep this narrow position as you ascend the scale.
4. Pull your lips in again on the last note. Try to feel the movement of vibrations from the mask on the high note to the chest on the low note.

ee

FIGURE 6-6. Exercise 6-5

EXERCISE 6-6

TRACK 20

1. Sing the descending scale using the word "yawn." Watch yourself in the mirror to achieve the narrowest position of the nasolabial folds. Remember the lift in the soft palate.

Yawn
(Hold the vowel "aw" until the end of last note, then say the "n")

FIGURE 6-7. Exercise 6-6

EXERCISE 6-7

TRACK 21

1. Sing the five-note scale starting on "ah."
2. Move toward "eu" on the top note.
3. Move back to "ah" on the lower notes.

Try to feel the narrower position in the throat on the top notes.

FIGURE 6-8. Exercise 6-7

Always remember that the goal is one fluid voice throughout your entire range. By blending through these changes of register, you mix the color and quality of one part of your voice into the other parts, so that really you could think of your entire voice as a vocal mixture.

CHAPTER 7

Diction

The human voice is the only musical instrument that uses words to communicate its message. How the music and text support each other has fascinated composers, lyricists, singers, and audiences for well over a thousand years. And hasn't everyone felt that feeling of frustration when they can't understand the words. How many times have you been surprised when you read the lyrics to a song you thought you understood? Learning how to articulate words clearly is important in almost all styles of singing in order to convey meaning, and it takes a little practice and awareness of the differences between speech and singing.

Vowels

Vowels are defined as sounds of speech having a continuous and uninterrupted airflow. They are often easier for a singer to grasp since they make up the bulk of your practice regimen. Most exercises use vowels exclusively in order to learn resonance and tone production, since a pure vowel can be sustained without moving any of the articulators. When singing the vowel within a word, however, singers often revert to common speech patterns and pronounce the vowel as they would when talking. The rhythmic differences in music demand that we extend words in unnatural lengths and patterns, and it's the vowels that will be affected by these changes.

Whenever you have to hold a word for a longer period of time in a song than you would in everyday speech, you'll need to sustain the tone of that note on the vowel rather than the consonant. The word *hold*, for example, is sung "hO – ld," not "hoLD." How you pronounce a sustained vowel can make or break both the beauty and the meaning of that word. The way the text is set to the music can also change natural rhythmic accents of speech. There may be times when the singer must accent a syllable in a word that wouldn't normally be accented in speech, but the singer must still make the word intelligible. In addition, singing lyrics presents the challenge of altering sound production according to the pitch. The same vowel cannot be sung in the same way on high C as it is on middle C, and the different vowels are practically impossible to tell apart when singing in a very high range.

The clear pronunciation of any vowel sound is closely related to the concept of resonance, which you read about in Chapter 5. Vowel tone is formed by the shape of the vocal tract, and in particular by the movement of the tongue to change that shape. The intent to say a certain vowel causes the tongue to move into a position that enables that sound. Slight variations of the tongue position will change the degree of openness in the throat and mouth, thereby altering the clarity and quality of the tone. Singers learn to feel and control these various positions in order to produce the clearest vowel tone.

Vowel Classification

The five English vowels are *a, e, i, o,* and *u.* Whereas some languages have pure vowel tones assigned to letters, English pronunciation includes many variations of these five letters. It's most helpful for singers to think in terms of vowel sounds rather than the actual letters. The same letter *a* has very different sounds in the words *cat, cape, call,* and *awe.* When you first learned to speak and read, vowels were usually defined phonetically as long or short, such as the long *a* in the word *bake* and the short *a* in the word *back.* Further distinctions to clarify and better define vowel sounds for singers depend on the position of the lips, tongue, jaw, and soft palate. These distinctions fall into three main categories:

- forward, central, and back
- close, mid, and open
- rounded and unrounded

Using these more refined descriptions, there are more than twenty vowel sounds represented by the five letters. The style of music will determine how precise you'll need to be in your pronunciation. Certainly a rock song won't demand the same clarity as choral music.

QUESTIONS

How do I know if my pronunciation is correct?
The most precise way to achieve accurate pronunciation is the use of the International Phonetic Alphabet (IPA). This is a phonetic alphabet that assigns a particular symbol to each different sound. It was established in 1886 to unify a systematic code of pronunciation in many languages, and it is still the best method to learn clear diction. You'll find a complete chart of these symbols in Appendix A.

Forward Vowels

Forward vowels, also called *front vowels*, are defined by the shape of the tongue. The intent to voice certain vowel sounds creates an arch in the tongue. The highest point of the arch is toward the front of the tongue in forward vowels. The forward vowels are listed in order of the height of the arch position:

- *ee* as in *meet*
- *i* as in *mitt*
- *ay* as in *mate*
- *eh* as in *met*
- *a* as in *mat*

Say these words and notice the position of your tongue. Be sure to keep the tip of the tongue touching the back of the bottom teeth and the lips in a neutral and relaxed position. The soft palate should be raised.

FIGURE 7-1.
Forward, central, and back vowels

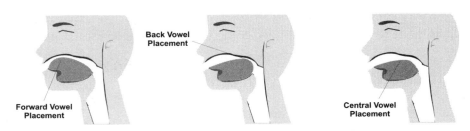

TONGUE POSITIONS OF VOWELS

Back Vowels

The back vowels, as you might guess, create the highest point of the arch in the back of the tongue. They are once again listed in order according to the height of the arch:

- *oo* as in *too*
- *oo* as in *took*
- *o* as in *go*

- *aw* as in *saw*
- *ah* as in *father* or *lot*

Notice the position of the tongue as you say each of these words. As with the front vowels, the tongue should touch the back of the bottom teeth and the soft palate is raised. The lips, however, are rounded forward to pronounce the back vowels.

ALERT!

You will find that *ah* as in *father* is usually listed as a back vowel, but it actually is unique enough to be considered in a separate category by itself. The tongue doesn't arch in the same way for *ah*, but rather lies in more of a flat position in the mouth and has a slight lengthwise groove down the center. Look in the mirror to see if you can identify the difference in this vowel.

Central Vowels

The arched shape is in the middle of the tongue for the central vowels. There are two vowel sounds using this position, but the most important consideration in this category is the stress of the syllable. A stressed syllable has a stronger emphasis than the other syllables surrounding it in the word. The other syllables may either have weaker stress or they may be unstressed altogether. The unstressed syllable in many words is sounded with a schwa, which is defined as a neutral vowel:

- *uh* as in *under*
- *ur* as in *her*
- *uh* (schwa) as in the first syllable of *above* or the second syllable of *sofa*

When singing central vowels, the jaw should be slightly relaxed and the lips can be neutral or somewhat rounded. The soft palate should be raised.

When singing any vowel, the tip of the tongue should touch the back of the bottom teeth. The tongue should always be forward in this way except when needed to pronounce certain consonants. It should then return to its regular forward placement, touching the teeth. It's a strong muscle and will close the back of the throat if allowed to move out of this position. Remember to check yourself in the mirror.

Close and Open Vowels

Vowels can also be defined by the height of their position, meaning the distance between the tongue and the roof of the mouth. If you look at the previous lists of vowel sounds, the vowels at the top of each list are more close, or high, and toward the bottom of each list the vowels are open, or low. For example, the words *meet* and *too* have close vowels and the words *mat* and *lot* have open vowels.

This way of categorizing a vowel affects the singer primarily in defining how to feel the opening in the mouth. Rather than thinking of opening the mouth from the front, use the method of inhalation discussed in Chapter 3. Imagine the beginning of a yawn and notice the release of tension in the jaw. Now pronounce the words in the previous lists and notice the sensation of a relaxed jaw. See if you can identify the distance between the tongue and the roof of the mouth.

Rounded and Unrounded Vowels

A vowel is rounded if the lips are forward in a rounded position. Unrounded vowels require a neutral placement of the lips. Often, beginning singers will open the lips into a wide horizontal position resembling a smile. While the feeling of a slight smile can help lift the soft palate and open the back of the throat, a wide smile will work against you by lowering the soft palate. When rounding the lips, be careful not to pull so far forward that you create tension. You can practice these positions in a mirror to check yourself.

FIGURE 7-2.
Smile position
is too wide

FIGURE 7-3.
Unrounded:
neutral position

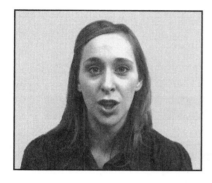

FIGURE 7-4.
Rounded
position

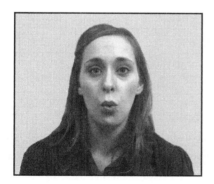

Usually the lips will be most rounded for the back vowels and unrounded for the front vowels. Try saying the word "boot" and notice the position of your lips that's necessary for the back vowel *oo*. Now say "bat" and see the lips move into the neutral position. Finally, say the word "beet" and check in the mirror to make sure that your lips have not moved into the horizontal smile position. If so, make the correction toward the neutral position of unrounded lips. Remember, your lips should not be held in a wide smile since it will affect the length needed in the vocal tract.

You might hear directors and teachers refer to a sound as bright or dark. Changing the degree of brightness in a vowel is accomplished by rounding the lips and shaping the tongue for an *oo* vowel to get a darker sound and opening the position slightly to an *ee* position for a brighter sound. The same vowel can have degrees of brightness or darkness. Broadway singers tend to use a much brighter sound than classical singers. The classical voice emphasizes a longer vertical position in the throat, which creates a darker sound. Be careful to avoid the extremes, however, as a sound that is too bright can be grating, and a sound that is too dark can be boring.

Sing the vowels "ee-ah-oo" on a single pitch and notice the changes of position in the tongue and lips as you move from one vowel to the next. Watch the positions in the mirror and then turn away from the mirror to get a better sense of the feeling of space in the mouth.

Diphthongs

A diphthong is a vowel sound that is actually composed of two pure vowels combined into one syllable by moving from the first vowel position to the second in a smooth transition. It's considered to be a single vowel unit. English has many diphthongs, while some other languages have none. Here are some of the more common examples:

Word	Diphthong	Vowel Combination
boy	oi or oy	aw + i
day	ai or ay	eh + ee
out	ou or ow	bright ah + oo
night	I	ah + ee
use	ew	ee + oo
owe	oa	oh + oo

In singing, diphthongs should be treated in much the same way you would sing a vowel followed by a consonant. Sing the syllable on the first vowel and then move to the second vowel position at the end of the beat. For example, if you have to sing the word "day" for two beats, hold "deh" as long as you can before moving to the "ee" at the end of the second beat. Try it, and then sing it again the wrong way, moving immediately to the ending "ee" as we do in speech. You'll hear right away the difference between DEH-ee and deh-EE.

Vowel Modification

In the lower notes and in the middle of your range, every word of the song should be clear and intelligible. As you sing higher in your range, however, you'll no longer be able to pronounce a vowel in the same way. The position and shape of the vocal tract must change in order to sing high notes, and this change will automatically adjust the vowel sound. As you approach and cross your passaggio, the larynx must remain low and the soft palate must rise a bit higher.

Pronunciation of a word on a high note (approaching and above passaggio) may adjust automatically if you are singing the note in the correct vertical position. If this is the case, your only job is to accept the sound you hear inside your head; don't try to force it to your concept of a more "correct" vowel pronunciation.

If, on the other hand, you find yourself unable to resist singing the vowel as you would speak it, you'll need to consciously narrow the sound. This means that you will have to think another vowel sound that may sound wrong in your head, but will achieve the length of the vocal tract needed for the high pitch. It actually ends up sounding like the original vowel when put in context with the word, and it certainly allows the space for a more beautiful tone. Exact adjustments to narrower vowels are personal to each singer, but some common modifications include the vowel *ah* moving toward *uh*, and *ee* modifying to the French vowel *eu*.

TRACK 23

Consonants

The remaining letters of the alphabet are consonants, but as with the vowels, there may be more than one sound for a single consonant. A consonant is defined as a sound of speech created by an interruption in the flow of air. Technically, a vowel is a period of tone, whereas a consonant is a period of noise since it actually stops the sound briefly. Articulation is the use of parts of the mouth and throat, called *articulators*, to clearly produce the consonant sounds. The consonant articulators are the tongue, lips, teeth, lower jaw, and palate. The glottis is an articulator for the consonant *h*.

Healthy singing always requires that you sing primarily on the vowel. Vowels give your voice musical tone and are the predominant part of each syllable. Try to speak a sentence without the vowel and you'll find it impossible to communicate. But on the other hand, take the same sentence and leave out all the consonants. This can be a good way to practice lines of your music, but obviously no words can be formed. The consonants need to be pronounced quickly and clearly to keep the lyrics intelligible without interrupting the beauty of the musical line.

Consonant Classification

Consonants are divided into identifiable categories according to three main sets of criteria. They can be classified by the articulator used to stop the airflow, by the way the interruption of air occurs, or by the voicing of the consonant. Each of these three methods of classification can be useful to know if you have any problems with articulation. If you practice saying and singing each of these sets of consonants, you can familiarize yourself with sounds and avoid some of the common problems for singers.

FACT

A standard guide for studying pronunciation is *The Singer's Manual of English Diction*, by Madeleine Marshall. This book offers a complete guide to clear enunciation of each letter and sound. It also lists rules for how to connect words smoothly and distinctly. This is an important reference book for any singer. Another great resource is *Diction for Singers* by Joan Wall.

Articulators

Look at this list of articulators and the sounds they produce. Practice saying each letter while feeling the place in your mouth or throat that identifies the point where the air is stopped.

Articulator	Sound
Both lips	p, b, m, w, wh
Upper teeth against lower lip	f, v
Tongue and upper teeth	th
Tip of tongue and hard palate	t, d, l, n
Body of tongue and hard palate	s, z, sh, zh
Tongue and soft palate	k, g, ng
Glottis	h
Sides of tongue and upper teeth	r

Voicing

Certain pairs of consonants are formed in the same way and use the same articulators, but one is voiced, or has vibration, and the other is not voiced. An unvoiced consonant can't make any sound by itself but will be heard as soon as its neighboring vowel is voiced.

Say the consonants in the following list and notice that you can't isolate the unvoiced half of the list. If you can say it, it's because there's a vowel following the sound. But you should be able to feel the humming vibration of the voiced consonants.

Voiced	Unvoiced
b (bat)	p (pat)
z (zoo)	s (so)
d (den)	t (ten)
g (give)	k (kit)
v (vast)	f (fast)
th (this)	th (thought)

Exercises

Exercises for articulation are some of the most enjoyable singing exercises. The first three exercises work the different articulators while maintaining a clear vowel tone. The other two exercises are called *tongue twisters* because the combinations of certain consonants are hard to manage when singing or speaking quickly. Many people have heard tongue twisters as children and laughed at how difficult and tangled the words can end up sounding. Practice these exercises slowly at first and then try to build up your speed.

EXERCISE 7-1

TRACK 24

1. While using your hands to hold your cheeks out, sing the following exercise. Make sure your tongue is touching the back of your bottom teeth.
2. Drop your hands and repeat the exercise with the feeling of puffing out the cheeks.

FIGURE 7-5. Hold your cheeks out for the first part of the exercise

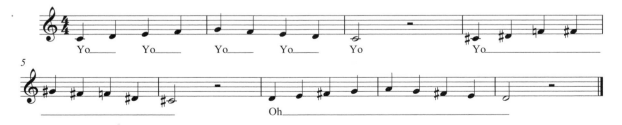

FIGURE 7-6. Exercise 7-1

EXERCISE 7-2

TRACK 25

1. Keeping the *oh* tone as open as possible, sing "lo-do" using only your tongue to form the *l* and the *d*. Keep your jaw still, which will force your tongue to do the work.
2. Repeat the exercise on "na-ta."
3. As you progress to "ya-ga," keep the front of your tongue against the back of your bottom teeth and your jaw still. Feel the movement in the back of the tongue to form the "ya" and the "ga".

FIGURE 7-7. Exercise 7-2

EXERCISE 7-3

TRACK 26

1. Alternate the syllables "be" and "de" and sing as evenly as possible.
2. While you are singing, massage your cheeks gently to prevent tension.
3. As indicated on the CD, drop your hands, change to the vowel *ee*, and continue the exercise.

FIGURE 7-8. Exercise 7-3

If you need to loosen your tongue at any time before or during these exercises, review the flexed tongue position included in the physical warmup section of Chapter 2. The tongue is a strong set of muscles and can easily get too tense when trying to sing the following tongue twisters.

EXERCISE 7-4

TRACK 27

1. Begin by speaking the phrase "red leather, yellow leather" very slowly.
2. Gradually build speed while keeping all the syllables even. As you get faster, begin to feel the accents on "red" and "yellow."
3. Sing the exercise while keeping these accents.

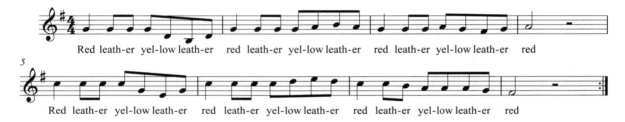

FIGURE 7-9. Exercise 7-4

EXERCISE 7-5

TRACK 28

1. Speak the phrase "they threw three thick things," slowly at first. Only go as fast as you can while maintaining accuracy with the words.
2. After you've practiced speaking the sentence, then try singing it. Notice the difference between the voiced *th* of "they" and the unvoiced *th* in the other words.

FIGURE 7-10. Exercise 7-5

There are many more phrases and sentences using famous tongue twisters that are fun to practice. You can even make up a melody of your own to go with words that are challenging to pronounce.

Common Problems

English is one of the hardest languages to pronounce easily and clearly while singing. Many singers favor Italian for the pure vowels in the language, making it much easier to maintain the quality of tone, but for the most part, we need to master English. Look through the following list of some common challenges to clear diction and try to apply them to your music:

- Don't voice the consonant too soon after a vowel. Elongate the vowel tone and then articulate the consonant quickly.
- Link words together in a phrase unless doing so changes the meaning of the second word. In other words, link "one note" but not "my ears," which could sound like "my years."
- Articulate the final consonant of the word.
- Sing only one consonant when double consonants are in a word. For example, sing only one *t* in the word "better."
- Soften any *r* that precedes a consonant or ends a word.
- Raise the tip of the tongue to the palate at the back of the top teeth for the consonant *l*. Don't let the double *ll* close the back of your throat.
- Use a glottal attack if necessary to articulate a word beginning with a vowel.
- Use the middle range of your voice for lyrics in pop music. The words will be clearer without getting a more classical sound.

Remember that the goal is to make your speech, whether spoken or sung, as natural as possible. Perfecting the quality of your speech shouldn't make you sound too formal or affected. Effective communication is always about reaching your audience and telling the story of the song. That means the words should be clearly understood, but never overemphasized in a way that sounds unnatural.

CHAPTER 8

Voice Classification

Your voice can be classified as a particular type depending on your range and the part of your voice that feels most comfortable while singing. Some people have a preference for the type of voice they'd like, but nature has already given you your best voice. Knowing your voice type helps you in choosing the songs you'd like to sing, but it's not important to classify your voice early in your training, since the goal is to achieve healthy vocal production in general. You may get an idea after reading this chapter which vocal type might be your best match.

Basic Vocal Types

The human voice is divided into six basic vocal types. Women's voices can be categorized as soprano, mezzo-soprano, or alto (also called *contralto*). Men's voices are classified as tenor, baritone, or bass. Within these six types are further divisions that apply primarily to classical voices. Your vocal type is determined by a number of factors, including range, passaggio, vocal color, and area of greatest comfort and power. There is crossover of these types and you may have a vocal quality that can be a combination of more than one category. For example, you could be a high baritone with tenor qualities.

FACT

Vocal types are also commonly divided into four parts: soprano, alto, tenor, and bass. Choral music often lists parts as SATB, which refers to these four parts. Similarly, most church hymns are divided into four parts. The mezzo-soprano and the baritone usually sing the alto and bass parts, respectively, or can choose which part to sing according to the range of the music.

Many voices can develop an impressive range and are certainly not limited by their vocal type. One of the most important aspects to consider in classification is not necessarily the full range but rather the tessitura, which is the part of your vocal range that feels most comfortable, has natural power and resonance, and sounds the best. When you are singing in your natural tessitura, there is an effortless feeling and the sense that you could sing for long periods of time without tiring. Stretching your voice to the outside extremes of your range may sound good for a few notes, but you might not be able to sustain a melody that rests only in those more stressful areas of your voice.

Another element to consider is vocal timbre. Timbre refers to the color or quality of your voice, as you learned in Chapter 5. Some voices sound rich and full while others might sound bright and clear. These differences in tone color help define the type of voice. Timbre can be a strong indicator of a vocal type if two singers have similar ranges but a different quality and sound in their voices.

Soprano

The soprano is the highest of the women's voice types. A typical soprano range is middle C through high C, two octaves above. A soprano can sing notes lower than middle C but will probably not have the strength or power that a lower voice type will have on the same note. Many sopranos can also sing well above high C, a range primarily heard in opera, but also in some pop riffs. A soprano's tessitura, or comfort range, is in the upper part of her range, not the lower or middle voice, which can be difficult to project.

A soprano has a strong head voice, and the tone color is usually bright and clear. There are some soprano voices, however, that are so full and rich they could be mistaken for a mezzo-soprano. A soprano's voice might be described as having the quality of a flute or a bell or a warm and velvety sound, depending on the individual voice. The soprano generally moves out of her chest voice and blends in her head voice beginning on E♭ just above middle C, and has a passaggio (passage to the next register) around the F or F♯ on the top line of the staff.

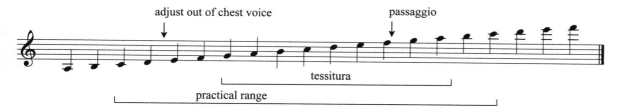

FIGURE 8-1. General soprano range and tessitura

Soprano Roles

Sopranos are often the leading roles in musical theater and opera. Musical theater roles include Maria in *West Side Story*, Sarah in *Guys and Dolls*, and Christine in *Phantom of the Opera*. Some soprano roles in opera are Mimi in *La Bohème*, Pamina in *The Magic Flute*, and Gilda in *Rigoletto*.

Some Famous Sopranos

There are far too many gifted sopranos to name, but if you are unfamiliar with some of these singers, it would be worthwhile to listen to them.

Classical sopranos:
- Joan Sutherland
- Maria Callas
- Montserrat Caballé
- Natalie Dessay
- Renée Fleming
- Beverly Sills

Musical theater sopranos:
- Julie Andrews
- Kristin Chenoweth
- Barbara Cook
- Rebecca Luker
- Gertrude Lawrence

Popular music sopranos:
- Mariah Carey
- Christina Aguilera
- Kate Bush
- Jessica Simpson
- Diana Ross

Mezzo-Soprano

The mezzo-soprano can have the same range as a soprano but is able to extend her voice to the lower notes beginning around A♭ below middle C. Her sound is warmer, richer, and darker than the soprano. The comfortable range for a mezzo is lower than that of a soprano, with a ringing quality and strength in the middle voice. While a mezzo may have a high C in her range, she wouldn't choose material that stays in that upper range for an extended period of time. She will blend out of chest voice and into head voice at the same middle E♭, but approaches passaggio at approximately E♭ or E (top space of the staff), a step lower than the soprano.

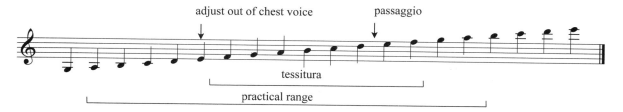

FIGURE 8-2. General mezzo-soprano range and tessitura

Mezzo-Soprano Roles

The mezzo roles may be leading ladies, but are often the earthier characters such as a best friend or a villainess. Some musical theater roles are Lilli in *Kiss Me, Kate*, Rizzo in *Grease*, and Nancy in *Oliver*. Opera roles include the lead character of Carmen in *Carmen*, Dalila in *Samson et Dalila*, and Rosina in *The Barber of Seville*.

Some Famous Mezzo-Sopranos

Mezzo-sopranos may typically be secondary roles, but the following women have stood out in this category and are certainly worth a listen.

Classical mezzo-sopranos:
- Marilyn Horne
- Cecilia Bartoli
- Frederica von Stade
- Olga Borodina

Musical theater mezzo-sopranos:
- Patti LuPone
- Audra McDonald
- Idina Menzel
- Ethel Merman
- Mary Martin

Popular music mezzo-sopranos:
- Aretha Franklin
- Bette Midler
- Judy Garland
- Sarah McLachlan
- Tina Turner
- Celine Dion
- Whitney Houston

Alto

The alto, or contralto, is the lowest of the female voices. An alto's range is generally E or F below middle C to G above the top line of the staff. The lower part of the middle voice is a comfortable part of her voice and has great resonance. The timbre is dark, warm, and rich. A true alto voice is considered to be somewhat rare and unusual, and there are fewer roles written for an alto. Realistically, there is crossover between the alto and mezzo because of a similarity of timbre and tessitura. The range differs by approximately one step for both general range and passaggio, and either voice type could handle most music written for a rich-sounding middle voice.

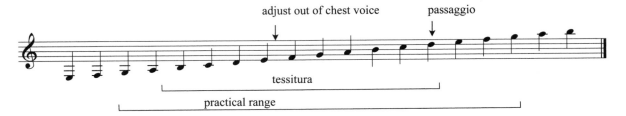

FIGURE 8-3. General alto range and tessitura

Alto Roles

As mentioned, alto roles are rare and really could be categorized much the same as mezzo roles. Both the mezzo and the alto sing the "belt" roles in musical theater. The lower range is used in musical theater roles such as Aurora in *Kiss of the Spider Woman*, Fraulein Schneider in *Cabaret*, and

Mama Rose in *Gypsy*. Opera roles include Erda in *Das Rheingold* and *Siegfried*, Olga in *Eugene Onegin*, and Maddalena in *Rigoletto*. Gilbert and Sullivan's operettas also regularly include an alto role, such as Ruth in *The Pirates of Penzance*.

Some Famous Altos

The alto voice is distinct and different. The following woman have managed to make that uniqueness work in their favor and are certainly worth your time to listen to.

Classical altos:
- Marion Anderson
- Ewa Podles
- Clara Butt

Musical theater altos:
- Lotte Lenya
- Ute Lemperer
- Lauren Bacall
- Jennifer Holliday

Popular music altos:
- Alicia Keys
- Annie Lennox
- Cher
- Amy Winehouse
- Anita Baker
- Karen Carpenter
- Tracy Chapman
- Queen Latifah

All examples of both roles and singers are only tiny representative lists of that category. Given the descriptions of vocal types, see if you can add some of your favorite singers to these lists. Listen mostly for vocal quality and not just for the range.

Tenor

The tenor is the highest of the male voices. The range is similar to that of the soprano but sounds an octave lower. The tenor voice has a brilliant and ringing quality with strength in the upper part of the range. Unlike the soprano, a tenor can carry the heavy registration up through the middle voice with very little transition until the passaggio, which occurs around F or F♯ on the top line of the treble staff. The tenor's passaggio notes are often considered to pose more difficulty than other voice types and he will need careful training and practice to achieve an elongated throat position and a smooth transition across the passaggio. The tenor quality has a good deal of head voice in his overall register mixture, and he might have trouble getting his voice to carry below middle E♭ on the treble staff.

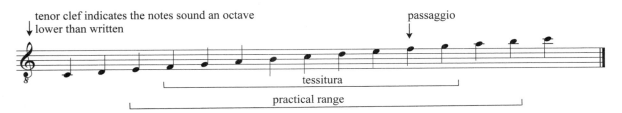

FIGURE 8-4. General tenor range and tessitura

Remember that his voice sounds an octave lower than the written range.

Tenor Roles

Tenors are often the leading men in theater and opera. It's a popular voice type that tends to get a great deal of attention from an audience. Think of the celebrity status of the Three Tenors. Some tenor roles in musical theater are Tony in *West Side Story*, Chris in *Miss Saigon*, Jean Valjean in *Les Misérables*, and Jesus in *Jesus Christ Superstar*. Opera roles include Pinkerton in *Madame Butterfly*, Radamés in *Aida*, Alfredo in *La Traviata*, and Edgardo in *Lucia di Lammermoor*.

Some Famous Tenors

These men have become standouts in the tenor range.

Classical tenors:
- Luciano Pavarotti
- Plácido Domingo
- José Carreras
- Enrico Caruso

Musical theater tenors:
- Michael Crawford
- Colm Wilkinson

Popular music tenors:
- Andrea Bocelli
- Elton John
- Jon Bon Jovi
- Justin Timberlake
- Usher
- Clay Aiken

Baritone

The baritone utilizes predominantly the middle range of the male voice and is probably the vocal category of most men. This voice type tends to have a rich, warm, and lyrical quality and sounds strong in the middle part of the range. The overall range is generally A below middle C (written in the treble staff, but sounding one octave lower) to G above the top line of the staff. This is the same range as the mezzo-soprano, only it sounds an octave lower. The natural passaggio is also similar to the mezzo, around E♭ to E on the top space if written in the treble staff.

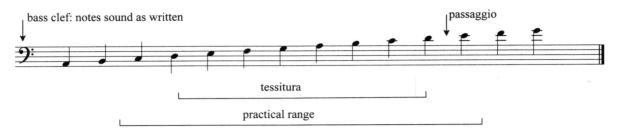

FIGURE 8-5. General baritone range and tessitura

ALERT!

Men's solo vocal music is written in the treble staff except in opera scores. The man's voice, however, sounds an octave lower than the pitch as written. Middle C written in the treble staff, for example, is actually sung on the pitch of C in the second space of the bass clef. See Chapter 12 for more information about reading vocal music.

Baritone Roles

Baritone roles in musical theater are the most plentiful of all the male vocal categories. Some roles are Beast in *Beauty and the Beast*, Billy Bigelow in *Carousel*, Dr. Frank-N-Furter in *The Rocky Horror Show*, and El Gallo in *The Fantasticks*. Representative opera roles are Don Giovanni in *Don Giovanni*, Figaro in *The Barber of Seville*, and Baron Scarpia in *Tosca*.

Some Famous Baritones

The following men are characteristic of the baritone voice and are worth a listen:

Classical baritones:
- Bryn Terfel
- Robert Merrill
- Thomas Hampson
- Sherrill Milnes

Musical theater baritones:
- Richard Kiley
- Nathan Lane
- Robert Goulet
- Alfred Drake
- Brian Stokes Mitchell

Popular music baritones:
- Josh Groban
- Frank Sinatra
- Nat King Cole
- Elvis Presley
- Barry Manilow
- Michael Feinstein

Bass

The bass is the lowest male voice. This voice type is rich and dark in tone color. It can have a heavy sound while still maintaining great ringing quality. The range is from low E or F to the E above middle C, with its greatest power and comfort in the octave below middle C and passaggio falling on D one step higher. Basses and baritones often share repertoire, and a newer classification of bass-baritone has become a popular description of the range of low male roles in theater.

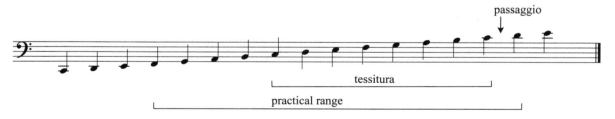

FIGURE 8-6. General bass range and tessitura

Bass Roles

The bass is often the villain, comedic character, or older man in theater and opera. Musical theater roles include Judd Fry in *Oklahoma*, Joe in *Showboat*, Audrey II in *Little Shop of Horrors*, and Arvide in *Guys and Dolls*. Some examples of operatic roles are Don Basilio in *The Barber of Seville*, Mephistopheles in *Faust*, and Hagen in *Götterdämmerung*. Most Gilbert and Sullivan operettas also have prominent bass roles.

Some Famous Basses

Often cast as kings, priests, villains, or smooth operators, these basses have made a name for themselves in their respective categories.

Classical basses:
- Samuel Ramey
- Boris Christoff
- Nicolai Ghiaurov
- Jerome Hines
- Ezio Pinza

Musical theater basses:
- Paul Robeson
- Thurl Ravenscroft
- Ezio Pinza

Popular music basses:
- Barry White
- Bill Medley

Finding Your Vocal Type

Don't feel you need to be in a hurry to classify your voice type. It's really best to train for a healthy voice in general and then notice the areas of your range where it feels most comfortable. Many voices can stretch to the outer ends of their range, but you shouldn't spend a lot of time there. A singer can have an exciting sound when a few notes are at the top or bottom of his or her range, but it can also sound pushed and just as uncomfortable for the audience as it is for the singer. More important, you can damage your voice with the constant strain of singing outside of your comfortable range. The predominant tessitura of the song should match your tessitura as a singer.

It's important that you choose material that allows you to stay within an easy range. It does no good to continually sing out of your range. In fact, it can do harm by weakening your voice and creating muscle memory of poor technique. Let your throat be your guide: if it feels bad, don't do it!

The term *tessitura* can also refer to the area of your song where most of the melody is written. If you look at your music, you'll notice that a large percentage of the notes are within one octave. That would be the tessitura of that music. Even if notes stretch above and below that octave, you can determine if this is good material for you if the tessitura is right for your voice.

Trying Out the Ranges

Listen to the CD and sing along as you look at the following scale. Track 29 demonstrates a general vocal range for men, followed by a vocal range for women.

TRACK 29

FIGURE 8-7. Sing along with this scale and mark your comfortable notes

As you sing along with the track, mark on the scale which notes feel comfortable for you. Then compare them with the following chart. This will give you an idea of which vocal type is the closest match at this stage in your training. As you continue to study and grow, your range and vocal quality will probably change, so don't be too quick to make any final decisions.

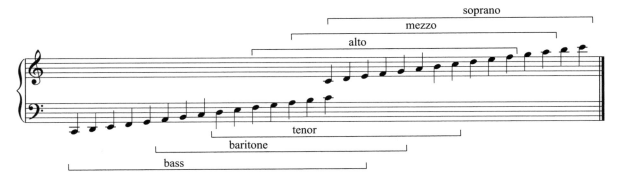

FIGURE 8-8. Match your comfortable notes to this chart

Knowing your vocal type is most important for choosing material to sing, deciding which roles may be appropriate for you, and for intelligently answering audition notices. Otherwise, you only need to know the range that shows off the best quality of your voice and feels the best for extensive singing.

CHAPTER 9

A Basic Voice Class

Now you've had a chance to try the exercises related to each separate area of concentration. In this chapter you'll be able to put them all together in one continuous practice session. Using the CD tracks, you can sing this basic group of exercises every day. Remember that you need constant repetition in order to build muscle memory. Soon you'll find that the body responds without as much effort or concentration. This chapter is your basic class, or warmup, but be sure you've read each of the previous chapters that relate to each section of the class.

Warmup Exercises

The first set of exercises is designed to warm up the body and the voice. Approach these exercises gently and without excessive force. Remember to use the posture and body support you learned in Chapter 2, and be sure to avoid rigidity or tension. These exercises will help you stay relaxed and limber. Feel free to stop and repeat them if you begin to feel any tension in the vocal exercises.

Read through the exercises of the physical warmup or just follow along with Track 31 on the CD.

Physical Warmup

EXERCISE 9-1

TRACK 31

1. Stand with your feet comfortably apart and lean over to touch your toes. Stretch over the right leg, then over the left leg, and back to center. Slowly roll up to a standing position.
2. Pull your shoulders up toward your ears, hold for three seconds, then release your shoulders down and relax. Repeat twice.
3. Slowly circle your head clockwise. Reverse the circle to counterclockwise. Center your head, lifting it up away from your shoulders.
4. Open your mouth as wide as possible, and then place the tip of your tongue behind your bottom front teeth. Press the middle of your tongue out in an arch shape while keeping the front of your tongue behind the teeth. Retract your tongue and close your mouth. Repeat twice. Gently move your jaw from side to side.

FIGURE 9-1.
Arched tongue

5. Place your hands on your ribs and breathe in until you feel the ribs expand on both sides, then slowly release. Breathe in again and feel the ribs in your back expand, then release slowly. Breathe into your belly and feel it expand, then release slowly. Repeat the breath in parallel plié position, arms forward in a circle as if holding a hoop straight out in front of you. Try to feel which muscles are working, especially the abdominals. (Refer to the breathing exercises in Chapter 3 if you need to check these positions.)

FIGURE 9-2. Plié with arms forward

Gentle Vocal Warmup

EXERCISE 9-2

TRACK 32

1. Hum through the lip trill in an easy range, then again as high as you can and as low as you can without creating any muscular tension. Keep an even flow of air throughout the exercise.

TRACK 33

2. Hum through the lip trill on octaves. Continue with the tongue trill (rolled *r*) on the descending sets. Remember to keep the air moving and to engage the abdominal muscles. Change to a hum on the octaves while trying to feel the vibration behind your nose. On the top note of each octave let your jaw open gently, keeping your lips closed.

3. Hum the five-note scale. Continue on the fourth set with a hum ascending the scale and "me" descending the scale. Try to keep the feeling of the hum forward in the mask and let the "ee" follow the same placement. Your mouth should remain almost closed for the descending "ee."

TRACK 35

4. Open your mouth to a comfortable position and then inhale through your mouth, as if you didn't want someone to see you yawning. Concentrate on the sensation and the cooler temperature of the air across the soft palate. After the inhalation, hold this open placement and exhale through your nose without lowering the yawn position. Repeat the yawn inhalation, exhale through your nose while maintaining the lifted soft palate and, after you feel the air through the nose, sigh out on "ha." Try to feel the same humming sensation from the previous exercise.

TRACK 36

5. Repeat the previous inhalation and exhalation. As you feel the air has started to flow through the nostrils, sigh "ha" on the descending pitch. Change the sigh to "hoo" (as in *noon*) as the pitch gets higher. The entire exercise should maintain the hum feeling.

TRACK 37

6. Using the same inhalation through the mouth and exhalation through the nose, sing the descending scales on "hoo." Repeat the exercise with "hoo-ee." The *h* is silent, but ensures that you have started the sound with air.

TRACK 38

7. Slide through the notes of your comfortable range on "ee." Think of imitating the sound of a siren. Remember to always begin the sound with a silent *h* and keep your lower jaw relaxed by focusing on the air across the roof of the mouth and the soft palate.

The warmup is an important part of your lesson, rehearsal, and performance. You'll need to make sure the air is moving evenly and that the muscles used in body support are engaged. These exercises will help to relieve tension that interferes with the voice and set up the proper placement.

Vocal Exercises

As you progress to the next set of exercises, try to be aware of the sensation in the roof of your mouth. Imagine the hard palate is a domed ceiling of a room you create inside your mouth. Also focus on the smile lines drawn from the outside of your nose to the corners of your mouth. Imagine adjusting those lines to be vertical and parallel, so that the middle of your face feels very long.

The vocal exercises in this lesson will be sung on the CD by both male and female voices. Since men and women sing in different octaves, you'll need to hear someone of the same gender singing the pitch as your reference note.

ALERT!

Remember to keep your lips and mouth in approximately the same position. Your lips should be forward but not pulled so much that you can see tension. Too much movement with the mouth will change the placement of the sound. Watch in a mirror to check yourself.

EXERCISE 9-3

TRACK 39

1. Keeping your lips forward and maintaining length in the center of your face, begin each set of this exercise with "ay" (as in *day*) and smoothly move the vowel tone toward "aw." Try to feel the vibration in the vicinity of the upper lip and nose, while holding the vertical throat position of "aw." Then continue through the vowel tones as indicated on the CD.

FIGURE 9-3. Keep the lips forward

ay   aw   ah

FIGURE 9-4. Exercise 9-3 Step 1

TRACK 40

2. Beginning on "ee," sing down the five-note scale. As you descend the scale, pull your lips into an *oo* position, while still singing the *ee* vowel. Keep this narrow position as you ascend the scale. Pull the lips in again on the last note. Try to feel the movement of vibrations from the mask on the high note to the chest on the low note.

FIGURE 9-5.
Mouth positions for
Exercise 9-3 Step 2

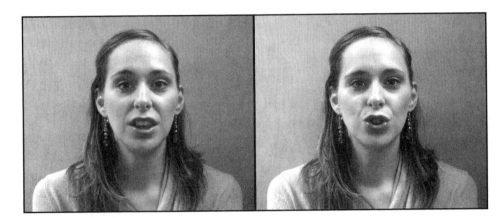

ee

(lips rounded)   (lips rounded)

FIGURE 9-6. Exercise 9-3 Step 2

TRACK 41

3. Curl your bottom lip around your lower teeth as you sing "ee" for the first three sets. Continue singing the same exercise with your lips forward for the next three sets.

FIGURE 9-7.
Mouth position
for Exercise 9-3
Step 3

ee_____

FIGURE 9-8. Exercise 9-3 Step 3

As indicated on the seventh set, change "ee" to "ah" in a smooth transition and continue descending the scale on "ah." In the lower notes of the scale, narrow the center lines of the face and use the French vowel *en* as demonstrated on the CD.

move smoothly from ee to ah

ee_____   ah_____

FIGURE 9-9. Exercise 9-3 Step 3 (continued)

4. Watch in the mirror to make sure that your mouth position stays long and narrow throughout the vowel changes. Your lips should be forward and away from your teeth. Begin with "hyoo," move to "oh," and finally "aw." Continue this exercise with the first sound "hyoo," but then sing "ay" (as in *day*), and finally "ee." Be sure to stay in the same position for "ay" and "ee" and don't spread your mouth into a wide smile.

FIGURE 9-10. Exercise 9-3 Step 4

5. Sing "yay-ee-oo-ah" on a single pitch. Try to feel the onset of "yay" in the hard palate; "ee" adds on the sensation of the tongue against the back of the bottom teeth; "oo" lengthens to add vibration in the chest; and finally "ah" is a cumulative combination of the first three vowels. Try not to lose the sensation of each vowel as you move to the next, but rather add each new placement sensation to the previous one.

6. Sing "ah" and continue to hold the tone while you pinch your nostrils closed with your thumb and forefinger. For this exercise, you should begin the tone on "ah" with your nostrils open. Then pinch your nostrils closed and continue to sing up the five-note scale. Release your nostrils while continuing to sing the highest note and check that the tone and sensation remain the same. While holding this open position, take a breath, re-attack the top note without pinching your nostrils, and continue down the scale. Change the vowel tones as you hear them on the CD.

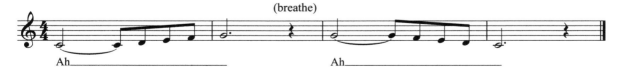

FIGURE 9-11. Exercise 9-3 Step 6

7. On the vowel *ee* begin the four-note ascending scale. As in the previous exercise, pinch your nostrils after starting the tone. Take your hand away while still holding the top note. The *ee* vowel should narrow its position toward *eu* as the pitch ascends. At the same time, the upper back teeth should lift to create a wider space between the upper and lower molars, giving the sensation of a square mouth. Hold this space open in the back while closing your lips in to descend the octave.

Ee

(round lips on bottom note)

FIGURE 9-12. Exercise 9-3 Step 7

8. Without allowing the tip of your tongue to leave the back of your lower teeth, sing "own-yee" on the descending scale as shown. Review the appoggio exercises in Chapter 3 and be sure to use the sensation of air gently pushing against the sternum.

own - yee   own - yee   own - yee   own - yee   own - yee

FIGURE 9-13. Exercise 9-3 Step 8

ESSENTIAL

Pinching your nostrils closed is a way to check the position of the soft palate. If the soft palate is high, the sound should remain the same whether your nostrils are open or closed. If your soft palate is lowered, you will have a nasal sound and will feel blocked when your nostrils are pinched closed. You can use this method to check the open position in your songs as well.

The exercises in this section will set placement and positions of the entire vocal mechanism to create the best resonance. They should feel comfortable in your body even if they require mental concentration and focus. Your body will eventually take on the positions without your even thinking about it.

High and Low Registers

Extending your range to higher and lower notes helps to develop both stretch and strength in your voice. You'll find that this work will not only extend your usable range, but also increase the power and control of the middle voice. The predominant range of your songs will be in the middle voice, which can have a richer quality when you have usable notes above and below it. Refer to Chapter 8 for more detailed information about range.

EXERCISE 9-4

TRACK 47

1. Sing the arpeggio on "ee." On the highest note, sit in plié position while lifting your top back teeth up toward the top of your ears. This creates a stretch in opposite directions. Also feel the appoggio, the lean of air against the sternum. In the higher notes, think of *ee* moving toward the French vowel *eu*. Try thinking of biting into an apple to open up on the top notes. Be sure to close again as the notes descend.

(plié)

Ee

FIGURE 9-14. Exercise 9-4 Step 1

TRACK 48

2. Sing "aw" on the five-note descending scale. Think of the dome shape in the roof of the mouth. Begin with the adjustment toward the French vowel *en* and open toward "aw" or "oh," whichever feels more comfortable, as you descend the scale.

Aw_____

FIGURE 9-15. Exercise 9-4 Step 2

TRACK 49

3. Sing the octaves on "aw." Begin the exercise on your lowest comfortable note. Try to feel the chest vibration against the sternum in the bottom note and keep this sensation as an anchor for the top note. Add the French *en* placement behind the nose on the top note.

Aw ____ (en) ____ aw   Aw ____ (en) ____ aw   Aw ____ (en) ____ aw

FIGURE 9-16. Exercise 9-4 Step 3

These exercises will stretch your voice and provide the more open position you need to comfortably reach high and low pitches. Be sure to use your judgment to determine when to stop the repetitions when it feels too high or too low for you. If you feel any strain at all, you'll create tension that will close your throat and back of your mouth. Tension is counterproductive to achieving your goals. It is better to increase the stretch and strength gradually.

Strengthen Forward Placement

The middle voice is often the most difficult register to achieve by feeling the forward placement it needs. You might be inclined to avoid this placement because it sounds very loud and brassy inside your head, but an element of this sound is necessary to project the voice to performance level. When your body learns to integrate this placement, you will be able to relieve any tension or pressure in the throat. Forward placement will provide the power and volume you need and will also develop your belt voice. Have fun with the exercises and play with the sound of a bratty child or a cat, as you've learned in previous exercises.

ALERT!

Be very careful to keep the soft palate in a high position for these exercises. These exercises are important but can cause strain in the throat if not done correctly. Always stop if you feel any discomfort, and reset the lifted soft palate position with the yawn inhalation.

EXERCISE 9-5

TRACK 50

1. Sing "meow" on the five-note descending scale.

Meow   meow   meow   meow   meow.

FIGURE 9-17. Exercise 9-5 Step 1

TRACK 51

2. Sing "meow" on the five-note descending scale and then continue one long "meow" across the ascending and descending scale.

Meow   meow   meow   meow   meow____

FIGURE 9-18. Exercise 9-5 Step 2

TRACK 52

3. Maintaining the same forward feeling of meow, sing "had" on the five-note scale. This exercise should sound like a bratty child saying "nya, nya."

had
hah

FIGURE 9-19. Exercise 9-5 Step 3

TRACK 53

4. Repeat the previous exercise, alternating the *ha* sound in "had" with other vowels as you hear them on the CD. Pronounce the vowels as you have in the earlier exercises, but try to keep the forward placement and sense of buzzing behind your nose.

TRACK 54

5. Sing the first three notes on "ha" (as in *had*) then move the vowel tone to "ah" as smoothly as possible for the remaining notes. Be sure you don't stop the air in order to change the vowel. Think of narrowing and lengthening the center of the face for the last lower note.

ha   ah

FIGURE 9-20. Exercise 9-5 Step 5

These exercises may sound ugly inside your head, but let yourself have fun with them. The main hurdle will be to let yourself sound loud and brassy inside your head. Don't judge the sound and stop, but rather let your recorder tell you if you sound like the CD. Singers often have to overcome feeling shy or silly to reach their goals.

Adding Consonants

In these exercises, your challenge is to maintain the placement of the vowel tones while adding a consonant to the syllable. Certain consonants will disrupt the open placement of the vowel, which requires a return to the proper position as quickly as possible. Other consonants will allow you to keep the vowel placement while using your tongue to make the consonant.

EXERCISE 9-6

TRACK 55

1. While holding your cheeks out, sing the following exercise. Make sure your tongue is touching the back of your bottom teeth. Drop your hands and repeat the exercise with the feeling of puffing out your cheeks.

FIGURE 9-21.
Hold the
cheeks out

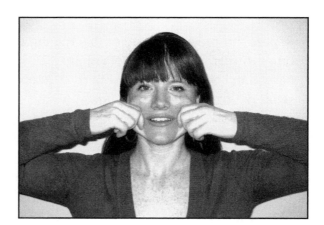

FIGURE 9-22. Exercise 9-6 Step 1

TRACK 56

2. Keeping the *oh* tone as open as possible, sing "lo-do" using only your tongue to form the *l* and the *d*. Keep your jaw still, which will force your tongue to do the work. Repeat the exercise on "na-ta." As you progress to "ya-ga," keep the front of your tongue against the back of your bottom teeth and your jaw still. Feel the movement in the back of your tongue to form the "ya" and the "ga."

lo_____ do_____ lo_____ do_____ lo_____ do_____ lo
na_____ ta_____ na_____ ta_____ na_____ ta_____ na
ya_____ ga_____ ya_____ ga_____ ya_____ ga_____ ya

FIGURE 9-23. Exercise 9-6 Step 2

TRACK 57

3. Alternate the syllables *be* and *de*, and sing as evenly as possible. While you are singing, massage your cheeks gently to prevent tension. As indicated on the CD, drop your hands, change to the vowel *ee*, and continue the exercise.

be de be de be de be de be de be de be de be de be

FIGURE 9-24. Exercise 9-6 Step 3

Flexibility

Developing flexibility in your voice allows you to sing the cadenzas of classical music and the riffs of popular music. In order to sing the following exercises, you will need to balance the concepts of maintaining support in the body while feeling lightness in the voice. If the vocal production is too heavy, the movement cannot be as flexible. When using your lighter voice, however, you'll need to concentrate even more on the forward placement of the previous exercises so the sound doesn't lose its resonance.

EXERCISE 9-7

TRACK 58

1. Sing this ascending exercise on "ee," changing to "ah" in the descending pattern. Concentrate on the beats of the scale degrees and accent these notes to gain speed and a fluid forward motion.

FIGURE 9-25. Exercise 9-7 Step 1

TRACK 59

2. As in the previous exercise, the ascending pattern should be sung on "ee" and the descending pattern on "ah." Listen to the accented notes, but also notice which portion of the exercise has a legato line.

FIGURE 9-26. Exercise 9-7 Step 2

During this section and throughout the entire lesson, you should try to periodically assess your progress. Make sure all the exercises feel physically comfortable. Watch yourself in the mirror to check for tension in the throat, face, mouth, and tongue. And finally, remember to record your sessions at regular intervals to see if you can hear the improvement. Don't worry if progress seems slow at times, and remain patient with the process.

After you complete the exercises in this chapter, you can continue working on your repertoire if you'd like. This set of exercises can stand alone as a lesson or serve as a warmup for rehearsal of a song. Feel free to use this lesson daily to increase your body's ability to retain the muscle memory of the exercises.

CHAPTER 10

Caring for Your Voice

The voice, by its very nature, is part of the human body. If your instrument, the voice, is part of the human body then it makes sense that to care for it is to care for the whole body. Most people treat their guitar, keyboard, drums, etc., with much greater care than they do the most primal instrument, the voice. Musicians usually won't leave an instrument out in the cold or rain, throw it around, or play it with a coating of debris all over it. But that's exactly what happens all the time with your voice. It's very easy to heap all sorts of abuses on your voice and not even be aware you're doing it. This chapter will identify some of the most common dangers to vocal health and how to avoid them.

Think Like an Athlete

If you think of your vocal training in the same way you would approach training your body for an athletic event, you'll be on the right track. Singing at performance level requires enormous stamina, with physical demands much the same as those put on any athlete. If you maintain proper vocal health and good general physical health, your voice should remain strong and usable for a lifetime. You'll know your voice is healthy and strong if you are able to sing on a daily basis without pain, discomfort, weakness, or strain. If you have no symptoms of discomfort, your voice is probably healthy. Conversely, if you feel any pain or discomfort, something is not right. Pain will act as your body's guide and you can be grateful to have this warning sign. If there were no pain, you would have no way of knowing you were doing something wrong. It's very important to know that pain is never okay. It's not something to work through to get stronger, but rather a signal that you're approaching the sound in a way that will cause damage. You can analyze your vocal health from both the viewpoint of vocal misuse and from that of basic health concerns.

Get a small notebook to carry with you. You can keep an ongoing journal of the times, places, and situations in which you felt any vocal discomfort. Note any behavior, food, drink, or medication preceding the difficulty. Look through the lists in this chapter to see if it's one of the common culprits.

If you feel any pain or discomfort while singing or your vocal sound is scratchy, hoarse, or just not at its best, you'll need to analyze what's wrong. To be sure, knowing how to treat your body kindly is a daunting task. Thousands of books and articles exist on the subject of basic health concerns, and a day doesn't go by that you can't hear some sort of health-related news. Health issues are also popular social and business talk. Musicians are forever comparing notes on the best way to deal with certain conditions that confront them, ranging from what to eat and drink to treating colds and other illness. The best way to determine what's true is to ask your own body.

Each person is different and might react differently to the same substance or situation. You'll need to get to know your voice by tracking which things affect you personally.

Misuse of Voice

Most of the problems singers encounter come from improper vocal production. Any harsh use of the voice is potentially damaging, especially if the action is repetitive. Seemingly innocent actions can produce severely detrimental results. Sometimes certain speech patterns can be even more troublesome than singing because of the constancy involved. Shouting and yelling are common problems, as is harsh coughing and clearing of the throat. Singing with tension or excessive volume and singing too high or low for your natural voice type can all be harmful.

Tension in the tongue, jaw, and throat are detrimental to healthy singing. Singers are often overly eager to attack the song with too much force. Think of focusing your energy by increasing concentration on the proper technique and approaching the material gently. Remember to keep your tongue forward. Eventually the muscles of the face, tongue, jaw, and throat respond by relaxing rather than tensing into forced positions.

Career and Lifestyle Habits

Certain careers have inherent dangers to the voice. Anyone who uses the voice in a harsh manner as part of his or her job or general lifestyle has extra challenges to overcome. Teachers, clergy, politicians, salespeople, dance (especially aerobics) instructors, wait staff in noisy or smoky restaurants, sports referees, cheerleaders, and anyone required to use the telephone constantly are some examples of those who face the hazards of vocal abuse.

Certain activities, although fun, can lead to vocal damage. A common problem is excessive yelling or screaming at sports events. This could mean the local game with all the crowd noise around you, or even a group watching television. Trying to talk over loud music at parties, clubs, or bars is another activity that can be extremely damaging to your voice. This can be a particularly difficult caveat, since singers are often very social people and find many potential contacts in the very places that might cause the problem. Many aspiring singers find jobs working in restaurants or bars, which is even worse since it's constant. In essence, any time you try to reach someone with your voice in a way that pushes it beyond its capacity, whether by excessive volume or force, you could be inviting trouble.

Singing Incorrectly

The only way to determine that your singing is incorrect is if it doesn't serve you. *Correct* and *incorrect* are not terms of value judgment about the sound of the voice, but rather evaluation of your vocal health. Many would-be singers have damaged their voices by attempting to sing songs or styles for which they are not yet prepared or that simply do not suit their voice, by design. The following list identifies common problems:

- Singing too loudly and pushing the voice
- Singing too much or for too long without periods of rest
- Singing for extended periods of time outside of your comfortable range
- Screaming or whispering
- Muscular tension in the tongue and jaw
- Muscular tension in the throat and neck
- Competing with any form of background noise

Your best defense is solid vocal technique. Practicing proper technique and using the exercises in the previous chapters will ensure that your body will develop muscle memory of the elements of safe vocal production. If you feel your voice tires easily or you have a vocally demanding job, review the yawning exercises, which will keep the larynx in a relaxed position. Be patient and train your voice as you would any other instrument.

Basic Health Concerns

Whatever affects your body will on some level affect your voice. You are your instrument and if you're tired, hungry, thirsty, under stress, or sick, your voice will be affected. You will need to determine which activities or substances affect you and in what way. Remember that everyone's different, but almost everyone can afford to pay close attention to the following health concerns.

Keep Your Body Hydrated

This is probably the most beneficial and immediate improvement you could make in your general health, which, of course, translates to your vocal health. Your body is made up of over 60 percent water and loses water daily just in normal functioning. Each person has different needs depending on their activity level, but singers tend to need more water than those with fewer demands on their bodies. It's important to keep the body, and thus your vocal cords, sufficiently hydrated throughout the day. Some phlegm is necessary and good for lubrication, but you want to keep it thin and watery. The general recommendation is eight to ten glasses of water a day.

Proper Nutrition

Your body will need a sound, balanced diet, with plenty of foods that will contribute to a more alkaline state. Acid in the body can have a profoundly negative effect on your general health and certainly on the delicate tissues of your vocal folds. In its more extreme state, acid reflux can permanently damage your voice. There are numerous books and articles outlining which foods are most helpful or harmful in maintaining a proper balance. Again, let your body be the judge of what's right for you.

It is also important to maintain a reasonable weight for your height and body type. It is not true that you will sing better with extra weight. In fact, just as being overweight would hamper any athlete's performance, the extra strain on your body will lessen your strength and endurance for singing.

Exercise

Daily exercise is important for general health and well-being, but performers need extra strength, endurance, and flexibility. Moderate exercise could include walking, jogging, dance, workouts at the gym, or any of your favorite sports. Swimming is wonderful exercise but often causes ear infections, a major handicap for a singer.

Exercise programs such as yoga and tai chi are excellent for strength, flexibility, and relaxation. They promote deep breathing, focused energy, and a calming release of tension, all characteristics of healthy singing. Pilates strengthens core muscles needed for proper body support of the voice.

Sleep

Most people need seven to eight hours of sleep each night. When you are rested you are able to concentrate and function at your best. Fatigue can cause you to overcompensate and push your voice beyond a healthy level or just not have enough energy to do the job.

Hormonal Changes

The body undergoes physical and emotional changes during puberty, pregnancy, menopause, and menstrual cycles. Some women experience vocal difficulties during their menstrual period due to extra swelling in tissues of the body, including the vocal folds. If you feel hoarseness, it means the vocal folds are unable to close together completely, and, if possible, you should consider a rest from singing for a day or two.

Emotional Well-Being

Perhaps the most important factor contributing to overall good health is a positive attitude. Tension is one of the greatest deterrents to developing your singing voice. Depression and anger will usually cause fairly extreme muscular tension, which can make freedom in your voice almost impossible. The throat will tighten to an almost closed position in crying, and anxiety affects almost every system of the body. A relaxed attitude and a sense of humor can render most challenges relatively minor.

Environmental Hazards

People react differently to environmental challenges. Exposure to outside elements isn't always in your control, but at least you can prepare some defense if you know what to look for. Once again, you will have to pay attention to which things affect you and your voice because you may respond differently than your friend or colleague. They could react to something that wouldn't bother you, and vice versa. The following list details many of the more common situations or substances that might cause a reaction:

- Weather conditions, such as extreme heat or cold, humidity or dryness can take their toll. Humidity can actually be good for many people, but some are affected adversely. A comfortable temperature and somewhat high moisture level are usually ideal.
- Buildings that are overheated or air-conditioned can be too dry. Similarly, climate control in cars, buses, trains, and airplanes will usually cause very dry air. It's best to keep the air moist in any enclosed space, especially in American buildings, known for being more airtight than those in other countries.
- Smoke and dust are both damaging to inhale and are more sources of overly dry conditions. This includes smoke in the air as well as tobacco or marijuana. Smoke is drying, whether it's yours or someone else's. Secondhand smoke has been proven to be just as damaging to your health as primary source smoke.
- Allergens can range from minor irritant to the cause of disease. You may already know substances that aggravate you, but you may experience an allergic reaction and not be aware of its source. Well-known allergens are dust, animal dander, pollen, various plants, perfume and hairspray, toxic fumes, and certain foods.

If you are traveling before a performance or audition, you may need to allow some extra time for your body to adjust to new environmental conditions. Changes in temperature, altitude, and air quality may cause your voice to react differently. Spend some time doing very gentle warmup exercises to get your voice acclimated to the new climate. The same advice is offered for athletes who must travel for games or competitions.

Food and Drink

Finding which foods and beverages your body can tolerate is an individual matter and can be extremely difficult to track, but sometimes even more difficult to change. Everyone has her or his particular favorites and you certainly don't want to eliminate them from your diet. You may find that if certain foods cause your voice to suffer, you could consider cutting them out of your diet only during times you'll be singing. Just be sure to watch how you feel in general, since something that causes discomfort in your voice may also be causing more general physical problems. At some point the consequences of eating or drinking something detrimental will outweigh the momentary pleasure. The usual symptoms to be aware of are too much mucous or phlegm in your throat and nasal cavities, hoarseness, coughing, having to clear your throat often, acidity, and lack of breath.

The most common food and drink offenders are:

- Dairy
- Chocolate
- Sugar
- Wheat
- Caffeine
- Soda and carbonated drinks
- Citrus juice
- Nuts

If this list includes items in your diet and you are healthy and free of symptoms, then count yourself lucky and have what you want. If you do suffer from any of the previous symptoms, try eliminating one item from the list for a few days and see how you feel. Not many can make drastic changes in lifelong habits and expect them to last. Just as with the vocal exercises and muscle memory, you'll need to be patient with yourself.

On the positive side, foods that are often helpful and soothing to your throat are apples, pineapple, garlic, honey (even though it's sugar), some lozenges, and slippery elm. Pineapple contains bromelain, an enzyme that is anti-inflammatory, which can reduce swelling, and it is good for digestion.

Drugs and Alcohol

These substances are doubly dangerous to your vocal health. Not only can they cause physical damage to your throat and entire vocal mechanism, but they also alter your mental awareness and perception. You may not even notice damage as it's happening, and certainly you won't be as alert. Performance is such a demanding physical activity that you'll need all the support you can give yourself. Unhappily, there are too many examples of ruined voices and careers due to drug or alcohol addiction. A singing career is both social and stressful, and peer pressure can be a powerful influence. It can be very easy to convince yourself to relax before you perform with this external help. Once again, make your decisions based on your willingness to accept the consequences.

Alcohol

Alcohol is both a depressant and a muscle relaxant, affecting the whole body. Sometimes even a small amount can lead to lowered awareness of pitch and vocal control. It is also drying to the membranes of the throat and larynx, which need to stay moist and lubricated. Finally, alcohol causes dilation of the blood vessels, resulting in a swelling of the vocal folds. The voice coarsens from the thickening of the vocal folds, which are potentially in danger of a hemorrhage. Beer and wine have a lower alcohol content than hard liquor but are still best taken in moderation and after a performance, not before it.

Drugs

Drugs and medications can have direct effects and side effects, which may alter your vocal production as well as your general ability to function. Illegal drugs, prescription, and over-the-counter medications are all capable of both causing damage and masking damage. They all bear potentially serious capacity to harm your voice.

Social Drugs

All social drugs, including marijuana, cocaine, heroin, crack, and many more, alter perception and change normal physical functions. In addition, if the substance is smoked, it's without a filter and poses an even greater drying effect than inhaling tobacco. Any chemically induced change in your awareness is damaging to the strength and concentration required for your best performance, as well as your physical and emotional health.

Medications

Aspirin and ibuprofen belong to the category of drugs called NSAIDs (nonsteroidal anti-inflammatory drugs) and are some of the most common over-the-counter drugs. They may lead to fluid retention and edema, and thus a swelling of the vocal folds. Since they are also blood thinners, there is danger of vocal fold hemorrhage.

Any medication, such as an antihistamine or decongestant, that's designed to help clear a runny nose will, by its very nature, dry your system. If you need one of these to relieve allergy symptoms, be sure to double your dose of daily water intake to keep sufficient moisture in the body.

Anesthetic sprays and lozenges are designed to numb the throat. This is one of the worst possible situations to create for yourself if you're trying to stay aware of your body's signals. Remember, pain can be valuable for tracking a problem and alerting your need for special care. Any substance that masks a problem or deadens pain is misrepresenting your physical state. Under these circumstances, you could easily convince yourself that you're healthy enough to push through the pain and as a result cause serious damage. If you have a sore throat, you shouldn't sing.

Signs of Abuse or Damage

Your warning signals may take different forms. In some cases you will feel pain. As previously stated, pain should never be ignored. It's a sign that something is wrong, not something to work through. Your vocal training is not a "no pain, no gain" situation. If you proceed in doing the action that is causing the pain, you can create serious or irreversible damage.

There are also some warning signs that aren't painful. You may just regard them as an annoyance, or maybe even so longstanding and familiar that you're not even aware of the message they're sending.

Warning Signs with Pain

A sore throat means that the tissues are swollen and inflamed. This usually is a result of illness, such as a cold or flu, but can be caused by misuse. It will always be your indication to stop singing and restrict talking as much as possible.

ALERT!

If a sore throat lasts more than a few days, or if you feel any intense pain in the mouth, throat, or chest, you should see a doctor. The more quickly you take care of an illness, the less chance it will cause any permanent vocal damage. Never sing with a sore throat!

Warning Signs with No Pain

There are also many serious conditions that do not trigger pain. You should pay careful attention to any frequency of these indications, since the results may be severe.

Excessive throat clearing can be a nervous habit or a sign that something is irritating the throat. It could be the result of some form of allergy, acid reflux, a reaction to an inhaled substance, overproduction of mucous and phlegm, incorrect use of the voice, or emotional anxiety. If the problem is constant, you might want to look through some of the previous sections of this chapter and begin tracking the source.

Hoarseness means the edges of the vocal folds are unable to vibrate properly. It could be mild, only lasting a few hours or a day, in which case you may have been singing either incorrectly or for too long. A short rest should take care of it. If it continues, however, it can be a serious indication of illness or any of the symptoms listed above with throat clearing. You must pay very careful attention to technique and be sure you're not singing incorrectly. With constant abuse the vocal folds can form lesions known as *nodes* or *nodules*. This condition is similar to any callous formed by friction or irritation. Although surgery was once a popular treatment for this condition, most doctors now will recommend vocal rest. Vocal rest means total silence—restriction from any talking or singing, sometimes for several months.

Laryngitis is severe inflammation of the tissues in the larynx. It may be caused by illness and infection or, once again, by any of the causes mentioned previously. Many people will experience laryngitis after yelling, screaming, or singing with excessive tension for long periods of time. Vocal rest is necessary to recover from laryngitis. You should definitely not try to talk or whisper while afflicted.

How to Protect Yourself

By now you should have a clear idea that vocal distress can come from illness, external sources, or misuse of the voice. You'll want to find some ways to defend yourself against these challenges. Your voice isn't an instrument you can return or replace if it's broken or damaged. It's much easier to protect and care for it now. Usually it's easier to think of what positive actions we can take rather than giving up what's been a long-term habit, comfortable, or pleasurable. As you look through this list, think of one or two actions you might adopt, and then keep adding to those as you're able:

- Drink at least eight to ten glasses of water daily.
- Use a humidifier to keep moisture in the air.
- Use saline spray rather than medicated spray for your nose.
- Get at least seven to eight hours of sleep.
- Keep a food journal to determine any possible patterns of allergy, discomfort, or time intervals necessary between eating and singing.
- Drink water and herbal tea at moderate temperature, neither too hot nor too cold.
- Get plenty of exercise, especially calming practices such as yoga.
- Practice proper vocal technique and build up beneficial muscle memory.

Moisture is one of a singer's best friends. Besides drinking plenty of water, you can also inhale steam. There are inhalers with molded plastic masks to guide the steam. Simply boiling water on the stove also works well, as does turning on a hot shower and filling the bathroom with steam.

The more serious you are about singing well, the more careful you need to be with your general physical health. Certainly no one is perfect in the quest for physical and vocal health, but if you can identify which things are helpful or harmful, you'll at least have that information. Then you can make decisions based on the immediacy of your vocal needs and your willingness to accept the consequences of those choices.

Restorative Exercises

If you feel that the regular set of exercises is too demanding and want to try something a little more soothing, here is a set of restorative exercises. Some of them you've seen in earlier chapters. Often the voice will feel better with these exercises. Just remember to use all the technique you learned in the previous exercises. It doesn't help to sing too lightly or to guard your voice, but a gentle approach to the exercises is always more helpful than a forceful approach. If your voice still feels raspy, breathy, or uncomfortable, you should probably rest.

EXERCISE 10-1

TRACK 60

1. Sing gently using "nin," then again using "naw."

nin nin nin nin   nin   nin nin nin nin   nin   nin nin nin nin   nin   nin nin nin nin   nin

FIGURE 10-1. Exercise 10-1

EXERCISE 10-2

TRACK 61

1. Sing "oo," imitating the tone of an owl.

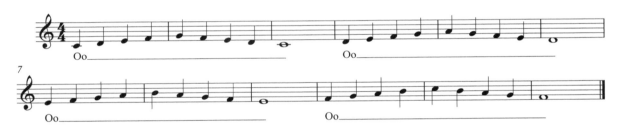

FIGURE 10-2. Exercise 10-2

EXERCISE 10-3

TRACK 62

1. Sing on "na" as in *nab*. Repeat this exercise with your comb and plastic bag, as in Exercise 4-2 in Chapter 4. Remember to use the hum and then "oo."

FIGURE 10-3. Exercise 10-3

CHAPTER 11

Musicianship

Good musicianship is a synthesis of many musical elements, including musicality, performance expression, and proficiency in theory and sight-singing. To be a truly great artist, the singer has to combine the technical and emotional aspects of music. If you listen to your favorite singers, you'll probably find you love the sound of their voice, but also how they phrase the music and deliver the emotional content of the lyrics. These singers need an understanding of the music they're singing in order to accomplish this.

The Basic Elements of Musicianship

The difference between a good musician and a great artist is the degree of musicianship she brings to her craft. *Musicianship* is a somewhat elusive term and can have varying definitions depending on your source. Some might use it to refer only to the technical aspects of training and a solid grasp of music theory. Others describe it as the ability to connect to the emotional and spiritual substance of the music. Considering that both elements are equally important in capturing the attention of the audience, or even experiencing the fulfillment of singing for your own enjoyment, you'll need to explore each side.

The technical requirements of great singing include clarity and proficiency in producing proper pitch and rhythm. A strong sense of accurate pitch is crucial. How many times have you heard complaints about singers being sharp (too high), flat (too low), or "pitchy" (off-pitch in either direction)? It should be the first thing you correct if there's a problem. You also need to work with the rhythm of the music until it becomes a part of your body. Singers use the whole body to sing and can keep a pulse in motion by maintaining the sense of an inner metronome. The ability to read music well is another skill included in most musicians' definition of musicianship.

The emotional connection to music is exhibited in the phrasing and dynamic levels of the lyrics. The composer writes some of this information and the rest is a result of your work with the dramatic interpretation of the words and music as a whole. You should begin with the information provided on the page so that you remain aware of the composer's intent. After that you can study the words as if they were an acting monologue.

Pitch

Pitch is actually an acoustical term referring to the frequency of the vibrations of sound waves. A note has a specific number of vibrations per second, which is the center of the pitch. Think of this as the bull's-eye, or center of a target. You can move to one or two of the closest rings around the center, but not much further, and still sound in tune.

FACT

The musical term for pitch is *intonation*. If someone says a singer has good intonation, then the pitch is accurately centered and clear for each note. Good intonation can also be referred to as "having a good ear." It's one of the most important elements of singing well.

Most people are able to hear pitch. But how many people do you know who claim they can't carry a tune? Often you'll hear someone say they are tone deaf if they feel they can't sing. True tone deafness, or amusia, is actually not a common occurrence. The ability to discern pitch in melodies can be trained and poor intonation can be corrected. Singing in tune is essential and probably the most basic skill you should perfect.

QUESTIONS

Do you need perfect pitch?
You don't need to have perfect pitch, also called *absolute pitch*. This is the ability to discern the specific frequency without hearing any other point of reference. Relative pitch is necessary, however, and can be learned. Hearing relative pitch means you can identify surrounding notes when given a reference note.

It will always be important to develop accuracy in your ability to hear relative pitch, no matter what style of music you sing. Relative pitch refers to hearing a particular note when given another note as a point of reference. If you hear a C played on the piano, for example, you will need to learn how to hear D, E, and any other note of a scale or melody in relation to that given note, C.

Ear Training

Learning to hear melodies and centered pitch is largely a matter of practice, training, and experience. The part of your brain that distinguishes pitch can be exercised just as any other mental function. The first level of training intonation is careful listening. You can't rush through a melody when you're beginning to study or if matching pitch is a challenge for you. Take it slowly so you can concentrate on each note and really focus on hearing the tone and then matching the pitch.

The elements of developing a good musical ear are the same no matter the level of experience:

- Listen
- Process the information
- Sing

These three steps are always present when singing in tune. Upon hearing a given pitch, your brain is able to process the information of the sound and internalize it. You can then match it exactly. You'll need to relax and let this happen slowly at first, and then sing the correct pitch by voicing what you've heard.

Matching Pitch

Spend some of your practice session just listening to a note, scale, or a short phrase. Notice if the pattern of notes is rising or falling and if one note is higher or lower than the next. You can try playing a single note on a piano or guitar and then singing the note. Do they match? If not, do you think you're higher or lower than the instrumental note? Try to adjust in each direction until you can determine how to find the center of the pitch. After training yourself to focus on specific notes, try matching a short phrase of a simple song such as a nursery rhyme.

EXERCISE 11-1

The next step of ear training should be to test your accuracy. Try recording your voice while you sing these exercises.

1. Play a note on the piano or guitar.
2. Listen carefully to the pitch so you can fully process the information.
3. Sing that note with the instrument.
4. Listen and feel the vibration of the two notes together to analyze your accuracy.

5. Sing higher than the instrument, and then sing lower than the instrument. Now return to the original pitch.
6. Listen to your recording to check yourself.

You can repeat these steps with a short scale (a set of sequential notes explained in Chapter 13) or a short melody phrase.

You can check your accuracy in matching pitch with the aid of software programs designed for this purpose. You can also test your ability to match single notes by using a digital chromatic tuner. This is an inexpensive instrument used primarily by instrumentalists and is available in music stores and on the Internet. It will read what note you're singing and show you if you're sharp or flat (above or below the pitch).

Intonation Problems

If you think you have trouble with pitch accuracy, it could be due to lack of training, lack of concentration and focus, rushing through the musical phrase, or it could be the result of improper vocal technique. Sometimes you can hear a pitch perfectly and match it accurately inside your head but still not reproduce the correct pitch frequency. Some of the technical problems that can contribute to a sharp or flat tone include:

- Physical tension
- Inadequate breath support
- Pushing your voice
- Vocal strain
- Raised larynx
- Lowered soft palate
- Lack of vertical position in the throat
- Singing material out of your range

Once again, you should record your voice to check your intonation. Listen to other singers and try to match those you think have a good sense of pitch. Let other people listen to you and give you feedback on the exactness of your pitch. If you are careful in the beginning of your training, you'll set a pattern for maintaining proper pitch when you are more experienced.

Intervals

An interval is the distance between two notes. The smallest interval between two notes in Western music is called a *semitone* or a *half step*. Two half steps are called a *whole step*, or sometimes just *a step*. A singer needs to hear this relationship between the notes in order to stay in tune and to develop sight-reading skills. Try to picture these steps as stair steps so that you'll have a clear visual image of them.

Hearing intervals is the same as hearing relative pitch. The intervals are based on a single given note, usually the lower note of the pair. The lower note is called *the root*, and the number of steps between the two notes, including the top and bottom note, provides the name for the interval. The distance from C to G, for example, is five steps and is called a *fifth*. C is the root note. If the two notes are sung separately, the interval is called *melodic*. If more than one vocalist sings the two notes simultaneously, the interval is called *harmonic*. For further information about intervals, see Chapter 12.

ALERT!

There are several different types of intervals you can study in music theory. The main purpose of these exercises is for you to hear and practice singing basic intervals so that you can feel the distance between the two pitches in your voice. You can learn more about how these intervals are created and interpreted in music theory books, including *The Everything® Reading Music Book with CD* by Marc Schonbrun.

Diatonic Intervals

TRACK 63

Diatonic intervals are based on the major scale described in Chapter 13. There are eight intervals in a major scale. Listen to the sound of the diatonic intervals.

FIGURE 11-1. Diatonic intervals

Chromatic Intervals

TRACK 64

The remaining intervals incorporate the half steps between the notes of the major scale. Listen to the sound of the chromatic intervals.

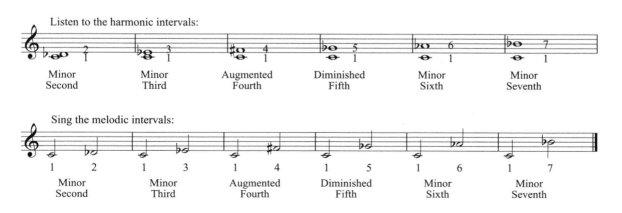

FIGURE 11-2. Chromatic intervals

TRACK 65

1. Sing along with the following exercise often enough to feel comfortable with these intervals.

2. Say the name of the interval so you associate the numbered distance with the sound of the interval.

3. See if you can identify intervals in songs you know. For instance, the first interval of "Twinkle, Twinkle, Little Star" is a fifth.

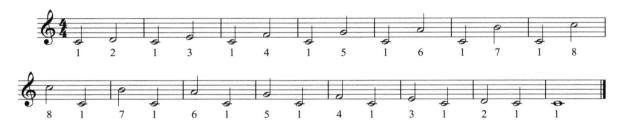

FIGURE 11-3. Exercise 11-2

Rhythm

Another important aspect of good musicianship is an understanding of singing in rhythm. Rhythm is basic to physical function and movement. You move and breathe in rhythm. Your heart even beats in rhythm. Feeling rhythm in music is both a natural, organic function and also a learned function depending on the complexity of the material.

The best way to feel the rhythm of the music you're singing is to move your body in time to the music. Play various styles of music and see if you can dance to each of them. How does your body respond differently to the different beats? Some music is very energetic and driving, and some is more lyrical and fluid. See if you can imagine situations or elements of nature to match the feel of each different style. Some beats will feel more like machinery, while others might be more like moving water. Now stand in place while tapping your foot or hand to the beat. Hopefully you can feel a sense of movement in your body without actually moving. This ability to feel rhythm is often called being "in the groove" or "in the pocket."

The underlying beat should always be present in your body. This is the structure on which you overlay the given rhythm written into the music. As you study the rhythmic notation of your song (explained in Chapter 12) you will hopefully be able to keep that steady pulse going under the pattern of notes you sing. It's helpful to use a metronome while practicing your music so that you can maintain a fixed tempo and rhythm in rehearsal.

Performance Notation

Most vocal music contains words and, just as in speech, the different levels of volume and the types of tone used will produce different effects. Usually the music gives you the information you need. The composer, or sometimes the publisher, will mark the music to establish the meaning and mood of the song. This performance notation, or expression markings, serve as a basic guide that the singer should follow to honor the intent of the composer. Through rehearsal, extra markings may be added to further enhance the meaning.

Dynamics

Dynamic markings indicate the desired level of volume. They are written above the vocal line of music so as not to interfere with the lyrics on the page. Dynamics range from very soft to very loud. Since there is no universal measure of what soft and loud mean, it remains up to the artist to interpret the level. The following markings are the most commonly used.

Marking	Dynamic Level	Meaning
pp	Pianissimo	Very soft
p	Piano	Soft
mp	Mezzo piano	Moderately soft
mf	Mezzo forte	Moderately loud
f	Forte	Loud
ff	Fortissimo	Very loud

Dynamics may also change over a phrase, getting gradually louder or gradually softer. These markings are often called *hairpins*, and are easy to identify since the widest point indicates that you should get louder and the smallest point indicates that you should get softer.

⊂	*crescendo* or *cresc.*	getting gradually louder
⊃	*decrescendo* or *decresc.*	getting gradually softer

Expression Markings

There are many symbols in notation to indicate a desired style of singing or attack of a particular note. They are too numerous to list here, but it's recommended that you have a music dictionary to check the additional terms you might see in your songs. Some of the most frequently used markings are the following:

Marking	Term	Meaning
♩ (with dot)	staccato	quick, detached
♩ (with accent)	accent	sharp attack
𝄐	fermata	hold the note
legato or *leg.*	legato	smoothly
dolce	dolce	sweetly
con brio	con brio	with vigor

If you pay attention to the details of performance notation, it will be much easier to interpret the meaning of the song. You should also be careful to follow natural accents of words unless otherwise indicated. Good musicianship demands that you make the music clear and accessible for your audience. Sometimes your own instincts will take care of this, but you should also be able to read the dynamic and expression markings that guide you to the strongest result.

CHAPTER 12

Reading Music

You don't need to read music to sing well, but the skill is practically mandatory to become a good musician. Singers and vocal teachers often concentrate on training the voice to the exclusion of learning basic music skills. Musicians who study any other instrument, however, are required to learn music notation in order to practice independently. In knowing how to read notation, you will learn music more easily and quickly, converse succinctly with your fellow musicians, and learn music independently without having to rely on someone else to teach you the song.

Music Notation

Think of music notation as a chart or map of how to make music come alive from ink on a page. It's easier to comprehend if you realize it's just another language to learn and, as with most languages, some of it is already familiar. If you analyze your ability to read English, you'll see that letters have sounds which, when combined in various ways, form other sounds and words, now able to take on meaning. As words form phrases and sentences they may develop deeper or even different meanings. The musical language is formed of similar elements. By creating written musical symbols, composers from other time periods or locations are able to express the concept of the sound they want and communicate with you, the singer. These symbols will give you information about pitch, rhythm, tempo, dynamics, articulation, expression, and phrasing. The information given on the printed page is your key to the composer's intent.

Pitch

When you speak of sound as high or low, you're referring to its pitch. Pitch is the tone you hear given a specific frequency, or number of vibrations per second, of sound waves. The frequency is measured in Hertz (Hz) and assigned to note names. The accepted twentieth-century standard of pitch establishes that A above middle C vibrates at 440 Hz, and is often referred to as *concert pitch*. Pitch is represented in music notation by notes, the staff, and the clef.

Staff

Modern notation uses a grid of five equidistant parallel lines called *the staff*. The five-line staff is a place to organize levels of pitch, and it is the standard staff for most instruments, including the voice. Notes are placed on the staff either on the lines or in the spaces between lines. The lines and spaces read from the bottom upward, as shown on the staff in Figure 12-1. Consecutive pitches would be read on alternating lines and spaces.

Lines   Spaces

FIGURE 12-1. Music staff

The staff can be extended by use of ledger lines, which are small extra lines that serve to increase the range on the staff, either above or below the set of five lines.

Ledger lines can be above or below the staff

FIGURE 12-2. Ledger lines

Clef

A clef is a symbol placed at the beginning of each staff to identify the position of a pitch. There are a number of different clefs, three of which are commonly used in modern notation, but usually only two are necessary for singers. In fact, most solo vocal music uses only one clef, the treble clef, so you should concentrate on mastering that one.

The treble clef is also called the *G clef* and identifies the placement of a particular pitch, called *G*, on the second line. Notice the curl of the clef around line two. From this point we are able to figure out the placement of the other pitches.

**FIGURE
12-3.**
Treble clef
and
bass clef

TREBLE CLEF   **BASS CLEF**

The bass clef, or F clef, is used for lower instruments and men's voices. A man needs to read in the bass clef for choral music but will use the treble clef for most solo material. The exception is the use of the bass clef for solo baritone and bass parts in opera and classical music. For all popular music a man actually sings the same pitch as the female singer, but it sounds an octave (eight notes) lower.

Notes

Each pitch is placed on the staff by a symbol called a *note*, comprised of a note head and a stem.

Stem   Note head

Note head   Stem

FIGURE 12-4. Notes

The vertical position of the note head on the staff identifies the particular pitch. In America, the letters A through G designate notes. Many other countries use a solfège system called "fixed *do*," and name these same notes *do, re, mi, fa, sol, la,* and *si,* where *do* is C, *re* is D, and so on.

FACT

Another sight-reading method, called "movable *do*," is also part of the solfège system. It uses the syllables *do, re, mi, fa, sol, la, ti,* but *do* can be moved to indicate the beginning tone of a different key. The relationship of the syllables to one another remains constant, but the starting point, *do,* could be any pitch.

TRACK 66

If a note is higher on the staff it's a higher pitch, and a lower note on the staff sounds lower in pitch.

Note One   Note Two   Note One   Note Two

FIGURE 12-5. Note one is higher in your voice than note two

The Treble Clef Notes

The treble clef includes the most important vocabulary you will need as a singer. Begin with one ledger line below the staff. This note is called *middle C* and it divides the grand staff (as you'll see later) and also the piano keyboard in half, with treble on the top and bass on the bottom. From note C you can count up consecutively, as shown in the example.

C   D   E   F   G   A   B   C   D   E   F   G

(middle C)

FIGURE 12-6. Notes in the treble staff

Many people find it useful to further divide the notes to make it more manageable to learn them. Look at the notes on the lines. Within the staff they are named E – G – B – D – F. If you use the sentence "**E**very **G**ood **B**oy **D**oes **F**ine," you'll have the key to remembering the line notes. They are the beginning letters of each word. The notes in the spaces are F – A – C – E and spell *face*.

Line Notes   Space Notes

Every **G**ood **B**oy **D**oes **F**ine   F - A - C - E

FIGURE 12-7. Line notes and space notes in the treble staff

Now sing these notes in the treble staff, naming each note as you sing the pitch.

FIGURE 12-8. C Major scale in treble staff

The Bass Clef Notes

The bass clef, also called an *F clef*, establishes the note F on the fourth line. Notice that the two dots of the clef are placed on either side of the fourth line. As stated previously, men will use this clef for the bass part in certain classical forms and in choral music. Otherwise men will use the treble clef and sing the same note as the female singer, but it will sound an octave lower.

FIGURE 12-9. Notes in the bass staff

The line notes of the bass clef, from the bottom up, are G – B – D – F – A and can be remembered using the sentence "**G**ood **B**oys **D**o **F**ine **A**lways." The space notes are A – C – E – G, "**A**ll **C**ows **E**at **G**rass." The first ledger line above the bass staff is the same middle C as the note you see on the first ledger line below the treble staff. When joined, the two staves (plural of staff) intersect at this point.

Line Notes

Space Notes

Good Boys Do Fine Always All Cows Eat Grass

FIGURE 12-10. Line notes and space notes in the bass staff

Now sing these notes in the bass staff, naming each note as you sing the pitch.

TRACK 68

C D E F G A B C

FIGURE 12-11. C Major scale in bass staff

The Grand Staff

The two staves together form the grand staff. For most practical purposes, the grand staff encompasses roughly the entire vocal range, collective of all male and female voices. Imagine the grand staff as one eleven-line staff. The eleventh line is the middle C ledger line between the two staves. Since the eye can't easily discern the placement of notes on eleven lines, the grand staff is separated with extra distance between the treble and bass ranges.

Music notation is continually evolving as a language. In previous centuries, the staff has had a varied number of lines and notes had different shapes. There were no bar lines, but other ways of indicating patterns of notes. Many twenty first-century composers feel constricted by modern notation and look for new ways to indicate sound. Some contemporary classical scores include a key diagram explaining new notation methods.

The middle C ledger line remains an equidistant space from the other lines of whichever staff it extends, which makes it appear to be two different pitches. Again, think of this note merely as the eleventh line between the two staves.

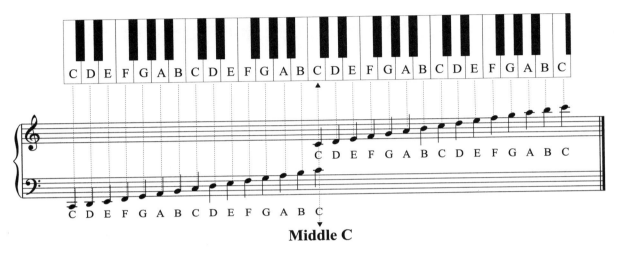

Middle C

FIGURE 12-12. Grand staff and corresponding notes on the keyboard

Notice the grand staff is connected on the left side with a vertical line and a brace. The grand staff is predominantly used for piano notation and indicates that one instrument plays both staves together. A pianist reads both staves simultaneously, with the right hand playing the treble notes and the left hand playing the bass notes. You can see in Figure 12-12 the placement of the corresponding notes on the piano keyboard. If you have a keyboard, try playing each of these notes as you name them. Sing the notes on pitch whenever they feel within your range.

Accidentals

Any pitch can be modified by using an accidental before a note. There are five accidentals: sharp, which raises a pitch by one half step; flat, which lowers a pitch by one half step; double sharp, which raises a pitch by two half steps; double flat, which lowers a pitch by two half steps; and natural, which returns the pitch to its original tone, or a white key on the piano. An accidental precedes the note in music notation, but comes after the note name when referring to the pitch, such as "C sharp."

FIGURE 12-13.
Accidentals

FIGURE 12-14.
Accidentals on the
piano keyboard

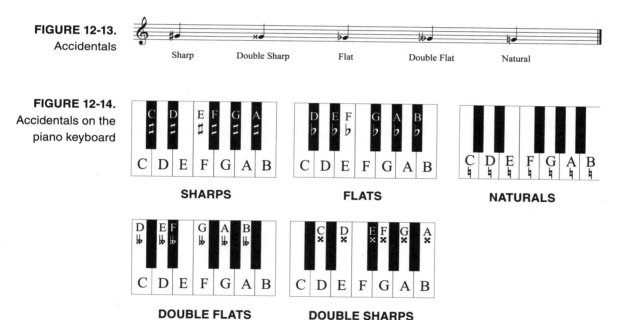

Enharmonics

The same pitch can have different names, which are called *enharmonic equivalents*. If you look at the piano keyboard, you'll see that C♯ is the same pitch as D♭. Every pitch has enharmonic equivalent notes and derives its name from the function it serves in music theory. Although not an exact analogy, this is much the same idea as a word having different meanings depending on its context in a sentence.

Each set of pitches has the same sound:

C♯ = D♭   D♯ = E♭   F♯ = G♭   A♯ = B♭   G♯ = A♭

FIGURE 12-15. Enharmonic equivalents

ALERT!

Learning to read music can be confusing at first, and this chapter is necessarily brief. For more information about reading music, take a look at *The Everything® Reading Music Book with CD* by Marc Schonbrun. You'll find much greater depth, a slower pace, and will have plenty of exercises for practice.

Sight-Singing Pitch

TRACK 69

The ability to sing music when seeing it for the first time requires that you are able to imagine the sound of the pitch in relation to other pitches. This ear training takes practice, but is crucial to good musicianship. Try using the system of assigning numbers to each note, since it's both easier to count with numbers and will also be needed to understand some basic theory in the next chapter. Although the numbers may start on any note, for now you should assign the number one to middle C. From C (one), count up consecutively to seven, which is B. The next note is C and becomes the number one again.

Try singing from middle C to the next C using the numbers as shown.

FIGURE 12-16. Sing this scale using the numbers indicated

Each number has a particular pitch, which will remain with that note even if the notes are not consecutive. A melody is formed by moving these notes into patterns that are not necessarily consecutive.

EXERCISE 12-1

TRACK 70

1. Try singing the following patterns. If a note is skipped, you should hum the missing note or notes to yourself to keep their place in the tonal line.
2. First sing the melody with the audible missing notes.
3. Then try just thinking these missing notes without actually voicing them.
4. Finally, sing the melody without the extra notes.

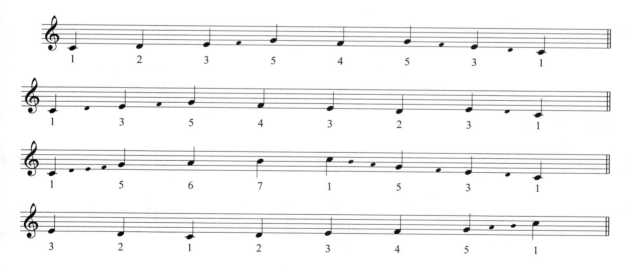

FIGURE 12-17. Sing these notes with the CD

Try to sing the notes again without the CD.

Intervals

By singing the previous exercise, you were able to feel distance from one note to another note. The distance between two notes is called *an interval*. The size of an interval is determined by counting from the letter name of one note to the letter name of another note. Both note names should be included in the count. The distance from A to C is a third, including A, B, and C. In the same way, A to D is a fourth, and C to G is a fifth. Singers work with intervals in all exercises and music and learn to feel that distance in the voice, just as the pianist feels a distance in the spread of the hand on the keyboard.

Look at the following intervals based on C as the lower note. First count the distance on the page, then practice hearing and singing these intervals. Eventually these intervals will be incorporated into memory. You can get more practice with intervals in Chapter 11.

TRACK 71

FIGURE 12-18. Intervals

Rhythm

Rhythm is the pattern of sound in time. It's made up of the duration, or length of time, of sounds and silences. Just as important as the designation of pitch, a note specifies how long it should be held. We refer to the measurement of musical time in beats. A beat is a pulse in a steady pattern, and it is most easily understood as the natural pulses in nature, such as your heartbeat or a regular walking or running pattern. In musical notation, the appearance of a note, as you'll see in the next section, will determine its duration.

Note Values

Look at the following chart for the key to recognizing note duration. Each type of note shown has a name and indicates the number of beats to hold the note. For a singer, that means voicing a single syllable for the length of the given note.

One of the best ways to learn the alphabet of this new language is the use of flash cards. Most music stores carry sets of flash cards that drill you on note names and durations. It's helpful to recognize these symbols as quickly as possible so that you won't have to count lines and spaces or stop to figure out how many beats a certain note contains.

FIGURE 12-19.
Note duration

Note	Name	Beats
𝅝	Whole note	4 beats
𝅗𝅥	Half note	2 beats
𝅘𝅥	Quarter note	1 beat
𝅘𝅥𝅮	Eighth note	½ beat
𝅘𝅥𝅯	Sixteenth note	¼ beat

In addition, any note can also have a dot placed after it, which will extend its time by one half of its value. In other words, a dotted half note (𝅗𝅥) is worth three beats, two for the half note plus one (half of two) added to it. Look at the following dotted notes.

FIGURE 12-20.
Dotted note
duration

Note	Name	Beats
 𝅝 .	Dotted whole note	6 beats
 𝅗𝅥 .	Dotted half note	3 beats
 ♩ .	Dotted quarter note	1½ beats
 ♪ .	Dotted eighth note	¾ beat

Rests

A rest is a period of silence, just as a note is a period of tone. In musical patterns, the silences are just as important as the sounded notes in order to establish rhythm and to break the monotony of steady sound. The rests have the same duration values as notes, and are shown in the following. As you can see, a dot can also follow a rest, extending its length by half of the value.

FIGURE 12-21.
Rests

Rest	Name	Beats
▬	Whole rest	4 beats or entire measure
 ▬	Half rest	2 beats
 𝄽	Quarter rest	1 beat
 𝄾	Eighth rest	½ beat
 𝄿	Sixteenth rest	¼ beat
 ▬ ▪	Dotted whole rest	6 beats

Ties

A tie is a curved line from one note to another consecutive note of the same pitch. The pitch must be the same but the notes could have any duration. When two notes are connected by a tie, or tied, you should extend the duration to include both notes by adding them together. You should not reattack the second note, but rather continue to sing through the length of the two notes together.

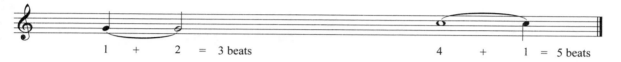

| 1 | + | 2 | = | 3 beats | | 4 | + | 1 | = | 5 beats |

FIGURE 12-22. A tie extends the note value

Rhythm Practice

Two things must happen simultaneously while you practice rhythm. First, you'll have to keep a steady beat with your hand or your foot. You can use your heartbeat or the tick of a clock as a pattern to follow. You can also purchase a metronome, an inexpensive instrument designed to keep a click at a steady rate. It has adjustable tempo settings that will allow you to speed up the exercises when you're comfortable.

EXERCISE 12-2

TRACK 72

1. After setting a steady beat with your hand or foot, you should speak the practice rhythms below on the syllable *bah*.
2. Your voice should hold the correct number of beats the note indicates while your foot or hand keeps the steady background beat. Remember that a rest is counted in silence.
3. Listen to the CD example, then sing or speak the rhythms on your own.

FIGURE 12-23. Exercise 12-2

Measures

A piece of music is organized into groupings of beats to make counting more manageable. The division into smaller units, called *measures* or *bars*, also serves to provide a natural accent on certain notes, usually the first note of each measure. This accented first beat of a measure is called the *downbeat*. Measures divide the staff with vertical lines, called *bar lines*, after a certain number of beats determined by the meter, as described in the next section.

FIGURE 12-24. Measures

Meter

This system of measurement and organization of patterns shown previously is called *meter*. Meter is indicated by a time signature, which looks like a fraction at the beginning of your music. The top number tells you how many beats are contained in a measure. The bottom number tells you what kind of note gets one beat. The lower number is representative of a note value as shown previously, so can only be 1 (whole note), 2 (half note), 4 (quarter note), 8 (eighth note), or 16 (sixteenth note). The quarter note and the eighth note are the two most common notes to get one beat. In other words, the bottom number is most often a four or an eight. Thus, ¾ meter, also called *¾ time*, has three beats in a measure and a quarter note gets one beat. When a measure is filled with three beats, a bar line is drawn and you start counting again with a new beat one. Any combination of notes that add up to three quarter notes is allowable, as shown here.

FIGURE 12-25. Meter

Putting It Together

Now you have all the necessary elements to begin reading music: pitch, duration, and meter. You'll need to separate these elements until they become more familiar. Look at the meter first for the most basic rhythmic information. Then you can decide whether to practice pitch or note duration, adding the next layer when one is mastered. The exercises will guide you through these steps.

Reading Rhythm First

EXERCISE 12-3

TRACK 13

1. Look at the meter to determine how many beats are in each measure and what kind of note gets one beat.
2. Without assigning pitch to the notes, count each measure using the method explained previously.
3. Be sure to keep a steady pulse rate with your hand or foot, and then voice the rhythmic values of the notes on the spoken or sung syllable, *bah*. The bar lines don't add any extra time to the count, so you should be voicing the syllables without gaps between measures. Begin with a tempo that allows you to maintain a steady rate.

FIGURE 12-26. Exercise 12-3

Reading Pitch First

TRACK 74

EXERCISE 12-4

1. Look at the previous exercise but concentrate on voicing the pitch of each note.
2. Try assigning numbers to the notes, with middle C as number one.
3. You can sing the pattern while filling in the missing notes silently, or you can read from note to note as individual intervals. Use whichever method is easier, but you'll probably find you use a combination of both.
4. Be sure to practice with the CD, and then again without it.

Simultaneous Pitch and Rhythm

TRACK 75

EXERCISE 12-5

1. Go back to Exercise 12-3, putting the parts together. Sing the notes on pitch, using any syllable, number names, or letter names.
2. This time sing the correct rhythm while maintaining proper pitch. Notice which element is easier for you, pitch or rhythm.
3. Keep repeating this exercise until it feels very easy to combine the two skills.

Tempo

The tempo of a piece of music is its rate of speed. How quickly or slowly you perform the music is usually indicated by the composer, but may be interpreted by the artist, director, or conductor, and is based on what is needed to best serve the performance of that particular piece. Tempo is indicated at the beginning of the music, or the beginning of a new section of music, in several different ways.

The most exact method of communicating the rate of speed is a metronome marking. As stated previously, the metronome measures tempo with a steady click representing the number of beats per minute. If a metronome marking is shown as ♩ = 100, that means there are 100 quarter note beats per minute. You should set the metronome to 100 to hear the click rate, and then tap the tempo along with it to determine how quickly you need to sing quarter notes, or the relative value of any other note.

Tempo Markings

Tempo may also be represented by generally accepted words or phrases stated at the beginning of the piece or at the beginning of a new section in the music. This method of tempo designation is most common, but less precise than a metronome marking. Descriptions of tempo can vary from person to person, or from one time period to another. Your definition of *slowly* might be quite different from your friend's concept of the same term. Most singers are, however, able to honor a relative tempo that should be acceptable. Sometimes in contemporary or popular music the tempo marking is in English, but more often, Italian terms are the norm. The following is a short list of the most commonly used Italian tempo markings:

- *Largo*: very slow, broad
- *Adagio*: slow, graceful
- *Andante*: walking pace
- *Moderato*: moderate
- *Allegretto*: slightly fast
- *Allegro*: fast, cheerful
- *Presto*: very fast, lively

As you can see, these are relative terms but still quite descriptive. The tempo markings allow for an interpretation of mood and character. Metronome markings are more exact but not as expressive. For this reason, many composers and publishers will use both methods together in the beginning of the music.

Tempo Changes

Tempo can also be changed during the course of the musical piece. The term *ritardando*, often seen as *ritard.* or *rit.*, means to get slower. *Accelerando*, or *accel.*, indicates the tempo should increase. After one of these terms of tempo change, *a tempo* designates a return to the original tempo.

Look through some examples of different styles of music and see if you can find the various markings. It's helpful to familiarize yourself with these terms in order to incorporate the information later in your music reading.

Practice

EXERCISE 12-6

TRACK 76

1. Look at the following piece of music. First determine the meter and then learn the melody, either pitch first or rhythm first.
2. After you're able to comfortably read with accuracy, you can then try to increase the tempo gradually.
3. If you find you start to make mistakes or hesitate at certain measures, slow it down again until the patterns are steady.
4. Be sure to try this exercise on your own first. Check with the CD afterward to see how well you did. Have fun!

FACT

"Simple Gifts" is a Shaker song written in 1848 by Elder Joseph Brackett, Jr. at a Shaker community in Maine. The Shakers are a religious group who developed their community as an offshoot of the Quaker denomination. The song was originally published in *The Gift To Be Simple: Shaker Rituals and Songs*, but is perhaps best known for Aaron Copland's adaptation in his ballet music, *Appalachian Spring*.

FIGURE 12-27.
Exercise 12-6

Simple Gifts

Shaker song

Elder Joseph Brackett, Jr.
(1797-1882)

Moderato ♩ = 100

mp

'Tis the gift to be sim - ple, 'tis the gift to be free, "Tis the

gift to come down where we ought to be, And

when we find our - selves in the place just right, 'Twill

be in the val - ley of love and de - light.

mf

When true sim - pli - ci - ty is gained, To

bow and to bend we shan't be a - shamed, To

turn, turn will be our de - light, 'Till by

turn - ing, turn - ing we come round right.

rit.

CHAPTER 13

Basic Music Theory

Music theory is the structure of songs you sing. A basic familiarity with the concepts of theory will allow the singer to perform a piece of music intelligently. The strongest musicians understand both the architecture and construction of the work they're building. Singers often concentrate on the voice because they are usually evaluated for the sound they produce, not their skills of musicianship. You'll need knowledge of theory, however, to develop and practice autonomously, communicate with your fellow musicians, and interpret the meaning of the music.

Key and Tonality

Key is the specific pitch that serves as a reference point of a melody or piece of music. The tones in the melody relate to that pitch as if it were "home," or the tonal center. Almost all Western music is tonal, which means it has a central note as a reference key. Some classical music of the twentieth century is atonal, meaning it was composed without a key, or tonal center. Atonal music is intentional and is not the same as singing out of pitch.

This reference pitch is called the *tonic*. The tonic is one tone, C for example, and serves as the name of the key. So if a song is in the key of C, C is the tonic, or central note, and all the notes of the melody will relate to C in some way. The other notes either move away from C, creating a sense of suspense, or they return to C as the goal of the melodic line, creating a sense of finality.

Don't confuse the word *key* in music theory with the keys on a piano or keyboard. Piano keys are a physical part of the instrument you press to hear a certain pitch. The key of a song is the central pitch and resulting set of notes used to form its melody.

Music has a key, but the singer, as an instrument, does not. Some singers think they have a key that is best for them, but really the piece of music has a key that best suits their voice. Depending on how the melody line is written, this could be any number of keys.

Scales

A scale is composed of the tones that relate to the tonic note. There are many different types of scales, but they all have ascending and descending notes in a consecutive order. Think of a scale as a palette of notes to draw from in making a melody. The majority of the colors, or notes, will come from this established palette, but a melody could borrow from outside of the specified scale.

FACT

The word *scale* comes from the Latin word *scala*, which means or "staircase," and the notes in the scale are called *steps*. A diatonic scale is a series of seven whole steps and half steps in a specific order. Any notes outside this grouping are called *chromatic notes*.

In most of the scales you'll be singing, this pattern of consecutive notes will begin and end on the tonic note and must use each of seven notes before the tonic is repeated. Remember the notes are named using the letters A through G. You can begin on any letter but then must continue in order and name each letter once until the initial letter is repeated. In this series of notes, the first note is the tonic and also the name of the key in which the piece of music is written. From one tonic to the next is an octave, or interval of eight notes.

In addition to letter names, the notes can be identified as the numbers one through seven. The numbers refer to scale degrees, or steps of the scale. There are many types of seven-note scales, but the two most commonly used scales in Western music are the major scale and the minor scale.

The Major Scale

TRACK 77

Look at the piano keyboard and identify the note C. If you count up from C to the next C, using all white keys on the piano, you'll have the formula for a major scale. Notice that there is no black note between E and F and between B and C. These are half steps and fall between the third and fourth notes and the seventh and eighth notes. All the rest are whole steps comprised of the two half steps formed by having a black key between two white keys. The resulting arrangement of consecutive steps is whole, whole, half, whole, whole, whole, half. This is the same formula you would apply to any starting note to create a major scale.

FIGURE 13-1.
Steps of the C major scale

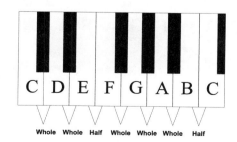

TRACK 78

If you start on the next note, D, and apply the same formula, you will need to adjust both F and C by raising them a half step. This allows the proper placement of half steps and whole steps. Remember that the half steps are between notes three and four and notes seven and eight. The numbered notes of the scale are called *scale degrees*.

FIGURE 13-2.
Steps of the D major scale

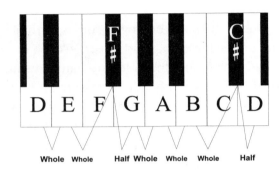

Minor Scales

If you begin with the sixth note of the major scale and play consecutive notes from that scale, you'll have the relative minor scale to the major key. A minor key is often described as having a more reflective, sad, or haunting mood. The arrangement of steps for the minor scale is whole, half, whole, whole, half, whole, whole. In this scale the half steps are between scale degrees two and three and between five and six. The relative minor scale of C major is A minor. Notice that A is the sixth note of the C major scale and begins the A minor scale.

TRACK 79

FIGURE 13-3.
Steps of the A minor scale

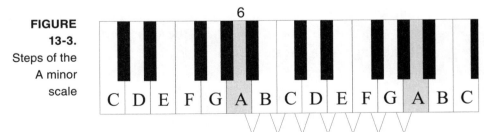

Listen to the difference between a melody in major and in minor. Knowing the key and its mood will help you interpret the song and make more accurate and powerful acting choices. A song in a minor key should probably not have a bright and airy delivery, just as a song in major would sound too dreary with a dark and somber attitude.

FACT

There are actually three different minor scales. The one described here is called *the natural minor scale*. If you're curious about learning more music theory, be sure to look at *The Everything® Reading Music Book with CD*. It's all explained there.

Key Signatures

The key of your song is represented by the key signature. A key signature is a set of varying numbers of sharps or flats and appears to the right of the clef at the beginning of each line of music. It determines the tonic and resulting scale notes. Each key signature has two possible scales: the major and the minor. Often you can determine whether a key is major or minor by looking at the final bass note, which is usually the tonic note and the name of the key.

Look at the following list of key signatures. You should start learning them so you'll be able to identify the key of the song you're singing. The key of the song is the most common question that musicians will ask of the singer. You'll need to know how to answer so you don't waste rehearsal time searching for your key. Concentrate first on the keys with the lowest number of sharps and flats, since they're used more frequently in popular music.

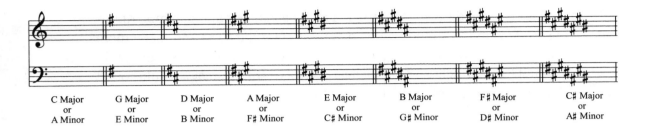

C Major	G Major	D Major	A Major	E Major	B Major	F# Major	C# Major
or	or	or	or	or	or	or	or
A Minor	E Minor	B Minor	F# Minor	C# Minor	G# Minor	D# Minor	A# Minor

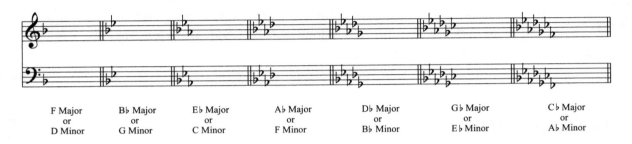

F Major	B♭ Major	E♭ Major	A♭ Major	D♭ Major	G♭ Major	C♭ Major
or	or	or	or	or	or	or
D Minor	G Minor	C Minor	F Minor	B♭ Minor	E♭ Minor	A♭ Minor

FIGURE 13-4. Key signatures

Transposition

If a song is too high or too low for you to sing comfortably, you can move the entire key of the music to fit in a more comfortable range. Changing the key, called *transposition*, will move the original scale up or down to a whole new scale, giving you a different palette of colors in your voice. You might change a key because you can't reach certain notes in the original key, or you could transpose the music to convey a different mood. A song with sultry lyrics would sound better in a lower key that requires you to use more of your chest register, resulting in an earthier sound than your head register. If you have a favorite song published in a key that doesn't suit the mood of the music in your voice, transposition is the answer.

When you transpose music you will need to change the notes and the key signature. This is easier to do by ear than on paper. Sing to yourself "Happy Birthday" or any simple children's tune. Now sing it again but start with a higher note. The entire song was raised to higher notes in order to keep the same melody. We do this all the time and don't really think about it. Look at the example of "Row, Row, Row Your Boat," first in the key of C and then in the key of D. Notice that the key signature changed and all the notes in the music are one step higher.

Row, Row, Row Your Boat

FIGURE 13-5. "Row, Row, Row Your Boat"

If you're going to an audition, never ask the accompanist to transpose the song for you. It's a very specific and challenging skill to transpose music while sight-reading. This request puts the accompanist on the spot, looks unprofessional, and you run the risk of less than perfect accompaniment, which will only hurt you and your audition, not the pianist. Instead, you should come prepared with music transposed to your correct key.

Transposing a song yourself will probably require further study. If you need to change the key of your music, you can get help from other musicians, your teacher, or your coach. There are also services on the Internet that offer song transposition for a small fee. Enter a search for "digital sheet music" or "music transposition" for a list of services. Also check the appendices of this book for a few specific Web sites.

Reading the Score

Many songs are written with a standard system of symbols that guide you through a sort of roadmap of the music. Without these symbols your music would be many pages longer, repeating information you can easily get from an earlier page.

Bar Lines

A single narrow bar line separates measures into readable units of time. A double bar line marks a new section of music. This could be a key change in the music or a significant change of mood or style. A heavy double bar line marks the end of the piece.

FIGURE 13-6. Bar lines

Repeat Signs

Using a repeat sign will avoid copying a set of measures. The dots to the right of the double bar line indicate the beginning of the repeat and the dots to the left of the double bar line mark the point at which you return to the beginning. If there is no beginning repeat sign, go back to the first measure of music. Once you've sung the repeated measures, continue the song.

FIGURE 13-7. Repeat signs

First and Second Endings

Another use of repeat signs is the bracketed first and second ending. After singing the measures contained under the first ending, return to the beginning repeat sign or the beginning of the song. If there is a second verse, sing that verse through the measure to the left of the first ending. Skip over the first ending and sing the measures contained under the second ending.

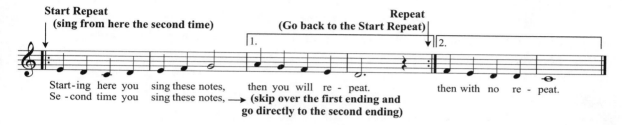

FIGURE 13-8. First and second endings

D.C., D.S., and Fine

D.C. stands for *da capo*, which means "from the head" in Italian. It means to repeat the song from the beginning. D.S. stands for *dal segno*, meaning "from the sign." D.S. indicates that you will repeat a section of music beginning with the D.S. symbol ✵. *Fine* (pronounced FEE-nay) is the Italian term for "end" and indicates the final ending with no repeat.

These symbols are used in some combination, giving you instructions about the route to take on the musical map. *D.C. al fine* means to repeat the song from the beginning and sing until you see the word *fine*. *D.S. al fine* means you return to the D.S. symbol and sing from that measure until the *fine*.

Coda

A coda is a short ending that is added to the regular body of the song, often called a *tag ending*. This separate ending is indicated with the coda sign and you would skip over measures to go directly to the coda when you see **To Coda** . *D.C. al Coda* means you repeat from the beginning of the piece, sing until **To Coda** , then skip to the coda symbol at the end. *D.S. al Coda* means you repeat from the D.S. symbol, sing until **To Coda** , then skip to the coda symbol and continue to sing to the end of the piece.

Rehearsal Letters

Vocal scores used in rehearsal settings with a director or conductor might have rehearsal marks as reference points for easier communication. The most common rehearsal marks are consecutive letters contained in a box. These letters indicate sections of music and offer an easily identifiable measure for review of a passage.

Most scores also have individual measure numbers. These serve as an additional way to locate a starting point for rehearsal. Sometimes measures are only numbered at the beginning of each line, so you'll have to count measures from that point if you need to begin in the middle of a line.

These symbols are all part of the language of music. Though not perfect, they can be extremely effective in guiding you through a vocal score. Take a look at some of your music and see if you can follow the map leading you to the different sections. After you are familiar with the terms, it's really much easier than turning many pages while trying to rehearse or perform.

CHAPTER 14

How to Practice

Practicing a new skill is the only way to incorporate it into your body as a habitual response. You need the repetition of an action to create muscle memory of that skill. When an action becomes an automatic part of you, you no longer have to think about every step of the process. Singing can be a lot of hard work, but if you think of this work as your time to have fun, the hours spent practicing can be the highlight of your day. In truth, the process of development is the most rewarding aspect of music. Try some of the tips in this chapter and approach your vocal exercises as you would a game.

Setting a Schedule

It's important to set up a schedule of practice to make sure you accomplish your goals. Repetition is crucial in training your body to respond to new habits, and you'll need to plan time for vocalizing. People respond differently to methods of scheduling, so you should be honest with yourself about the best approach. If you respond best to a set routine, you might want to actually write practice times in your calendar. Or you may prefer a more spontaneous system of practicing whenever you find the opportunity. Either way, be honest with yourself and respect your personal inclinations so that you can achieve the end result with minimal frustration.

How Often?

Ideally, some time should be spent each day on learning your craft. It's fine to vocalize every day if you'd like, or you could spend some days practicing your breathing exercises, reading and studying, or listening to other singers. Reading Chapter 9 of this book while listening to the accompanying CD is a good way to review the singing exercises on a day you're not able to vocalize.

When?

Any time of the day is acceptable for vocalizing. You'll need to listen to your own body to determine if you're a morning person or more comfortable later in the day. You may need a slightly longer stretch and warmup session in the morning to ensure that your body is alert. Many singers prefer vocalizing later in the day because of their performance schedules.

You should also try to remain aware of other people around you and be considerate of their schedules as well. In general, very early in the morning or late at night are times to avoid because of noise levels. It's important that you feel free to use full volume for certain exercises, so choose your time accordingly.

How Long?

The length of your practice session depends on your level of expertise. If you're a beginner, it's best to limit each session to fifteen or twenty minutes and spend time feeling the sensation of each exercise. When you become comfortable with short intervals, you can increase your time to thirty minutes. After you have some experience and feel at ease, an hour a day is ideal.

Always stop your practice session if you feel any strain or discomfort. You may just need to rest. If you are particularly tired or under excessive stress, your time is better spent in listening to exercises or studying your music theory. It's easy to push your voice past its limits if you're tired, and if you do, you'll end up doing more harm than good.

As with any practice, some time is better than nothing. If you only have five minutes, don't try to speed through the exercises. Do one or two exercises carefully so that it's time well spent. If you feel each session has to be perfectly timed and organized, you may avoid your practice altogether. It's better to achieve a small amount than to miss an entire day because it's not the perfect scenario. In contrast, be careful of getting so excited about your new skills that you overdo it and cause both vocal and emotional fatigue.

Where?

Any place you feel comfortable, relaxed, and free of tension is a good place to practice. If you practice at home, it's best to have a supportive environment. If this isn't the case, then find times you can be alone. Singing in the bathroom is a famous cliché, but the bright acoustics of the sound can be helpful.

You can sing in your car, but if you live in a dense traffic area be aware of any tension you may feel while driving. Any emotionally neutral space, such as a room in a school, church, or rehearsal studio, is especially good. These places are free of outside distractions and also require that you make some prior plan or commitment to your practice sessions. If you live or travel in a rural area, try vocalizing outdoors. It's fun to experiment with the sound of your voice in different environments and learn what various acoustic situations offer.

A Practice Routine

A basic lesson and practice session is provided in Chapter 9. Whenever possible, you should work through the entire lesson. You can also isolate exercises in the previous chapters for particular problems. No matter which material you choose for your session, be sure to start with the basic exercises first and then progress to the more difficult ones. The exercises that set up the proper placement of sound most easily are the ones you should repeat in order to reinforce the muscle memory. After completing the exercises, you can move on to practicing sections of your song.

The following list of equipment includes items that may be helpful or necessary, depending on the type of practice session you've planned:

- Piano, guitar, or some pitched instrument for reference notes
- CD player for your lesson or accompaniment tracks
- Tape recorder or digital recorder
- Mirror
- Music and a pencil to mark the music
- Notebook for practice log and rehearsal notes

Never skip your warmup before vocalization. The physical exercises and stretches you've learned will help to relax your body. Tension is definitely counterproductive to good vocal training. Take a moment to check your posture and alignment before singing and then check again at intervals throughout your practice session. Anytime you feel the slightest stress or strain, take a short break to stretch and refocus your energy.

Repertoire

The last part of your lesson or rehearsal time is spent on working with the material you want to sing. You may have several songs you'd like to learn, but limit each practice session to one piece if you're new to singing. There's so much information to synthesize in each phrase that it would be overwhelming and unproductive if you try to do too much at once.

Breaking It Down

Rehearsal is most productive if you break down the song into manageable units. It's always tempting to just sing through the whole song, but then it's too easy to gloss over difficult sections. A good length of music to practice in one session might be eight measures. Begin with single notes or intervals and then work complete phrases that would be sung on one breath. As sections become comfortable, you can attach them until the whole song is complete.

You don't have to rehearse phrases from the beginning of the song to the end or in any particular order. One trick to try is working on the end of the song first. Keep working backward through the song until you're at the beginning. You'll always be comfortable with the ending, which is sometimes more difficult material, because you've worked it more than any other section.

Studying the Song

When learning a new song, it's best to take your time and be as thorough as possible. If you don't go through the following steps, you'll risk learning the piece incorrectly. It's always harder to go back and change wrong notes than to learn it accurately the first time.

It can be helpful to hear the song before starting to work on it. If the song is recorded, or if you can play it on an instrument, listen to the melody and the structure. After a few times listening, however, you should put it away. It's tempting to copy what someone else has done with the song when the goal is really to find a way to make it your own. The recording artist probably changed some of what you see written, and it's too easy to follow what you hear rather than what you see on the page.

Work carefully through the following steps, first at a slower tempo, and then gradually increase the speed to performance tempo. If needed, practice only one or two steps each day.

1. Study the rhythm of each phrase as written. Speak the rhythm using a syllable such as *bah*.
2. Study the melody as written. Look carefully at the intervals and how the melodic structure relates to the words. If you play piano or some other instrument, play the melody of the phrase.
3. Speak the lyrics first as you would in normal speech, then again in the correct rhythm of the phrase. Be sure you know the meaning of each word and how to pronounce it.
4. Analyze the lyrics for natural breath phrases. How would you speak the phrases? Take a breath when you would naturally do so in speech. Remember that a rest in the music is also a place to take a breath. Write a check or apostrophe in the music to signify the breath marks.
5. Sing the melody in rhythm on a vowel tone that feels comfortable. Try singing the phrase several times using different vowels. Notice what changes in vocal register might occur at certain intervals.
6. Sing the melody and rhythm using only the vowel sounds of each syllable of each word. Now the vowel sounds are changing with each syllable as opposed to singing the melody on a single vowel sound.
7. Sing the melody and rhythm with the lyric line added. Keep the same vowel positions you felt in the previous step, just adding consonants to make the word clearly understood.
8. Add dynamics to the phrase. Notice what markings are written in the music to give the phrase a musical shape.
9. Connect phrases into full musical segments until you're able to sing the whole song. Sing through the entire piece to feel what level of endurance is needed.

When you feel ready, you should practice with accompaniment. This could be with your coach or teacher, or you may have recorded tracks for the song. Recorded tracks, which are instrumental versions of the song with no vocals, are helpful to hear the music. This type of accompaniment, however, may limit your capacity to develop phrasing choices that will make the song more personal and interesting.

Creating Good Habits

The best way to strengthen any new skill is to use constant repetition. Repetition is necessary for the body to incorporate muscle memory. It can also be a helpful tool to develop discipline and productive work habits.

FACT

It has been said that "slow practice makes fast learning." *Learning* to practice small segments of music with patience has significant benefits in the quality of your work. You'll feel more confident when you've mastered difficult passages in the music and consequently won't spend the rest of the piece in dread of that section.

The following list offers suggestions for creating some good work habits and maintaining motivation. What works best for you will depend on your personality and lifestyle:

- Set aside the same time each day for your practice.
- Enter your practice time in your calendar.
- Practice any time you feel you want to sing.
- Keep sessions short enough to leave you wanting more.
- Repeat phrases until they feel comfortable.
- Break down the music into small segments.
- Give extra attention to difficult phrases.
- Memorize phrases.
- Make a game of singing a phrase three times correctly before allowing yourself to move on.
- Reward yourself for your practice.

There is great satisfaction in achieving goals. Make a set of short-term goals that will be fun and easy to accomplish. This will encourage you to continue your study. Taking these small steps will actually speed up your learning process far more than jumping too quickly into a difficult project.

Mental Practice

Another method of practice is to spend time thinking through the process of singing. The use of mental imagery will increase your understanding of the exercises and the song. Try to imagine the sensation of lifting your soft palate or supporting the sound with your body. In your mind, sing through the exercises and feel the physical requirements for each set. Silently pronounce the words of your song and hear the rhythm of the syllables.

This practice can begin as a restful meditation. Feel the breath and let it quiet your mind before you begin the more active imagery exercises. Then think through each step as if you were singing the music. When you imagine the correct positions or the phrasing of a musical line, you'll discover a heightened awareness of what it feels like to sing.

Singing is accomplished in large part due to mental imagery. You can't reach inside and touch or move the parts of the vocal mechanism. But you are able to move each of these muscles by imagining certain positions. You are able to focus and direct sound vibrations to create volume, ring, and clarity in the voice. Spending some of your practice time in silent mental rehearsal can give you a deeper awareness of the physical action.

Attitude

So many children are forced to practice against their will that the very word has become a negative concept. Your practice time can actually be one of the most positive aspects of your daily life. This is the time you've set aside for yourself to accomplish something challenging, rewarding, and fun. Focusing your energy in practice sessions creates a mental state that allows you to go beyond your everyday concerns.

If you experience any setbacks or plateaus in your progress, don't worry too much. Sometimes you just need to rest and process the information you're learning. Stay aware of your body and never push yourself if you're sick or overly tired. Your time will be better spent listening to other singers and watching singers on video. Observing others will heighten your awareness and can often renew enthusiasm.

The most important aspect of creating productive practice time is to customize your methods to suit your unique personality. If you enjoy practicing, you'll want to continue. Make it work for you and your needs rather than feeling you have to follow a prescribed pattern or convention. Keep in mind that singing can be a lifelong process and evolution and there's really no such thing as "perfect" in music.

Learning a Song

TRACK 81

Try out the steps listed in the earlier "Studying the Song" section to learn a section of this music. You can check yourself with the CD, but see how many steps you can accomplish on your own first.

FIGURE 14-1.
"Evening Prayer"

CHAPTER 15

Finding a Teacher

Finding the right vocal teacher is an important and challenging decision. Some people are lucky enough to meet their best possible teacher easily and quickly. Others may spend a great deal of time and money in their search for the perfect match of teacher and student. If you're a beginning singer it can be extremely confusing to know what you need, who to trust, and which information is most helpful. This chapter will help you understand what to look for and how to evaluate a teacher and a lesson.

Do You Need a Teacher?

All singers, from beginners through professionals, can benefit from a teacher's guidance. Whether you need basic training or fine-tuning, an outside ear is necessary. What you hear inside your head is not the same sound that is heard by others on the outside. A qualified teacher can accurately assess what is required to help you find your best voice. Your teacher can give you a push when you need it, guidance, and feedback. Private vocal lessons are invaluable if you want to develop in a strong and healthy manner. Most experienced singers and professionals agree they need to check in often with their teachers and coaches.

Everyone can benefit from guidance in learning this complex instrument. You may be lucky enough to have a good voice already, but solid technique is needed to keep yourself healthy for a lifetime of singing. A teacher will streamline the learning process and keep you on track. You could potentially save years of trial and error, not to mention the risk of damaging your voice. It's a wise choice to utilize the background and knowledge of other more experienced singers, and not feel you have to reinvent the wheel.

Types of Teachers

There are two basic categories of vocal training: voice teachers and vocal coaches. You will most likely benefit from studying with a teacher until you have more experience. The teacher and the coach cover different needs of the student and have different skills to offer.

The Voice Teacher

A teacher will actually train you to sing by giving you step-by-step instruction. The purpose of your lessons will be to learn vocal technique and to prepare the voice for singing the songs you choose, also called *repertoire*. You will probably spend most of your lesson time working with exercises designed to develop the instrument. You can expect both breathing and vocal exercises that will increase your strength, endurance, and flexibility. Some teachers will work exclusively with exercises until your voice is ready to handle the challenges of a song. Others might incorporate a certain repertoire into the lesson as a chance to apply exercises to the actual music you want to sing. A voice teacher may have varying degrees of piano skills or accompaniment expertise, but this shouldn't affect your evaluation. The teacher's function is not as an accompanist, but rather to guide your vocal technique.

FACT

Often students feel they should study with a teacher of the same gender, but this needn't be a factor in your choice. It's important that the teacher understands the voice, not that she has the same voice type. Some teachers may be known for training particular classifications of voices well, even though they aren't necessarily that same voice type. In other words, for example, a teacher doesn't have to be a tenor to train a tenor.

The Vocal Coach

A vocal coach has a different function and is best utilized when you already have a certain level of competence as a singer. The coach will help you prepare material for performance or auditions by offering feedback on the presentation of the song. This could include analysis of the emotional content of the lyrics, dramatic interpretation and acting choices, diction and enunciation, musical phrasing, and all the aspects of performance that make the music come alive. A coach should be a qualified pianist and provide accompaniment for your music. He should also have a broad knowledge of repertoire, for the purpose of preparing the songs you bring to him as well as offering suggestions of new material.

What to Expect of a Teacher

It may be hard to assess a teacher if you're new to singing and voice lessons. You won't know what to expect from a lesson and have no previous experience to guide you in your decision. Even singers who may have some previous familiarity with vocal training can have a difficult time determining if a teacher is right for them.

Some aspects for you to consider are the same as those needed to determine the worth of any close relationship. The teacher-student relationship will be subjected to issues of confidence, vulnerability, power, and trust. You should feel that you can trust your teacher with your emotional well-being as well as your vocal instruction. Listen to your own instincts regarding the match of your two personalities. There is a psychological chemistry between teacher and student that is necessary to fully cooperate in the learning process.

Technical Expertise

The teacher should have a solid understanding of the voice and knowledge of vocal pedagogy. There should be evidence in a teacher's explanations of the vocal mechanism and the exercises that she thoroughly knows the subject she is teaching. This may be in the form of clear and concise verbal descriptions or even charts of vocal anatomy.

Also your teacher should have been or presently be a professional singer. No one can really understand an instrument without having played it, and hopefully played it well.

Often the best voice teachers are singers who were not able to depend solely on a natural gift at an early age. A singer who has encountered the same or similar difficulties will be more likely to know how to correct them and will understand the process. Such teachers are often more methodical in their approach because they've been there.

Evidence of basic musicianship is important for you to correctly learn material and connect the feeling of your voice to the musical line. You will also benefit from someone who is solidly grounded in classical work. Popular styles of singing are potentially damaging to the voice but can be managed with a strong foundation of classical study. Don't be afraid to sing classical repertoire such as basic art songs and arias. This material will strengthen your voice for later musical choices.

Exercises should be clear and achievable and they should cover several important concepts: breath management, using air for the onset of sound, the vertical position of the throat, and forward placement. As you work with the exercises in this book, you'll become familiar with these basic categories and learn to recognize them even when slightly altered. There are hundreds of vocal exercises used by various teachers, but usually the intent is toward the same goal of a strong and healthy voice. These exercises should be organized in a systematic approach so as not to be overwhelming.

Personal Characteristics

The most important element of the student-teacher relationship is trust. In addition to trust in your teacher's knowledge of the voice and ability to train you, you must also feel a more personal trust and know that he has your best interest at heart. He may challenge you to keep raising your level of learning but should be supportive and caring as well. You're served best by an honest teacher, not one who offers false praise. At the same time, the corrections should never be insulting or demoralizing.

ALERT!

Beware of any teacher who seems to have a particular agenda to prove. You'll want someone who allows and encourages your individuality. The goal is not to sound exactly like every other singer coming out of that vocal studio.

Your lesson should be fun and uplifting to keep your joy in the music alive. A sense of humor on both sides goes a long way toward easing any frustration or awkwardness you may experience. The best teachers of any subject matter are the people who love that subject and are excited to share the information. Their enthusiasm is infectious and will help you enjoy the process of study, not just the end result.

Practical Considerations

There are certain matters of a practical nature that you should consider in your choice of teachers. At times you may be willing to make some sacrifices to study with the instructor best suited to your needs. This isn't always possible, however, and your choice shouldn't cause unnecessary stress. Make sure your prospective teacher's policies and fees are agreeable with your lifestyle:

- The location should be clean, safe, and within a reasonable range of your home.
- You should be able to find a mutually compatible schedule for your lessons.
- Ask if you have to commit to a lesson package or if you may schedule individual lessons.
- The fee for your lesson should be affordable and within your budget. In smaller communities a lesson might range from $25 to $50, whereas teachers in large metropolitan areas usually charge anywhere from $75 to $250 for hourly lessons.
- Check on the teacher's payment policies before you begin lessons. Does she expect to be paid up front monthly or by the lesson? What form of payment is acceptable—cash, check, or credit card?
- What is the cancellation policy and do you have to pay for missed lessons?

In addition to these considerations, you can ask the teacher if she will allow you to record the lesson. It's helpful to hear yourself and the corrections, and also you'll have the recording for practice between lessons.

Evaluating a First Lesson

When you take your first lesson with a new teacher, you'll need to evaluate whether this is a good match for your needs. You may have your own set of criteria to consider in addition to these suggestions. The first lesson can give you most of the information you need to make a decision.

The Lesson

The teacher should have a professional working environment, even if it's in a part of her home. This will include a tuned piano or a keyboard, a mirror, and a tape recorder or some other recording method.

A lesson usually consists of exercises first and then a song on which you want to work. Exercises, called vocalises, warm up the voice and teach elements of technique. The exercises should be explained clearly, utilizing images that help you understand what to do. It's customary to stand during a lesson in order to assure proper support and posture. If you need to sit, it should be on the edge of a chair with a straight spine.

After warming up with exercises, it's helpful to work on a song that will integrate what your body is learning and incorporating as muscle memory. A large vocal library of sheet music in the studio is a benefit when looking for new material to sing. When learning a new song, technique should be addressed first, then musicality and interpretation.

You will need to analyze how you feel during and after the lesson. There should never, under any circumstances, be pain or discomfort. If you feel any pain from singing, the teacher should treat it as a serious matter that must be corrected. You should like what you feel and hear in the corrections you make. Most students also feel a sense of physical elation from a good lesson due to vibration from the musical tones, increased oxygen in the body, and openness in the throat.

The Teacher

Your teacher should give you his full attention during your lesson and remain patient with your development. Corrections are more helpful when phrased in a positive manner rather than continually focusing on what might be wrong. The purpose of corrections is to learn what will best serve the voice and its demands.

A professional attitude is important in a teacher. This includes respect for the student and the learning process. You should never feel insulted or belittled in any way. If you feel uncomfortable with the teacher physically or emotionally, look for someone else.

Your teacher should have a working knowledge of the style you want to sing and suggestions of specific pieces for your voice. His knowledge of your chosen genre and basic musicianship are some of the factors to consider when making your final decision. Often teachers specialize in specific genres of music and won't have an extensive knowledge of all styles.

Feel free to ask a new teacher for names of present or prior students. You can then check to see if you like their voices and if they sing in a similar style to your desired goal. If you know any of these students, you can check with them to see how they feel about their lessons.

Are You a Good Student?

You can also evaluate what it takes to be a good student. The responsibility for learning a new skill is ultimately your own. The challenge of learning to sing well is best approached as a partnership between you and your teacher. Most teachers appreciate a student who:

- Is eager to learn
- Is attentive during the lesson
- Accepts constructive criticism
- Remains focused and calm
- Is dedicated and consistent
- Asks questions
- Practices
- Respects the teacher's time and place

Try to be as prepared as possible for each lesson so you don't waste time and money. You can also plan to bring the following items with you to your lesson:

- A notebook and pencil (Use pencil on your music to allow for changes.)
- Two copies of the music you'd like to sing, one for yourself and one for the teacher
- A cassette tape and recorder, a digital recorder, or a blank CD if your teacher offers that recording option

Learning a new subject, especially one as personal as singing, can cause a certain amount of agitation, shyness, and defensiveness. Try to think past these emotions so you can concentrate on the task at hand. The teacher's job is much easier and more fun when the student is open and willing to work hard.

Where to Look for a Teacher

The best way to find a new teacher is through a personal recommendation. Ask your friends and colleagues if they know of good vocal instructors. Also feel free to ask any singer whose voice you like. They'd most likely be flattered and happy to offer suggestions. If you don't know anyone who studies singing, or if you've moved to a new community, you can look to outside sources. Check the music department of local colleges or universities for suggestions of recommended teachers. Often vocal instructors teach privately outside of the school setting. Church or community choirs are an excellent source of information as well. Choral directors and participating singers usually know teachers in the area. Teachers often advertise on bulletin boards in schools, community centers, and music stores, as well as the classified ads of newspapers and magazines. And don't forget about the option of searching the Internet. You can enter the search criteria of "voice teacher" and the name of your community, or look for lists of instructors on sites such as Craigslist.

Making a Decision

You may not find a teacher who fits all of the requirements you've set for yourself. Just as in any relationship, there may be compromises you make because you benefit from other qualities that seem more important. If you find a teacher who feels like a perfect match for your needs at this time, don't worry if one or two elements are missing. It's important, however, not to compromise on trust, vocal comfort with no pain, and a sense of progress.

Never feel obligated to stay with a teacher who doesn't suit you. You may feel a lack of personal chemistry, emotional tension, or you may dislike the direction your voice is taking. If a teacher encourages you to keep working through any pain, definitely look for someone new. Also keep looking if you feel this teacher doesn't understand you, your voice, and what you'd like to achieve. If you're unsure about the situation, a fair analysis would be your sense of progress within one or two months, if not immediately.

Once you've found a teacher you like, you should plan to take lessons at a fairly constant rate as often as your budget allows. Most students find that one lesson per week promotes a steady growth in the voice and gives enough time between lessons to practice. After studying for a length of time, you can determine if you'd like to stay with your present teacher because you continue to make progress, or you may be ready to move on to a new teacher and new challenges. If you are working as a professional singer or teaching others, you should never end your study of the voice. This is a life-long pursuit with new challenges at every level of expertise. Hopefully the satisfaction you derive from singing will encourage a desire for continuous study and growth.

CHAPTER 16

Expression

Singing is storytelling. Music is capable of representing people, places, and situations, but also can express a full range of moods and emotions. The desire to communicate an idea or a feeling through music is usually what attracts singers to their art. Singing expressively in a way that tells the story of the song is the primary goal of almost every singer. The previous chapters have dealt with issues of vocal technique and musicianship, which give you the framework to express yourself without the worry of how your voice sounds. This chapter will look at some methods of analyzing your music to best express its meaning and emotional content.

Interpreting Your Music

After you have learned your song and worked out some of the technical concerns, you'll need to address the content of the music and lyrics. Matters of interpretation are some of the most important elements of the song and each singer should be willing to spend some time with this step of the process. Your emotional connection to the music and ability to portray the sentiment of the lyrics are what count most with the audience, given that there are no glaring problems of vocal technique. First study the song technically, using the exercises you've learned in the previous chapters. When you feel comfortable vocally, then begin with the steps outlined in this chapter.

Musical Instructions

The composer provides some of the information you'll need when you first look at your music. Depending on what style you're singing, it may be very important to honor what the composer has written. Classical and theater music often give you very detailed instructions within the music, but you have more leeway in popular music. Interpreting whatever expression notation you find in the score, however, is your first step in analyzing dramatic interpretation. You might find details regarding tempo, dynamics, style, and articulation. Some performance markings are described in Chapter 11 if you need to review them. It's a necessarily short and therefore incomplete list, so you'll probably want to look up expression and performance notation in a music dictionary as you encounter specific markings you haven't learned yet.

FACT

Expression markings in the music cover tempo (rate of speed), dynamics (volume), style (emotional mood), and articulation (method of attack). These offer important information regarding the composer's intent about how you should approach the piece of music. Musicians frequently use a music dictionary to look up unfamiliar markings. You can find small and inexpensive dictionaries to keep with your music.

Standard performance notation is usually written in Italian, but occasionally you'll see these markings in the composer's native language. Most singers become familiar with basic Italian terms since they're used so frequently. For example, the term *Largo*, meaning "very slow," at the beginning of a piece tells you it's a ballad, not a peppy up-tempo. If you see *crescendo*, or *cresc.*, you'll need to sing increasingly louder throughout the phrase it marks, so there's probably increased emotion at this point. Issues of tempo and volume give a clue as to the emotional state of the singer's character. Someone who is upset and agitated will probably sing faster and louder at that moment than someone who is calm and peaceful.

EXERCISE 16-1

1. Look through any piece of music and try to find all of the performance notation. This will include dynamics, tempo, style, and articulation (notated on specific notes). If there are any terms you don't know, look them up.
2. Does this give you information about the song and the character? If you can, assign a mood to the song as described by these expression markings.

Most people don't even notice this information when they're beginning to sing. As you get more accustomed to learning new music, you'll begin to see these clues when you read the music for the first time. Your eyes will pick up what you know and filter out what you don't know, so make a point of looking for these markings in your songs. You might also want to pay attention to some aspects you don't have as much control over but still give you information about the mood. Look at the key and whether it's major or minor. Some composers write in particular keys to represent a mood they assign to that key. Also note if there are dissonant, or clashing, notes that will help you determine a mood of discomfort or edginess.

Lyrics

The words you're singing are the determining factor in any dramatic interpretation. It's best to separate the lyrics from the music so that you can look at the words clearly without being influenced by what the music is doing. Hopefully the melodic line of the music and the emotional intent of the lyrics will match, but sometimes they don't. If you don't feel that the music and words say the same thing, you'll have to decide how to interpret the line and what to emphasize. In most cases, you'll want to follow the meaning and accents of the words and assume that the melodic line will take care of itself.

EXERCISE 16-2

1. Write the lyrics of your song, including all punctuation, on a separate piece of paper so that you can see only the words with no music attached.
2. Read them aloud as if this were a poem or a monologue. Keep reading until you get a sense of what you are saying and hear the rhythm of the words. Be sure to look carefully at the commas and periods. These tell you where to pause and take a breath.
3. Listen to how you naturally phrase each line as you would in speech, and notice where you breathe. Place a check mark at each place you take a breath.
4. When you feel comfortable with the flow of the words, write the check marks in your music so you'll remember where to breathe when you're singing.

Exercise 16-2 gives you the first steps of phrasing by hearing the rhythm of the words and establishing your breath marks. After completing this exercise, you can further analyze the words to ensure that you really understand what they're saying.

Text Analysis

EXERCISE 16-3

Using the same page of lyrics from Exercise 16-2, complete the following steps:

1. Understand the vocabulary. Do you know the meaning of every word you're singing? Sometimes a song written in another era uses slang or popular words from that time period that are no longer in use. Or there may be other words you've never encountered and are unsure of their meaning. Be sure to look them up in the dictionary. When performing, you are the character singing the song as if you had written it yourself. Nobody would use words they don't know and run the risk of misinterpretation.

2. Paraphrase the story of the song. Retell the same story given in the lyrics but now use your own words, speaking exactly in the way you would talk as if this were your own story. It doesn't matter if it doesn't sound poetic; just tell the story. Don't use the same words as written in the lyrics—make them your own.

3. Say it in one sentence. Reduce your paraphrased story to one sentence that sums it up. Be strict about using only one sentence, but try to get the essence of the story in that sentence. This final step will be your statement of what the song is about.

When you've completed these steps, go back to the original words and read them aloud again. Notice how much more depth and understanding you are able to give the lyrics after making them your own. An added benefit is that you may have practically memorized the song lyrics by this time!

Acting the Song

Any song is a story to be told. The singer is really a storyteller who is able to use music to enhance the meaning and feeling of the story. You should always look at your song in the first person. In other words, think "I" or "me" when describing this story to yourself. If the lyrics are "I love him," then you shouldn't interpret this line as "she loves him," because this is looking at the story from the outside. Instead, you need to become this character in your imagination and pretend that you are actually the woman saying, "I love him." In the eyes of the audience, you are that woman. And the more you believe it at that moment, the more the audience will believe you.

Your emotional connection to the song depends on how strongly you can relate to the character singing those words. Any good actor (and singers are actors) will spend time doing a character analysis so that he might live within the character and as an external judge. It's easier to do this if you choose material that feels like you and says something you would like to say. But whether or not you relate immediately to the content of the lyrics, you can usually figure it out by going through the steps of a character analysis.

Listen to some of your favorite songs and singers. After reading this chapter, see if you can identify what steps they may have taken to get the end result. Listen for song form, phrasing, and emotional connection to the words. Can you hear the story they're telling?

Character Analysis

As you work through these steps, remember to think in the first person. Don't judge from the outside. The work you do in this section will pay off significantly. Being able to communicate well is the mark of a professional singer. Your emotional connection to the song is ultimately what your audience wants to see and hear, and separates a star from just another singer.

1. Who are you? Create a biography and be as complete as possible. Remember to incorporate any information you're already given in the written words. Try to include details about your name, where you grew up, what your childhood was like, your educational background, your job, your friendships, your love relationships, and anything else you might want to know about yourself.

2. Where are you right now, as the song is beginning? Be specific and really see it. Are you indoors or outdoors, at a club or at home, at work or school?

3. Who are you talking to? This is very important and you must be specific. See a particular person, not a generalized "someone." If the song is general and not directed to one person, or if you're talking to yourself in the

lyrics, try to create a story that would demand you say this to someone outside of yourself, even if it's you in the mirror. If you talk to yourself, you run the risk of internalizing the song rather than opening it up to your audience. If you talk to someone else, the intent is clearer for your listeners.

4. What do you need or want from that person? Is it some kind of response or a definite action? Remember, in real life we say things to people for a reason.

5. What's in your way? Why can't you have what you want? The story is basically over once you get what you're after, so be sure to build in a conflict to overcome, even if it isn't immediately apparent in the lyrics.

6. What are you doing to get what you need or want? What method are you using to achieve your goal? Make this an action verb, such as *pleading, tricking, seducing,* or *humoring.* These are just examples—think of an action that's appropriate for your character in this song.

7. What just happened the moment before you started to sing? What triggered your need to say these words? Were you praised, insulted, or ignored? Create a scene in your mind that will allow you to go to the emotional place of this song in an instant.

You can spend weeks developing these answers, or you may know most of this information immediately. You can go through these steps many times and find that you can always deepen your connection to the songs you sing.

FACT

Performers who have become famous for singing a particular song find that they have to sing that same song in concert many times throughout their career. It may be ten or twenty years after first recording a song, and still the audience wants to hear it. The singer can use these steps in the character analysis and find new, fresh ways to say the same words just by changing the imaginary story and character.

Once you've completed your analysis, go back to the song and say the words aloud. Feel free to try out several different stories and situations for the same song if it doesn't seem right. When your imaginary story fits the song, you might experience a feeling of freedom. The song seems to flow from the right place and you're no longer worried about it. You might even find the places where the character would take liberties with the music by adding improvisations or embellishments to certain notes.

Musical Shape

Your song has an overall form and shape that's usually regular and symmetrical. Imagine it's a piece of architecture you have to design. Most of the design has been taken care of by the composer who created the piece. There is an overall song structure, which may include sections such as verse and chorus. Within each individual section there are phrases that make up the section. The song as a whole has an arc, or a pattern of highs and lows. The height of the arc is usually, but not always, near the end of the song. This is the point of the highest level of emotion and will probably demand more power from the singer. You can try making a graph of your song, as many composers do, to identify the high points and low points of intensity so that you can gauge the amount of physical effort needed throughout the song.

It's very common when starting out to give equal emphasis to each note and word, with no change of dynamics. All English words have stressed syllables and unstressed syllables that should be honored in singing as well as speech. Equal accents on every syllable create a strangely robotic sound that's unnatural. Try speaking a sentence using equal stress on each syllable and you'll hear the problem.

Within each section, there is also an arc of some sort. No musical line should be entirely even, as this would sound more like a robot singing than a person. Once you've found the shape of the section, look to the individual phrase for another arc. The shaping of each phrase isn't necessarily wide and dramatic. It may be subtle, but it must be there. Once again, think of your natural speech patterns. Each phrase you speak has a rise and fall of pitch so as not to sound monotone. Music always has a sense of movement, even if you are singing the same note. Looking for these natural patterns is called *styling* or *phrasing*, and it can be approached technically and emotionally. Analyzing the architecture of the music along with the character and story line offers a complete method of rehearsing your song. The structure and syntax of the words and music give valuable technical information, but your emotional connection to the song is what makes it unique and special.

Practicing a Song

Look at the song "All Through the Night." Use this piece to go through the exercises and analyses. Try out different technical choices and story lines. It's a traditional Welsh folk tune, which allows it to be more adaptable to interpretation.

All Through The Night
Sleep, my child, and peace attend thee,
All through the night;
Guardian angels ever 'round thee,
All through the night.
Soft the drowsy hours are creeping,
Hill and vale in slumber steeping,
I, my loving vigil keeping,
All through the night.

1. Study the lyrics. Look first at the words of the song and write them on a separate page. Writing by hand tends to bring the song closer to you than typing the words.

   Remember to look at the punctuation for phrasing and breath marks. Speak the words in the most natural way possible and look them up if you don't know them. Try emphasizing different words and listen to the way it changes the meaning.

   Now go to the story and the character. Build your first story around a parent's lullaby to a baby. Do the complete character analysis. Later, change the story and imagine you're saying these words at a funeral. This character will have a very different emotional response to the words. If

TRACK 82

you can think of more story possibilities, you'll find each brings about a different phrasing of the words.

2. Study the music. Look at the form and identify the phrases. Look for all the performance notation and write any notes you might need to remember the meaning of each marking. Listen to the melody and decide how well it suits the words to determine if the music will help you with phrasing. You can try singing the melody without the words first, then add the words. The song is short, so spend time with each phrase and mark the shape you'd like to hear.

FIGURE 16-1.
"All Through the Night"

All Through the Night

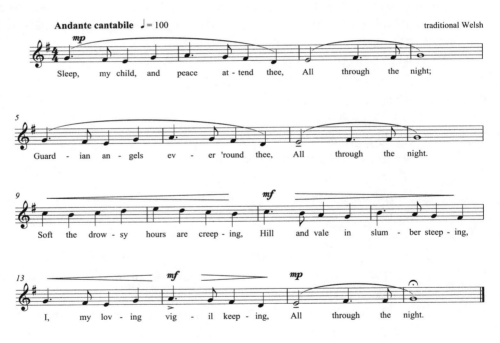

After practicing this song, pick one of your own. Spend time going through the steps. The biggest danger most singers face is rushing through the music trying to get the end result too quickly. It's easy to hear in your mind the way you'd like to sing the song, but you won't achieve that goal if you gloss over proper rehearsal. With practice, your song might sound even better than you originally imagined because you truly made it your own.

CHAPTER 17

Performance

Singing in public is one of the most exciting challenges imaginable. It's a common reaction to be both thrilled and terrified by the experience. Amateur and professional singers alike have to deal with their emotional response to public performance, and they have discovered various methods to ensure a good performance. If you keep in mind that the primary goal of singing is communication, whether it's with a small gathering or a large audience, performing becomes an act of sharing rather than presentation.

Preparation

The best insurance you can have for a good performance is solid preparation. There are many levels of preparation to consider, and the more thorough you can be with these steps, the more comfortable you'll be onstage or in the studio. When you're well prepared, you can be free to concentrate on the main purpose of performing, which is to communicate openly with your audience. No singer is able to focus properly on that goal if she is worried about her vocal technique, her memory of song lyrics or set list, how to move, what to wear, and the seemingly endless list of potential problems onstage. Take a moment to write down some of your own particular concerns about performance and keep this list in your notebook. Tackle each item on the list slowly and thoroughly until you feel you've addressed each one to your best ability. When you feel you are able, look for an opportunity to get onstage.

Vocal Technique

Solid vocal technique can't be rushed, but you can at least make sure you're on track with regular exercises and voice lessons. If you feel that your present level of technique affords you a comfortable and pleasing vocal range to use in your repertoire, you will probably want to try it out with an audience. Performing can be a great teacher, informing you of which technical aspects of your singing voice have become a part of your body in secure muscle memory and which still need more practice. Nervousness onstage may cause some lapse in even the best technique. Did your breathing get shallow? Did you crack on a high note? Use the experience to strengthen your knowledge and resolve to work harder on that facet of your training.

Rehearsal

You'll need plenty of rehearsal time in order to feel comfortable onstage and give the best performance. The more time you spend working with your songs, the better you'll know them and understand what you want to say with each piece of music. Be sure to go through the steps outlined in Chapter 16 to discover the story of the song and your emotional connection to it. Also review Chapter 14 regarding good rehearsal habits. Remember to first isolate portions of the song so that you don't gloss over problem areas, but also save ample time to continually sing through the entire piece. This is the only way to identify issues of stamina, breath management, and energy preservation. Finally you should pretend you're in performance in order to practice what it takes to get through each complete song. Remember, you won't be able to stop and fix something in front of an audience.

You should plan time to work with your accompanist and whoever else will be with you onstage during performance. Sessions with the accompanist and your vocal coach prior to the performance date are well worth the time and money. This is the time to decide on the arrangement of the song and to hear exactly what your accompaniment will sound like. If you're singing with prerecorded tracks, take them to your coach to use during a practice session. At the very least, sing your material for friends who will give you honest and constructive feedback.

Warmup

On the day of performance, be sure to allow adequate time to warm up your voice and your body. If you're not feeling well, you should allot extra time to vocalize slowly and gently. Unfortunately, personal experience is the only way to know how long you'll need to vocalize. You shouldn't sing too much on the day of a performance, since you might overtire your voice. But you do need to vocalize enough to make sure your body remembers all the vocal positions needed for your repertoire.

ALERT!

Be sure to get plenty of rest during your rehearsal period and before your performance. You'll need to be alert to manage the physical exertion needed onstage. Remember to treat yourself well, since you are the instrument as well as the performer.

You should definitely work through some of the stretches for your body listed in Chapters 2 and 9. It's very important to stay relaxed and free of excess tension, which will close off your voice. You might want to add in time for meditation, which provides a calming influence as well as a way to strengthen mental focus and clarity. Then proceed to your vocalises, continuing to sing until you feel your voice is clear and open. Sometimes the hardest thing to do is to make yourself stop at this point and not overdo the preparation. This can tire your body as well as make you more anxious. Relax and know that you're as ready as you can be at this time.

You can also add to your warmup routine some time for mental visualization. Picture yourself walking onstage, seeing your audience, connecting emotionally with your scene partner, or imaginary scene partner if you're singing solo, and singing to the best of your ability. This exercise can be very powerful as a way to rehearse on the day of performance.

Choosing Material

If you're cast in a theatrical production, your songs have already been chosen for you. But if you're going to perform in a concert or club setting, you'll probably need to choose your own songs. Making decisions about repertoire can seem overwhelming, since there's a wealth of great music in every genre. Here are some guidelines to get you started:

- You should like the song. It's very hard to do a good job with a song that doesn't appeal to you. There are so many wonderful songs available that there's never any need to sing something you don't like unless it's for a good cause.
- The song should be comfortable in your voice. Look at the range to determine if all the notes will be manageable. If the song has notes that are too high or too low, look to see if there's a way you can alter the melody to make it fall within your comfortable range. If not, look for another song. Performance isn't the time to stretch to the outer limits of your voice, but rather a time to show what you already do well. Save the challenging material for lessons and exercises until it's ready.
- The tempo and dynamics should be within your control. Songs that are very fast and wordy may be difficult to articulate while maintaining accurate rhythm, whereas slow ballads may have long phrases that are hard to manage on one breath.

- The tessitura of the song should allow you to articulate the words clearly and distinctly. The entire song should be within your range, but the majority of the notes you're singing should feel easy and comfortable. If too much of the melody lies in your highest or lowest notes, your voice will tire more quickly, and you'll probably sound strained. Change the key of the song to match your own tessitura.
- You should feel a strong emotional connection to the lyrics of the song. Your job is to tell the story, and you'll need to really understand what you're saying and feeling. If the song doesn't move you, it probably won't move your audience either. Make sure the lyrics are within your range of experience and maturity to be believable.

Finding material that's appropriate for you is an art and will probably take some experimentation. Look at the lyrics first to determine if the song is a match for you. The singer is always the storyteller and you must feel that the message and sentiment of the story are worth sharing. As you find a song you like, rehearse it using the steps you've learned. Then decide if you want to keep the song in your repertoire or move on to the next choice.

Finding Your Individuality

Each singer is completely unique by nature, but often, new performers will try to imitate famous singers they admire. Some people work very hard to be just like someone else, figuring that will guarantee success for them as well. By the time they achieve their goal that particular passing fad may be over or, even worse, there may be an overabundance of copies stamped out of the same mold. The only way to really make a lasting impression as a performer is to find and celebrate your own distinct individuality.

You may already know what qualities make you unique. If not, ask your friends to assign a few adjectives to your personality and physical demeanor. If the same adjective keeps coming up, there's probably some truth to it. Do you like the response? If not, you'll need to make a bolder statement about which qualities you'd like to portray. The main thing is to be truthful and honest with yourself, because you may have to wear this image for a long time. The easiest way to establish a strong self-image is to be yourself, since no two people are exactly the same.

Discovering your individuality will also help guide your choice of repertoire. The dramatic material you choose says something about you as a performer. The content of the song could be a direct statement about who you are and what you believe, or a more delicate approach to show the many colors of your personality.

Singing Onstage

After you've studied your vocal technique, chosen your material, and rehearsed your songs, it's time to try out your new skills with an audience. Performance, no matter the level, is an important goal to synthesize all the elements of learning to sing. It requires confidence, courage, and a willingness to expose your emotional self to a group of friends and strangers. This sort of vulnerability is most effective when you can find a balance between confidence and humility. The extremes can turn to boastfulness or self-denigration, neither of which is an appealing personality characteristic onstage.

The job of a performer is to move the audience. One excellent method of helping an audience to feel a particular emotion or reaction is to feel it or imagine it yourself. But you should always remember that you're there for the audience; try not to get so involved in your own private world onstage that you lose sight of the goal. It requires practice to find the right level of immersion into the character of the song without losing sight of certain practical considerations and basic communication skills.

FACT

Experiment with focus and concentration in front of other people. Only practice will determine what percentage of your focus you'll need to give to vocal technique and staging and what percentage will be spent in acting and communication concerns. This ratio will change from song to song and also generally with experience.

The strongest scenario for a good performance is that you're able to give the most concentration possible to acting the song and telling the story. The goal of rehearsal is to commit the technical issues to muscle memory in order to free you to sing with emotion. The more deeply you're able to genuinely feel the meaning of the song, the more easily you can transmit emotion to the audience and guide them to the world of that story.

Focus

You can regard the question of focus from two different angles. The first issue is that you'll need to maintain an internal focus and concentration that carries you through each song and through an entire performance. Ask yourself why you are singing that song and what you hope to convey. You could answer this question based on your own set of reasons or from the standpoint of a character you are playing. Knowing why you're there helps to keep you centered, calm, and able to think clearly if anything unexpected happens during a performance.

The other matter of focus in performance is the question of where to look while singing. Do you look directly at people as you do when speaking to them, or should you look somewhere else? The answer really depends on the style of music you're singing and the performance venue. If you're in a musical, you'll most often be singing to your scene partner. If you're singing in concert, you should keep your gaze at about the eye level of your audience rather than above their heads. A good rule is to never close your eyes completely for longer than a few seconds. It's natural to close them for a moment while thinking or remembering, but if you leave them closed you'll shut out your audience. The expression in your eyes is the clearest indication of who you are and what you're feeling.

Some genres of music are very presentational in their performance style. You should take this into account and follow convention to a degree, but always keep in mind that you're talking to someone when you're singing. If you don't, there's no point in having an audience.

Review the acting exercises in Chapter 16 to determine your imaginary scene partner and then *really* sing to that person. If you pretend the person is standing right in front of you, you'll actually take in the whole audience. If you believe what you're saying, they'll also believe you. Feel free to shift the focus and direction of your eyes just as you would in a real conversation.

Movement

The amount and type of movement onstage also depends on the style of music you're singing and the performance situation. Most singers wonder what they should do with their hands. If you're holding a microphone, the problem is half solved, but you still have one more hand. The best answer is to express yourself as naturally as you would when speaking to someone. Practice your song as a monologue, as you did in your acting exercises, and notice what happens with your hands when you relate the story. You can also try walking around while you rehearse your song and check to see what physical response feels comfortable and fits the music. Be careful that you're not too still, or you may look like a terrified statue. But you should also contain the movement enough that it's not distracting. When in doubt, you should stand in one place and gesture naturally with your hands. There is more power and strength in stillness than in frenetic movement.

EXERCISE 17-1

1. Try singing your song as if you were in a silent movie. Use big gestures and exaggerated portrayals of emotion.
2. Then sing the song again and make yourself stand absolutely still. Don't move your head or your hands.
3. Now go back to what you consider a normal presentation of the song. The two previous extremes of movement will help you decide on a comfortable balance.

Walking onstage and movement between songs can be very telling about your level of self-confidence and comfort with your audience. Even if you don't feel confident, you can convince your audience that you're at home onstage by walking and holding yourself with good posture and a straight body alignment. This is not the time to slump! Look again at the posture exercises in Chapter 2. Use these exercises to rehearse and again as your preperformance warmup. You should never apologize for being onstage, either literally or nonverbally with insecure body language.

ALERT!

What you wear onstage can affect how you feel. If you have a choice, you should dress in something that is comfortable and allows you to move freely, is flattering so that you'll feel you look your best, and is appropriate to the style of music you're singing.

EXERCISE 17-2

1. Practice making an entrance onstage. Pretend that the announcer has just introduced you, and you walk onto the stage as you hear the applause. You know the audience likes you and wants to be there with you. You have an important secret to tell them and can't wait to share it. You feel very proud and honored to be with your audience. This is you at your best!

Sometimes you'll be choreographed to move or dance in specific ways. Choreography can be reassuring since it removes the problem of deciding what to do. But it also adds the challenge of singing in positions that are difficult, physically exhausting, or that take you out of your best alignment. Be sure to keep the feeling of an anchor in your body while moving. Using the appoggio technique, imagine a vocal anchor in your sternum. This will steady the air pressure and keep the sound from pressing in your throat.

In general, try to examine your physical movement in everyday life. The more aware you become of your natural patterns, the more you can learn to adopt these habits onstage as well. Conversely, learning to move well onstage can make beneficial changes in your daily behavior.

Practice your performance with a video camera. You can record yourself during rehearsal and again during your show. It's hard to be objective when watching yourself the first few times, but try to use these recordings as a chance to see both what you like and what needs extra work. Studying yourself is the best way to streamline rehearsal for the next performance.

Stage Fright

Almost everyone has experienced some sort of stage fright at some time in her life. It might have had such an impact that it continues to cause anxiety, or even keep you from singing in public altogether. It's natural to be nervous when performing, especially if you're new to singing onstage. Just knowing that it's a natural response can be helpful. But you might need some extra tools to help you deal with performance nerves.

- Anxiety is emotional energy. Don't try to tell yourself not to feel scared. Instead, turn the feeling into positive energy by imagining that it's just excitement you're experiencing. Feeling your energy is the only way to have a good performance.
- Breathe! Breathe! Breathe!
- Forget trying to be perfect. No one is, and no performance is. There will be "mistakes" that can be turned to your advantage if treated with humor and lightness. Let any mistake be a chance to learn something for next time.
- Imagine that this is your party and you invited these people as your guests. It's your job as host of the party to make everyone comfortable. Turn it around so that it's not about you, but about them.
- Focus on your acting partner, real or imaginary. Let your partner lead you to your strongest emotional connection and your need to tell this story.
- Many singers are actually shy in everyday life. Let your performance be a chance to take on a stage persona of someone who's outgoing

and self-assured. If you pretend to be this character onstage, no one will be the wiser, except maybe your closest friends.

- Make sure you're prepared. Everyone gets nervous if they're unsure of what they're doing. Know what you're singing, where to go onstage, the order of your songs, and how to approach the music with your best vocal technique.

- Practice performing. It's really the only way to conquer your fears. The more you do something, the easier and more comfortable it can become for you. Sometimes it's just the unknown that's frightening, and when you're familiar with the routine, you can channel the energy more easily.

Remember, if you're too calm, your performance will probably be boring. The best performers are fueled by high energy, and it's up to you to decide how to interpret that energy. If you think the feelings come from fear, you might block your communication with the audience. But if you believe the rush of adrenaline is due to anticipation, excitement, and eagerness to share with your friends, you'll probably have great stage presence.

Using a Microphone

Singing with a microphone is standard practice in most styles of music. There are some situations in which you might be fitted with a body microphone, controlled by an offstage engineer. Most of the time, however, you'll be required to use a hand-held microphone, so you should spend at least one full rehearsal getting used to the technique.

A microphone is meant to enhance the volume of voice so that you can be heard over amplified instruments. It's not meant to correct faults or let you get lazy in your vocal technique. But you can learn to use the mic to your advantage.

Microphone Dos

Look at this list of ways you can work with a microphone:

- Adjust the height of the stand before you begin to sing. If you have a sound check before your show, you may be able to set it then. The height will depend on the type and strength of the microphone, but try it at chin level so you don't cover your face.
- Make sure the mic is turned on. Some microphones have a button or switch on the side. Others are automatically on if they're plugged in.
- Practice taking the microphone in and out of the stand so it doesn't get caught during a performance.
- Hold the mic about 2 or 3 inches from your mouth for a basic level of sound.
- Hold the mic in the center so it stays balanced in your hand.
- Sing into the microphone. If you have to turn your head, remember to move the mic so that it stays in the same position in front of your mouth.
- Hold the mic close to your mouth for low notes and when you want the sound to be warm and intimate.
- Hold the mic further away for high notes or if you are much louder than other singers or instruments.
- Think of the mic as an extension of your vocal tract, not a foreign object.
- Practice special effects of varying distance from your mouth and using vocal sounds that would otherwise be too low in volume without a microphone.

QUESTIONS

Should I buy a microphone?
Sometimes a singer is required to provide a microphone for performance. It's a good idea to have your own mic for such events and also for general practice. The most popular standard vocal mic is made by Shure and is called the SM58. It has good quality and is extremely durable.

Microphone Don'ts

You may need some practice time to get used to your microphone. Try to avoid these common problems:

- Don't hold the microphone in front of a speaker. This will cause feedback, which is a piercing squeal.
- Holding the mic too close to your mouth will make your voice sound muffled and unclear.
- If you hold the mic too far away from your mouth, it won't pick up your voice at all.
- Don't turn your head away from the microphone while you're singing.
- Be careful with your diction when using words with b and p since they can make a popping noise on the microphone. Similarly, c, s, and z can cause the microphone to pick up sibilance and hissing sounds. Hold the mic more toward your chin if this is a problem.
- Don't hold the microphone in front of your face. This will block the audience's view of your face, making it more difficult for them to connect with you.

Make sure you have some time to practice with your microphone. If you've never used one, it can be surprising initially. At first, just sing with correct vocal technique and adjust the mic as needed. After you're comfortable, play with some of the special effects you can get using a microphone.

Enjoy Yourself

Performance is the culmination of all the work and effort you've expended to be at your best as a vocalist. Preparation is the key to a good performance and enjoyable experience. It can't be stressed enough that you need to spend time doing your homework, exercising your vocal technique, and rehearsing your material. After you feel fully prepared, then the biggest challenge is to walk out onto the stage and let go of your inner critic. Performing is about being in the moment and not about overanalyzing or monitoring your actions. If you're watching yourself, you've forgotten your audience. Of course, you should be aware of what you're doing in order to learn for the next experience, but while onstage, enjoy yourself and the audience you're leading through the stories you tell.

CHAPTER 18

Performance and Career Opportunities

Once you've decided to sing in public, there are limitless possibilities if you use a little imagination. If you're getting good feedback when you sing and people are telling you that you should be a singer, that's a good indication to look for places to try out your skill. Or if you're shy and would like to use singing as a way to overcome fears and challenge yourself, there are places to start that won't be as difficult as you might imagine. Look through some of the ideas in this chapter and see if anything appeals to your sense of adventure.

Choir

Singing in a choir is an ideal setting for many people. The most immediate advantage of choral singing is the support you get from singing in a group. If there are others around you singing the same thing you're singing, you can feel more secure in your body, your voice, and your knowledge of the music. It can be a great learning experience if you're still a little shaky in trying out your new skills.

FACT

Most churches and synagogues have some sort of choir. There may even be professional jobs available as section leaders. Church choirs have the advantage of accepting anyone who wants to sing. You might also find secular choirs in your town. These choirs may hold auditions or may also accept anyone who wants to join. Look for more information in Chapter 19.

Choral singing can also be a serious challenge and a way to develop your musicianship. Learning how to blend with other voices requires certain technical adjustments so that your solo voice doesn't stand out from the rest of the voices around you. Many choirs require sight-reading skills and provide an excellent venue to practice. The material you're singing may also be more difficult than you might choose on your own and will give you exposure to new types of music you might not have sung otherwise. You also need to be exact in choral singing and sing the material precisely as written, again so that your voice blends with the others.

Choirs are a great choice for offering built-in support for your singing. Any situation in which people come together to do a single activity can be extremely valuable and uplifting. The sensation of singing together with other people and being part of the harmony created by many voices can be exciting and quite intense. Even if you think you might prefer solo singing, this is an experience no singer should miss.

Community Groups

Community singing groups are usually a lot of fun and provide some of the same benefits as choir singing. Often a community group has a particular thrust which is the reason they formed originally. That could mean there's a certain kind of music in which they specialize, or maybe even a cohesive subject matter of the music. Or the unifying factor could be the people themselves, such as groups that are specifically for just men or just women. They may be small groups or could be quite large.

The list of possibilities for these types of groups is practically endless. You might find a barbershop quartet, which is four men singing close harmony. Similarly there are girl groups, which are often three-part harmony.

Singing harmony with a group or choir does have certain requirements. The most important thing is that you sing on pitch. It's an absolute necessity that your pitch is accurate when you're combining voices to make a chord. You'll also need some basic musicianship skills to get along more easily and quickly in rehearsal.

Glee clubs are another example of groups defined by the people who join. They are often school groups, and may be offered as part of a college curriculum or later as an alumni group. Some of these school-based glee clubs, such as the Yale Glee Club, have become quite famous for their high level of musicianship. The Harvard Glee Club, formed in 1858, is the oldest college choral group and has included many famous musicians. Some schools have several groups spread out through the country for alumni participation.

There are groups formed for both the subject matter and the people involved, such as nationalistic singing groups. You may find a German group, for example, composed of German people in the community, people who enjoy German culture and music, or those who have that heritage in common. The music would probably be sung in German, but possibly in English translation as well to make the group more accessible to the general community. A famous example of national choral groups is the multitude of Welsh male choirs.

Other subject-oriented music groups could be based on periods of music history, such as early music groups, Renaissance, or Baroque groups. Some of these groups started out as a small get-together of friends and grew into professional singing groups who specialize in that style of music. Or perhaps one person's vision could be the creative force in forming the group as well as finding the material and directing the music. There are many historically based groups, such as the Tallis Scholars, Chanticleer, and Anonymous 4. And there's always Christmas caroling, which is dependent on the season, but lots of fun and a chance to try out your choral skills.

Musical Theater

Musical theater is a popular outlet for performers in the smallest towns and largest cities. The professional standard of this genre is traditionally considered to be Broadway musicals in New York City. Once a show has had its first professional run, either on or off Broadway, it's then usually available to be performed in national tours and open to anyone who can pay for the rights. Both schools and community groups enjoy producing one or many musicals every year and can offer an excellent opportunity for you to perform. Many people perform in musicals as a regular and fulfilling hobby for a lifetime, and some find they enjoy it so much that they move to a professional setting in which it can become a full-time career. Careers in musical theater are very competitive and often involve touring with a show for long periods of time. To make a livable wage in musical theater, you would probably have to live in a major city, such as New York.

Community and school musicals are almost always volunteer positions. Usually there is an audition to see if you can be cast and in which role. Getting a role means you will need to look and sound like the character in the show and have a strong enough singing voice to project in the theater. Often the leading roles are cast with people known to the director of the show or who already have some kind of track record. The best place to get started in musical theater is the ensemble, also called *chorus*, to see if you like the experience and can manage a demanding schedule of rehearsals and performances. It can be disruptive to your regular lifestyle, but many find it to be so enjoyable that it doesn't matter.

Musical theater offers a well-rounded experience in singing, acting, and dancing. Singers have the opportunity to learn both solo and ensemble music, some of which may already be familiar to you. The musical director can guide you in learning new vocal techniques and dramatic interpretation of the songs. It's a great chance to learn how to combine acting and singing, something necessary for all types of music. You can read more about the musical theater experience in Chapter 20.

Classical

Singing classical repertoire is a more demanding choice of career or hobby. Classical music is often more complex musically because it isn't written with the intent of being sung by thousands of people as is popular music. For this reason, the material is often very beautiful and satisfying to sing. Accomplishing a pleasing sound in this genre is one of the most rewarding experiences for many singers and marks a level of competence in your vocal technique. Some classical music is beautiful for its simplicity rather than intricacy, but still requires a clear and supported vocal quality.

Because of the demanding nature of this music, you would have to be quite serious about your vocal studies and committed to working in private lessons with a teacher and a coach. Daily practice is necessary to develop sufficient ability to handle more intricate and strenuous singing. Classical music is generally not amplified, so you'll have to have strength and good technique to project your voice to the audience.

FACT

Professional singers are those who are paid for their singing. An amateur is defined as a volunteer and is unpaid. There need not be any difference in the abilities, technical expertise, or talent of the two categories. There are certainly amateur singers who are equally or more able than some professional singers. The distinction is only one of career choice and payment.

Careers in classical vocal music may include opera, recital, recording, chamber groups, and professional church work. There are many opportunities to sing on an amateur level in any of the preceding categories.

Jazz and Standards

One of the most popular categories of singing is what's referred to as *standards*. Standards is a somewhat confusing term in that there are songs that are generally understood as belonging to this genre but they may come from musicals and movie soundtracks, jazz, or pop music. One defining feature is the number of times singers choose to perform or record these songs. The material is usually, but not always, well known.

Some examples of jazz standards include "Take the 'A' Train," "Satin Doll," and "Take Five." Songs originally from Broadway musicals are "All the Things You Are," "Some Enchanted Evening," and "The Impossible Dream." A song like "My Romance" is an example of a song that was originally in the musical *Jumbo* but became a favorite of jazz players and was recorded by many singers. Popular music, such as "Perfidia" or "Yesterday," are considered standards now, but were once the popular music of their time. You'd find recordings of these songs in the listings of Vocals, Vocalists, and Easy Listening.

Bands

One of the biggest dreams of many singers is to sing in a band. Various styles include rock, pop, country, folk, or almost any popular genre of music. The lead singer of a band tends to get the most publicity, but backup singers can also become well known. Singing with a band could mean that you put together an original band composed of people you know, or you might audition for an existing band. Established bands have been known to hire new singers who then lead the band to greater popularity or even fame.

Most bands have three to six members with one lead singer and several instrumentalists who may sing harmonies. Most bands will need to record their music in order to promote themselves and usually tour frequently to either make a name for a new band or keep an existing band in public awareness. It can be a difficult and disruptive lifestyle, but also perfectly suited to singers with a sense of adventure and wanderlust. Some or all band members will also need to develop strong business skills to go along with their musical skills. In the past, the primary goal was to sign with a record label, but more and more bands are now independent and manage their own careers.

Some singers work with bands that are put together for an event, such as a wedding or party. These jobs are called *club dates* and require the singer to know a selection of popular songs from four or five genres. Singers learn a sort of code to communicate with the other band members during a song, since these jobs rarely have any rehearsal.

Band singers may or may not have any vocal training. Of course, it's always helpful to develop your technique no matter what style you sing in order to maintain a healthy voice for a lifetime. Many band singers abuse their voices but have a chance to rest between concerts or gigs. One of the main requirements of the singer is high energy. This energy can lead to pushing the voice to extreme levels and drastically shorten or end a promising career. Learning how to protect yourself is a must for singing in a band. You can figure out in rehearsal whether a particular song or style of singing will damage your voice. For more details about this type of performance, read Chapter 21.

Clubs and Lounges

Clubs are primarily a venue for singers of all different genres to make a name for themselves. Singing regularly in a club means that your audience can find you and you can develop a fan base. Clubs usually specialize in a particular style of music so that the public knows where to hear new acts within that genre. The most common types of clubs are dance, rock, more generalized pop, jazz, folk, and cabaret, which caters mostly to standards.

Singing in a club is almost always amplified and sometimes you have to provide your own equipment, such as a microphone and amplifier. Most singers would not consider working in clubs as a goal in itself, but rather a means to some other goal. You can build repertoire by trying out songs on a live audience. This will help determine if you want to keep that song and possibly record it. Once you've recorded enough music for a CD, you can also use clubs as a place to sell your music and expand your fan base.

Singing in cocktail lounges is somewhat more low-key, but can provide steady work for many years. The style is predominately standards and in the easy listening category. You may find you can develop a regular audience, but often lounges have a transient clientele, especially in hotels. Singers working in lounges usually accompany themselves on piano and are amplified at a fairly low level. The establishment provides the equipment. The performer may receive a salary plus tips or work for tips only. Some people have managed long careers in this type of work, and others find it's a good second job and outlet for regular performing.

Commercial and Industrial Work

Some companies hire singers to record their commercials for radio, television, and Internet advertising. These musical advertisements are referred to as *jingles* and the singers are called *jingle singers*. Jingle singers need to be strong musicians with good sight-reading ability and usually have clear voices and good diction so that all the words are easily understood. These singers are hired to record material that they learn on the spot. They might even sing harmony by ear, meaning they use their musical knowledge to hear what notes to sing rather than reading a previously composed line of music.

Jingle singers are highly skilled and able to work quickly, but are also usually very well paid. Because this is such a lucrative career, it's also highly competitive. A small group of people tend to work most of the available jobs because the producers of the commercials get to know them and know they can count on them to deliver a good job in a short period of time.

Large companies may also hire singers to work live performances during expos, trade shows, and other promotional activities. These jobs are called *industrials* and are also quite lucrative. Singers who work industrials usually have to travel around the country to whatever location the company requires. Some singers may be hired by one or two companies regularly and have a fairly steady income. It can be a fun chance to sing and is good for outgoing people who like to socialize and act as representatives of a business. The downside is that it's not a particularly creative form of singing.

Create Your Own Venue

If you could make a list of all the places you've heard people sing, you'd be surprised at the number of opportunities you can create for yourself. It's easy to get caught up in the rules or the "right way" to approach a new career. But if you let yourself imagine all the possibilities without editing your ideas, you may find situations arise that you hadn't anticipated. Places such as nursing homes and hospitals appreciate musicians who can volunteer their services. In large communities there may even be organizations willing to pay for these services. Groups and businesses frequently plan entertainment as part of meetings or dinners. Schools and clubs are often open to showcasing new singers. Depending on your location, you might even be able to sing on a street corner or public area and put out a hat for tips. Churches, community centers, and parks are all potential places to perform.

Look at the following list of ways to find performance opportunities, but also see if you can think of some more ideas particular to your own situation:

- Audition notices in trade papers, such as *Backstage* and *Variety*
- Magazine and newspaper ads
- Bulletin boards
- Colleges in town or alumni groups
- Internet search
- Music Web sites such as MySpace.com
- Word of mouth

The most important thing is that you're trying to find some opportunity to perform. This is the only way to figure out if singing is something you'd like to have as part of your life, whether as a hobby, part-time work, or a full-time career. If you love to sing but think you might not like performing your music, keep trying some of the other ideas you might not have already exhausted. There's usually a way to sing if you love it. And ultimately, if you discover you don't like any type of performance, there can still be great satisfaction in singing for your own pleasure in the privacy of your own home.

CHAPTER 19

Choral Singing

Singing in a choir can be one of the most musically rewarding experiences for a singer. There's nothing quite like the sensation of being part of a chord formed by human voices. It can be a demanding job and serious career choice, or it can be strictly for fun, a chance to improve your musical skills, and time spent with like-minded people. In this chapter you'll learn what it means to sing in harmony and how to prepare yourself for potential opportunities.

What Is Choral Singing?

Choral singing goes by several different names, all meaning basically the same thing. You may hear the terms *choir, chorus, chorale, ensemble, harmony,* or *part-singing.* All indicate that a number of people are singing together at the same time but on different musical lines. In one single passage of music there is a division of parts, all of which are sung together to form that one passage. One part may sing the basic melody of the music while the other parts sing the harmony, which are complementary lines of music that make up the chords. The easiest analogy is to think of an orchestra or band. There are many different types of instruments, such as violins, flutes, trumpets, and percussion, which may all play at once but not exactly the same notes. As well as having its own musical line, each instrument also has its own distinct range and timbre, but the goal is that they blend in one harmonious whole. The notes they play create chords that are constantly moving and changing, all the while shaping the melody you hear.

Just as in the orchestra, there may be more than one person on a single part. The most common division of voices in a choir is four parts: soprano, alto, tenor, and bass (listed from highest voice to lowest voice). If there are only four people singing, each sings one of these lines. But if there are sixteen people, four people sing the soprano part, four sing the alto part, and so on. Large choirs may consist of well over 100 people singing up to ten or more different parts. Voices also have individual timbre and range, but choral singers work toward unifying their collective sound so that no one voice will stand out.

Types of Choirs

Choirs range from very casual gatherings to large professional choirs who record and perform regularly. The basic concept is the same in any circumstance, but the level of expertise may differ. A group of friends singing Christmas carols in harmony is a casual event and rarely involves rehearsal. A professional choir such as the Mormon Tabernacle Choir, on the other hand, is very demanding and involves more training for a serious career choice on the part of the singer. Any time you sing with a number of other people, however, you'll probably be singing in harmony and using the same techniques necessary for any ensemble singing. The types of groups and their personnel are as limitless as the imagination of those forming them.

Church Choirs

Almost all churches have some sort of choir. Some are small and basic because of their parish size. Others are on a professional level and may be quite large. Most church choirs have a policy of accepting anyone who wants to sing and then directing singers toward a more homogenous sound during rehearsal. Professional singers are often hired to join larger church choirs in order to support the sound. They may be hired as section leaders or cantors to lead the congregation.

Rehearsals are usually held on a weekday evening and again before the service. Attendance is voluntary but expected if you sing in the service. Often the organist of the church is also the choir director and runs the rehearsal. Sight-reading is certainly helpful but usually not mandatory. If you don't read music, you'll be learning your part by ear, which means you listen to it and then remember the music, reading only the words. The material is almost always religious in content, but some churches have incorporated appropriate folk music into their services.

Community Choirs

Community choirs are also voluntary. Some may even require that you pay a fee to join in order to defray some of their costs. Like church choirs, they may be quite casual or very advanced in vocal expertise and choice of repertoire. Repertoire may be either sacred or secular, but these choirs are not based on any particular religion.

There is so much sacred music written for choral settings that it would be hard to avoid this material. Most community choir members are singing for the choral experience and the beauty of the music, not for any particular worship service as in church choirs.

These choirs generally have one choral conductor leading the group, possibly an assistant conductor, and a rehearsal accompanist. They may perform with piano, organ, or orchestra. Many choirs also sing a cappella, which means without accompaniment. Some choirs are exclusively a cappella while others may choose sections of the concert to be unaccompanied.

Professional Choirs

Professional choirs may be fairly large vocal ensembles made up of trained singers and musicians. Performances are usually in concert venues or theaters, and admission is charged for concert tickets. Singers are chosen by auditioning for choral sections when openings are available. The audition may include submission of a demo CD, which is a recording of the prospective chorister singing an appropriate passage from choral repertoire. A professional choir may tour for a period of time and will probably record their music.

Singers in a professional choir should have a certain level of vocal training and musical skills. Each singer needs to learn and be responsible for her part without depending on the conductor to teach parts. The conductor's responsibility is to the ensemble, not to each individual singer. Some choirs also use soloists from within the ensemble if solo parts are written in the music.

Other Choral Categories

Choirs may be constructed according to the gender of the singers, the content of music, location, or performance genre. Sometimes ensembles are classified by their size as well, such as trio, quartet, quintet, or chamber group, all of which are smaller than large choirs.

Gender

Choral groups are most often mixed gender, with vocal divisions of soprano, alto, tenor, and bass. Soprano and alto refer to the high and low women's parts respectively. Tenor and bass are the high and low men's parts. This is shown on the music as the abbreviations SATB to represent these four parts. If these parts are subdivided, numbers indicate the range within the part. The number one is the higher part and two is the lower part. In the soprano part, for example, there may be a soprano one and a soprano two. Sopranos are hired in the ensemble as a particular part depending on their comfortable range. The number and type of parts are reflected in the lettered abbreviations, such as SSAATTBB, which indicates that all four parts are subdivided.

Some choirs are all male or all female. The musical arrangements would then bear the symbols to reflect those parts. For instance, the letters TTB indicate a male choir with two tenor parts and one bass part. There may be a female choir divided into SSAA, meaning there are two soprano parts, soprano one and soprano two, and two alto parts, alto one and alto two. The abbreviations are listed on the music under the title of the piece.

Content

A choir can be created for the purpose of singing a particular type of music. The musical distinction of the group could be based on an historical period, such as Renaissance music or Baroque music. Or the mission of the choir could be the singing of certain cultural or nationalistic material. Some groups even specialize in the music of one particular composer, such as Bach or Handel. The formation of such a choir may stem from the vision of one leader, or from an existing group who sing together and decide to formalize their association.

Location

The physical location of the singers in a choir may determine the choir's existence. Examples of these choirs may be the glee club in a school or a community choir. Schools are a particularly good source if you're looking for a choir to join. Most middle schools, high schools, and colleges have a glee club or specific types of choirs. Some become quite well known due to state and national competitions. High schools are also beginning to offer show choirs, which involve movement, dance, and sets. Sometimes the alumni association of a college is able to encourage graduates to form a choir to continue the spirit of that school and offer an outlet for choral singers. Community choirs are, as the name suggests, based on a certain location. They have been known to unify a community in a positive way, and they offer people a chance to meet people outside of their regular group of friends or coworkers.

FACT

Examples of school and community choirs include the Harvard Glee Club, the Yale Glee Club, the Cornell University Chorus, the New York City Master Chorale, and the San Francisco Symphony Chorus.

Performance Genre

The style of music can be a defining factor of a choir. Specific genres may include classical, popular, jazz, and gospel. Vocal jazz groups can be found in almost every city and can offer more experienced singers a challenging form of harmony. The music is fun, but often more difficult to sing than some other choral works. Many of these groups record their music and have moved to a professional level.

Gospel choirs are fun for both participants and audience members. This style of music is often rousing, inspirational, and lively. The repertoire is based mostly on material from African-American spirituals and Christian hymns, all arranged in a way that makes the performance active, exciting, and very energetic. There are usually soloists within the choir who serve as lead singers. Gospel choirs have always had a strong following, but they became especially popular after the film *Sister Act*.

ESSENTIAL

If you're interested in choral music, you should listen to CDs or download examples of music by the groups already mentioned. Searching for choral music on the Internet will provide many additional suggestions of excellent choirs and harmony groups. As you listen, see if you can pick out individual parts. It's a great way to train your ear for part-singing.

You can also listen to excellent vocal harmony in popular groups such as the Beach Boys, the Four Seasons, the Beatles, Simon and Garfunkel, Indigo Girls, and Dixie Chicks.

Vocal Requirements

Singing choral music requires certain specific vocal skills that differ from solo singing. Some basic technique that's important for all singers is particularly crucial for choral singers. The major difference is, by definition, the fact that you're singing with other people. The goal is a blended and uniform sound, and the ensemble nature of choral singing demands that each singer is aware of how to be part of a group. This is not the time to stand out.

- Blending your voice with others means that you'll need to be aware of vocal dynamics and not sing significantly louder or softer than those around you. If one voice stands out from the group, the entire balance of sound is disrupted. Most good choral singers will never sing at their greatest level of volume, because it's almost impossible to unify very loud voices. But you also can't sing so softly that you don't contribute your voice to the group. Each voice is needed to properly balance the sound.
- Your pitch must be accurate. A solo singer has a small amount of leeway with the center of the pitch, but a choral singer has to be exact. If one singer is out of tune, the entire vocal chord is affected negatively. Each pitch must be approached cleanly. Good intonation is an absolute necessity for singing in harmony.
- You'll need to hear and hold your own line of music. Many singers have trouble maintaining a different harmonic line when they hear the other voices around them, especially if they aren't singing the melody. It's very easy to drift to another line of music if that's what stands out to your ear. Learn to listen very closely to those who share your part, and then listen for the whole ensemble chord to hear if you're blending.
- You should be able to sight-read your music. Good musicianship is an important skill for choral singers, since it would be tedious and almost impossible to learn everything you'll need to know by ear. Most professional rehearsals don't involve teaching each line of music, but rather concentrate on perfecting the overall sound of the ensemble.

- Clear diction is especially important in ensemble music. When more people are singing together, it becomes harder for the audience to hear each word distinctly. Articulation is very strict in choral music. Good vowel production is crucial to the unification of overtones, and vowel sounds must match exactly for proper tuning.

ALERT!

Most choirs have a similar set of rules: be on time for rehearsal, little or no absence in the rehearsal schedule, know your part and mark your music, no talking while other sections are working, eyes on the conductor, and no perfume or hairspray, as these can affect singers with allergies. You're there to work, but it can be one of the most rewarding and enjoyable jobs you can have.

Exercises

It can be difficult to practice singing a harmonic line of music by yourself if you have nobody to monitor you. The first step is to learn your own line, but after that you'll have to check it against the other part. These exercises will help you practice, but you should probably record yourself to see how well you're doing.

Singing in Thirds

EXERCISE 19-1

TRACK 83

1. Sing this phrase several times. After you know it, sing the phrase with the other part.

Part One

FIGURE 19-1. Exercise 19-1 Step 1

TRACK 84

2. Now switch to the other phrase. First sing it a few times until you know it, and then with the other part on Track 83.

Part Two

FIGURE 19-2. Exercise 19-1 Step 2

Longer Phrases

EXERCISE 19-2

TRACK 85

1. As before, sing part one several times first. After you know it, sing with the other part.

The Riddle

FIGURE 19-3. Exercise 19-2 Step 1

2. Now switch to part two. First sing it a few times until you know it, and then with the other part on Track 85.

The Riddle

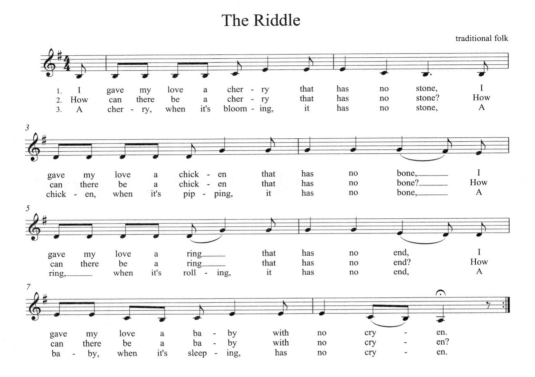

traditional folk

1. I gave my love a cher - ry that has no stone, I
2. How can there be a cher - ry that has no stone? How
3. A cher - ry, when it's bloom - ing, it has no stone,

gave my love a chick - en that has no bone,_____ I
can there be a chick - en that has no bone?_____ How
chick - en, when it's pip - ping, it has no bone,_____ A

gave my love a ring_____ that has no end, I
can there be a ring_____ that has no end? How
ring,_____ when it's roll - ing, it has no end, A

gave my love a ba - by with no cry - en.
can there be a ba - by with no cry - en?
ba - by, when it's sleep - ing, has no cry - en.

FIGURE 19-4. Exercise 19-2 Step 2

Choral Score in Four Parts

Look at the following music written for an SATB choir. This is a harmonized hymn called a *chorale*, composed by J. S. Bach. You may find his chorales, as well as many other pieces of ensemble music, written in two different ways. The first score is written on two staves, each containing two parts. The second score has four staves of music, each with one individual vocal line.

Two Staves

The upper staff shows the two women's vocal parts. The soprano line is shown by notes with the stems up and the alto line is shown by notes with the stems down. The lower staff has a similar division: the tenor line with stems up and the bass line with stems down. This is the standard format for a hymn or carol. Compare each part with the score in Figure 19-6 and you'll see that they are exactly the same.

FIGURE 19-5.
Bach Chorale
on two staves

Four Staves

Now look at the same piece of music with the same four vocal divisions, but further separated into one part per staff. This is much easier for the singer to read but, to save paper, not always the way you'll find your choral music. The more intricate the individual choral line, the more likely it will be published in this style.

FIGURE 19-6.
Bach Chorale on
four staves

TRACK 87
TRACK 88
TRACK 89
TRACK 90
TRACK 91

Listen to each of the four tracks and then learn the part that feels appropriate for your vocal range. Once you feel comfortable with your part, try singing it with the four voices together. Record yourself to check for accuracy. If you want extra practice, try the other parts as well. The best way to practice, however, is to sing the exercise with other people. Ask some of your friends to join you and each take a different part. Once you all know your vocal lines and can sing together, leave out the CD track and try it a cappella.

Learning how to sing in harmony is important, not only for singing in a choir, but also for singing backup vocals in a band, recording your own harmony when creating a CD demo, or singing in the ensemble of a musical theater production. Often people are hired in these situations and find themselves challenged by the ensemble lines of music more than the solo lines. If you can find a choral situation in which to practice these skills, you'll be more comfortable when you find you need to harmonize.

CHAPTER 20

Theater

Theater is an exciting venue for singers, offering a wide variety of opportunities. Music in theater can take many forms, including opera and Broadway musicals, but the unifying factor is always that a story is told utilizing singing and acting. Singers particularly enjoy this outlet for the expression of a wide range of emotions they might not find in any other genre. Since a story is usually the central focus of theatrical singing, the singer needs to be an actor as well, with an ability to portray a character. Singing in live theater requires talent, stage presence, physical stamina, energy, and a particular set of skills that can be studied and practiced.

Musical Theater

Musical theater is a sort of heightened form of theater that incorporates singing, acting, and dancing. This form of theater, often referred to as "a musical," tells a story by using scenes of spoken dialogue as in a play, but additionally features aspects of the story told in music and dance. Musical scenes generally represent intense emotion in the story line, explanation of a segment of the story itself, or internal reflection about how a character feels. Music and dance are a method of telling the story in a different way than by words alone.

The written material of a musical includes the script of spoken dialogue, just as in a play, the lyrics to the songs, and the music. The music and lyrics together form the score of the musical, and the spoken dialogue, in script form, is called *the book*. In published musicals, you'll usually find the book and lyrics together in one script. The score is published separately, either as a full theatrical score or as a shorter collection of music called *vocal selections*, which contains the prominent songs. When you buy the music book from a musical theater piece, it's usually the vocal selections.

Be careful when you buy the vocal selections for a musical. The book may not include all of the songs you want, and the songs may be in a different key than that of the original score. The key is often changed to make the song easier to play and sing, and more accessible to the general public. On the plus side, the vocal selections are less expensive and more readily available.

The presentation of a musical requires the cooperative efforts of a producer, director, musical director, choreographer, costumer, stage set designer, and actors. Depending on the budget and level of production, these may be separate people filling these roles, or one person may have to take on several functions. All aspects are important to a finished presentation, since the audience needs to be transported to another believable place and time.

The musical director of a show has many functions to coordinate the vocal music with the staging and choreography, as well as with the band or orchestra. This includes preshow planning, arranging music, leading vocal rehearsals, and conducting the orchestra. Often this leaves very little time to help each individual singer with his or her vocal part. Usually the first rehearsals are spent learning your part, but it's up to you to return to the next rehearsal with that day's work memorized and ready to stage. Any issues of vocal technique should be taken to your vocal coach, whereas the musical director might comment on styling, expression, and phrasing.

Vocal Style in Musical Theater

The style of singing in a musical has certain uniform factors, but the particulars often depend on the style of the show itself. Musicals may be referred to as *standard*, which are older, established shows, or *contemporary*, which generally have an updated musical feel but still tell a theatrical story. Contemporary musicals usually have a score best served by rock and pop voices, whereas the traditional standard musical is best served by a trained classical voice.

All musicals require that the singer portray a character in a story and act in a way that makes the character both believable and larger than life. This is a fine line to draw as both actor and singer. Some singers are tempted to push too hard in creating a character and lose the subtlety necessary to make that character believable. High energy is required to act in a musical, but that doesn't mean overacting. If you push yourself emotionally as a character, you'll probably push vocally as well. Ironically, the result is a weaker sound and a damaged voice. Remember, pushing your voice out in an effort to project will eventually cause damage. If you get a note from the director that you need to be louder, remember that volume comes from forward placement and the proper position of the resonating cavities. Practice your songs with the forward placement exercises in Chapter 9 to get more volume.

A particular challenge for musical theater performers is the need to dance and sing at the same time. Hopefully the choreographer has taken into account the physical demands of singing, but there are times when stage movement makes it difficult to hold a steady tone. If you use the appoggio technique and make sure that you have an anchor for your voice in your sternum and abdominal muscles, you will be able to support the air pressure even in different positions. Be sure to practice your choreography and singing together so you can have time to adjust to any potential conflict between movement and voice.

Musical theater voices usually have a very bright timbre that might sound somewhat brassy. It's important for the voice to have carrying power, so singers tend to utilize forward placement in the mask to get the volume they need. If the soft palate is lowered, the tone may become nasal as well. Be sure to keep the soft palate lifted if you want to reduce the nasality. The technique of belting is frequently associated with musical theater and its use is assumed in some of the repertoire. Most casting of musicals tends to favor voices with volume, clarity of sound, accurate pitch, and emotional expression. These attributes are often more important than beauty or richness of vocal quality. Ideally in musical theater, the character portrayal always comes first, which means that the vocal sound should represent that character rather than sacrifice the character to vocal beauty.

FACT

Musical theater voices that are classically trained are referred to as *legit*, which stands for "legitimate" singing. This term may refer to the vocal type of the singer or the musical that is written for classically trained voices. Some musicals may use both legit voices for leading roles and more stylized vocal types for the character roles.

The type of role in which you're cast will determine what vocal style you'll need. Lead roles may be more contained and proper, depending, of course, on the particular show. Supporting roles are often called *character roles* and may be funny, earthy, and energetic. Your physical type will determine in part which type of role is best for you. You should try to be realistic about the role that suits you so that you'll know what kind of material to prepare for an audition. If you have any doubt, ask your friends if you're more the elegant leading type or the comic character type. If you think you may be either, decide which one would be more fun for you and then play it up. Musical theater is a business of typecasting, even if you think you have a wide range. When you see musicals onstage or on film, ask yourself which role is most appropriate for your physical appearance, not just your vocal type.

The Musical Audition

Singers get roles in a musical from a sort of interview called an *audition*. This is your chance to show your vocal abilities and stage personality. When you audition or try out for a musical, you'll need to prepare certain things ahead of time. How to best prepare depends on where you are auditioning and for what level of theater. If you aim for thorough preparation, however, you'll look professional no matter what the situation.

What to Sing

The most important factor in deciding on your audition material is that you like what you're singing and connect to it emotionally. You have a very short time to show who you are and what you can do. Ideally, the song should show vocal range as well as emotional range, so you'll need to look at both the music and the lyrics to decide on a piece. Choose lyrics first that agree with your character type and are fun to express. Then look at the music to make sure it's in a comfortable range. An audition is the time to show off what you do best, not what you're working on or your greatest challenge.

Musical theater singers develop a collection of songs called a *book*, containing material they like to sing for auditions. Your book should include only your best material and should have variety. Take your book with you to an audition in case the musical director wants to hear something other than the song you chose to sing. It's a good sign if someone wants to hear more.

Audition material should always come from a musical theater repertoire. The only exception is when the audition notice specifies that you sing something else, such as rock, folk, or gospel. You should begin filling your book with two contrasting songs, a ballad and an up-tempo piece. Ballads are slow and often pensive or emotional. Up-tempo songs have a faster tempo and a bright, funny, or ironic sentiment. After preparing those two selections, you can add a contemporary song or something from a popular genre, since many current musicals require that style.

Many audition notices state that you should sing sixteen bars (measures) of your song. You can start from the beginning of your vocal part and sing sixteen bars, or you could count the sixteen bars backward from the end of the song. That would ensure a good ending. Whatever segment (called a *cut*) you choose, it should ideally have a beginning, middle, and end both lyrically and musically. If you are unaccustomed to choosing a sixteen-bar cut of your song, you should ask a coach or teacher to help you.

What to Wear

Your audition attire should be neat, clean, and flattering to your body type. It's usually a good idea to wear clothes that are somewhat fitted and not too baggy so that the casting director can see your body. Your auditioners are looking to see if you're a match for the character in the musical. Avoid the extremes of overly dressy, which looks like you're trying too hard, or too casual, which looks like you don't care about the audition. Some people try to dress appropriately for the particular musical of that audition, but you shouldn't look as if you're wearing a costume. A hint of the character is enough. If you audition regularly, you might want to have an outfit set aside that's always clean and ready to go.

FACT

You can find audition notices in various places, depending on the size of the community. You might see signs on bulletin boards in schools, churches, and community centers, or there may be advertisements in local newspapers. Large cities have trade papers listing auditions for the week. Well-known trade papers include *Backstage* and *Variety*. You can also search the Internet for listings in *Playbill*, *Backstage*, or Actors' Equity Association.

What to Bring

If you are auditioning in a large community, you'll need a picture and resume. The picture should be 8 by 10 inches and may be a headshot or full-body picture. Your resume of past theatrical experience and training should be cut to the same size and attached to the back of the picture. If you live in a smaller community, the director may simply ask you to write a short list of any previous experience.

You should bring your book, containing your music repertoire, with you to the audition and give it to the accompanist, open to the page of the song you want to sing. Try to limit the number of pages in each song and bring copies that will lay flat on the piano stand. Many people put their music in a ring binder and have it copied or taped to read like the pages of a book. You can also tape the edges of your music together to fold out into one long flat page, but don't exceed three pages if using this method. The music should be in the correct key. If you need to transpose the song, be sure that it's written out completely, preferably in a computer program for music notation, in the new key for the accompanist. You should never ask the accompanist to play your music in a key different from what's written. The accompanist is sight-reading the music, and if he makes a mistake, it will hurt your audition.

If you have enough music prepared that you're able to make a choice of what to sing, choose a song that's most similar to the show for which you're auditioning. Don't sing material from the show you're auditioning for unless someone asks you for it. The best choice would be music from another show by the same composer. If you're auditioning for *Oklahoma!* for example, you could sing music from *South Pacific* since the two shows are both written by Rodgers and Hammerstein. If you only have a basic ballad and up-tempo, however, it's better to sing material you're comfortable with rather than rush to prepare something that won't be well rehearsed by the audition. Be sure to look at Appendix B for a list of songs you might want to consider.

Depending on the musical and the particular audition, you should also be prepared with clothing and shoes appropriate for a dance or movement portion of the audition. You may also be asked to present a monologue to show your acting skills.

ESSENTIAL

If you're interested in pursuing musical theater, you should consider taking lessons in acting, dance, and stage movement, as well as your voice lessons. Performers who can act, dance, and sing are called a *triple threat* and usually are able to get more work than those who are skilled in only one area.

Focus

When you are ready to sing your song at the audition, go to the center of the room and face the casting directors, or whoever is holding the audition. After giving a nod to the accompanist to begin playing, you'll need to use your imagination and pretend that you are singing to a scene partner right in front of you. (Don't look directly at your audience of auditioners unless you're asked to do this.) Make sure your imaginary scene partner is at eye level and not too high or low. Your audience should be able to see the expression in your eyes as you sing. Look again at the exercises in Chapter 16 to review aspects of dramatic interpretation.

Some Famous Musicals

There are far too many well-known musicals to offer a comprehensive list, but singers interested in musical theater should do some research and get to know as many famous musicals as possible. There are dozens of excellent books about musical theater and also many musicals available on video and DVD that you can rent. Here is a short list of some representative musicals:

Standard musicals:
- *South Pacific*
- *Oklahoma!*
- *Showboat*
- *Annie Get Your Gun*
- *The Sound of Music*
- *West Side Story*
- *Guys and Dolls*
- *Anything Goes*

Contemporary musicals:

- *Cats*
- *The Producers*
- *The Phantom of the Opera*
- *Rent*
- *Beauty and the Beast*
- *Les Misérables*
- *Chicago*

Some important musicals also cross over to classical treatments and have been performed within both musical theater and opera. Composers such as Leonard Bernstein and Stephen Sondheim have written theatrical works, including *Candide, Sweeney Todd*, and *A Little Night Music*, that work equally well on Broadway or in an opera house.

Classical Music Theater

Classical music theater includes opera, operetta, and light opera, as well as numerous divisions within these genres. The production elements are similar to those of musical theater, but generally on a larger scale. As in musical theater, the purpose of opera is to tell a story. There are several distinguishing points, however, that differentiate opera from musical theater. Opera is usually defined as a work that is through-composed, meaning that the dramatic content is entirely sung. There are a few exceptions of spoken dialogue within an opera, but most operas use a style form called *recitative* instead. Recitative is a scene that is sung in a more conversational rhythm and may convey necessary dramatic information in the story. It takes the place of the spoken dialogue that's used in musical theater. The convention of a song in musical theater is called an *aria* in opera, and it is set apart from the less melodic recitative as an independent musical structure.

In opera, the vocal quality of singers is more important than their ability to act, whereas acting usually comes first in musical theater. There is a movement toward more realistic acting in opera, but still the voice itself is the chief concern. An opera audience is often more eager to hear the particular singer they love than to see the opera on its own merit, and opera stars command great respect. The acting style in opera tends to be grand and larger than life, and the actual stages are larger as well. Opera singers do not use amplification and must fill an entire opera house without the help of a microphone. (In large venues, musical theater singers are amplified by microphones attached to their clothing or hair. Smaller theaters depend on the "unplugged" version of the singer's voice.)

The vocal style is quite different in opera and musical theater. Opera singers are classically trained, usually for many years, before attempting to sing an opera. The training is almost always as steady and rigorous as that of an athlete training for the Olympics. An operatic singer needs more vertical length in the throat, which demands lift in the soft palate and lowering of the larynx. The lowered soft palate would produce a far too nasal sound for opera. Singers interested in pursuing opera should begin gradually learning specific operatic roles under the guidance of a qualified teacher and coach. Listen to some of these operas and operettas for vocal quality and operatic style.

- *La Bohème*
- *Aida*
- *The Marriage of Figaro*
- *Carmen*
- *The Pirates of Penzance*
- *Naughty Marietta*

Qualities of Theater Singing

Look through the following list of what you'll need to sing in theater. You may find that a particular show or even a particular community doesn't demand all of these requirements, or you may find you need some skills not on this list. This is just a starting point for you to consider as an approach to theatrical singing:

- Accurate pitch
- Clear and distinct enunciation
- Volume
- Forward placement in the mask

- Expressive phrasing and clear dramatic interpretation
- Ability to sing melodies without pop styling
- Character portrayal through acting
- Dancing
- High level of energy to maintain several hours of performance

You should spend some time listening to theatrical singers. Check out the lists in Chapter 8 of the many fine singers of both musical theater and opera. When you become familiar with their voices, you can better understand the qualities necessary for performance in each genre.

Theatrical singing is very demanding. It requires long hours of training and rehearsal, often with little response or monetary reward. It can also be a fulfilling and almost addictive form of artistic expression. If you want to be a singer, working in a musical can be one of the most valuable experiences you can have, no matter what genre you finally choose. You'll learn that singing is about communicating and telling a story, and have a chance to sing some of the finest vocal material written.

CHAPTER 21

Popular Styles

Popular music is a general term that encompasses many different styles and genres. It has the largest listening audience and is the predominant music you hear on the radio and in public places such as restaurants and stores. Popular music shares as a unifying factor among its many genres a general appeal for a wide range of people. For the most part, you're able to sing along with popular music, which makes it accessible to the general public. Popular music is the form most people know best and what most people want to sing.

Jazz

Jazz is generally the most musically complex genre of the popular styles, requiring jazz singers to be very strong musicians. The musicianship and styling of the music are far more important in singing jazz than a particular vocal quality. There are many fine jazz singers with widely differing vocal timbre, range, and clarity, but all have the ability to phrase the music in a way that demonstrates an understanding of the song's structure, rhythm, and chord progression. Vocalists often imitate various instruments, especially horns, to create the unique sound of jazz.

Jazz, which now has many subgenres, has its origin in African-American music of the early twentieth century. It incorporates spirituals and blues, and depends heavily on forceful rhythm, syncopation, call and response, and improvisation. Sometimes the improvisation takes a form called *scat singing*, in which the singer uses nonsense syllables instead of words and improvises both melody and rhythm with these syllables. This enables the singer to express the music as one of the instrumentalists, and in fact many jazz vocalists style their part to sound similar to that of a horn. Working as an ensemble member with the rest of the jazz instrumentalists is one of the most important factors in establishing yourself as a jazz singer. This can be a little intimidating for a newcomer, but challenging, fun, and exciting as you get more experienced.

Jazz vocals are meant to take liberty with the written music and break some of the traditional rules of phrasing. Singers will rarely sing exactly what's on the page. It's expected to find new and different ways to present a standard melody while keeping the form and chord structure of that melody in mind.

Listen to some of these great jazz vocalists to get an idea of the style:

- Louis Armstrong
- Ella Fitzgerald
- Mel Tormé
- Billie Holiday
- Sarah Vaughn
- Bobby McFerrin

Standards

Popular music in the category of standards, also called *jazz standards*, pulls its repertoire from a variety of sources. Standard music consists of songs that have endured over time and that are repeatedly performed and recorded, thus becoming very familiar to the public. The songs are not necessarily jazz pieces originally or composed by jazz musicians, but may come from Broadway musicals, film music, or another pop genre. Theater music has supplied the collection of standards with many songs that are now far better known than the musicals from which they originated.

The basic repertoire of standards is referred to as the Great American Songbook. This isn't a set book with a table of contents, or even a definite list of songs, but rather a loosely agreed-upon collection of songs considered worthy of inclusion. Some of the major composers considered to be part of the Great American Songbook include Cole Porter, George Gershwin, Irving Berlin, Duke Ellington, Richard Rodgers, Harold Arlen, Johnny Mercer, and Jerome Kern.

There is a good deal of crossover between jazz singers and singers of standards. The main difference is the degree to which the singer phrases the music as an instrumentalist. A vocalist singing standards gives more weight to the lyric as an expression of verbal meaning rather than using the actual sound of the words to create a vocal instrument in the fashion of a jazz singer. Two different singers may not interpret the same piece of music in the same way. One singer may also cover both categories.

You'll need to use some of the same techniques for approaching standards as those discussed in Chapter 16. Popular styling allows a great deal of freedom, and you should explore possibilities of interpretation to make the song your own by altering the music as written. Approach the song first by speaking the lyric in order to determine the phrasing you like. This may alter the given rhythm, which is fine as long as you don't add or subtract measures without warning your fellow musicians. The lyrics are important in this genre, so be sure to enunciate each word clearly. You should keep the song within a comfortable range for your voice in order to make the words intelligible.

As with all of these popular music categories, there are dozens of fine singers to check out. This is by no means a definitive list, but rather a starting point.

- Harry Connick, Jr.
- Judy Garland
- Frank Sinatra
- Bing Crosby
- Barbra Streisand
- Peggy Lee
- Tony Bennett
- Nat "King" Cole
- Natalie Cole
- Michael Feinstein
- Karrin Allyson

Rock

Rock music is defined by high-energy vocals with prominent guitar, bass, and drums in the accompaniment. There may be other instruments in the band as well, such as keyboard and synthesizer, but these first three instruments provide the core of the sound called the rhythm section. Rock music has a driving rhythm, almost entirely in 4/4 or 12/8 meter, and accents the backbeat (beats two and four in each measure) with a snare drum. Rock music may be acoustic, but is more often electric and heavily amplified. There are dozens of subgenres, including progressive, metal, psychedelic, acid, punk, glam, grunge, and folk rock. Bands may be mainstream or alternative, which means they don't get mainstream airplay.

Rock grew out of the rock 'n' roll style, which got its start in the 1950s and drew heavily from blues and country music. It originated as a synthesis of certain styles that had previously been perceived as specifically white or African-American. The rock 'n' roll music of the 1950s continued to change and evolve into numerous subgenres, and by the 1960s there was a marked difference in the sound, form, and content of the increasingly electric rock genre. The multitude of styles all retained the essential core energy that still defines all rock music.

Rock bands usually have one lead singer. The most important vocal quality is strong energy, and because of the power and forcefulness of the sound, singers very frequently push their voices to a dangerous level. Many rock singers have suffered at least some vocal damage in their careers. Screaming is frequently used in loud rock music, whereas softer rock groups can have a gentler vocal approach. Clear diction is not always an important issue and might sound too formal for the electric rock sound, depending on the genre or the band you are trying to emulate.

ALERT!

A common hazard in singing rock music is some degree of hearing loss. Almost all rock is electric and is usually amplified to high levels that are dangerous to your ears. Whether singing with a band or frequently attending rock concerts, you should protect your ears with earplugs. If you lose your hearing, you won't be able to sing on pitch.

Here is a short list of famous rock musicians and bands:

- The Rolling Stones
- Led Zeppelin
- Frank Zappa
- The Beatles
- Queen
- Nirvana
- Joan Jett
- Janis Joplin
- Stone Temple Pilots
- Evanescence

Country

Country music encompasses many different styles, but in general it is one of the largest selling categories of popular music. Country got its start in the American South in the early twentieth century and spread to worldwide acceptance. Some subgenres include Nashville Sound, cowboy western, bluegrass, Outlaw, country-pop, and country-rock.

Country vocal sound tends to have a forward placement with varying degrees of nasality depending on the subgenre style. When singing country music, stay within your lower and middle range and allow for a somewhat lowered soft palate to gain the nasal quality needed. As with all popular styles, the vocals shouldn't sound too formal and proper. The performance style is sincere, direct, and conversational, since the message of much of this music concerns personal stories and painful situations.

FACT

Country singers often use a vocal styling that became popular in other genres as well. When moving from one register to another, they allow a complete change in the voice called *popping the register*. This is also the sound of yodeling heard in cowboy country styles. The popped register originated because singers didn't know how to blend the voice, but it eventually became the accepted sound of country and folk vocalists.

As you listen to these singers, notice the wide variation of styles under the umbrella genre of country music.

- Patsy Cline
- Hank Williams
- Willie Nelson
- Dolly Parton
- Johnny Cash
- Glen Campbell
- Tanya Tucker
- LeAnn Rimes

- Shania Twain
- Reba McEntire
- Carrie Underwood
- Lyle Lovett

R & B, Hip-Hop, Gospel

Rhythm and blues, usually called R & B, originated as an African-American genre of the twentieth century and incorporates elements of blues, jazz, and gospel. It evolved to contemporary R & B, which includes some disco, as well as soul and funk. R & B crosses over to hip-hop, which adds strong rhythmic emphasis on the lyrics. These two genres are now so closely related that they are considered one category in the *Billboard* charts.

Gospel singing also had its roots in African-American music of the South. Its lyrical content is religious in nature, primarily Christian, and bases its musical character on the traditional African folk method of call and response. The response is often stretched out and ornamented with blue notes.

FACT

Blues is a style of music that came from African-American spirituals and folk music and eventually evolved as the basis for many popular genres. It uses a "blues" scale, which has flattened third, fifth, and seventh notes of a major scale. These flat notes are referred to as "blue notes." The musical form is usually twelve bars long. Blues can also refer to the mood of a song with lyrics about pain and hardship.

The vocal style is clear and bright, which means there's an emphasis on forward placement in the mask and slightly lower soft palate position. Phrasing usually includes plenty of embellishment and ornamentation of held notes. Any note with a duration longer than two or three beats is usually embellished with moving notes called a *melisma*. A melisma is a single syllable that is turned into a run of notes rather than holding the same pitch. It comes originally from the chants of early music and Indian ragas, but gained its present popularity from gospel singers and gospel-pop. Melismatic singing is a particularly identifiable feature of gospel, R & B, and hip-hop.

A raga is a melodic pattern within Indian classical music. It uses harmonies and modal structure not contained in Western music. Each raga contains a collection of phrases and patterns which convey specific emotional content and coloring. The color and personality of a raga can be adapted for melismatic phrases.

Listen to these well-known singers for examples of these vocal styles:

- Aretha Franklin
- Anita Baker
- Whitney Houston
- Alicia Keys
- Lenny Kravitz
- Mary J. Blige
- Diana Ross
- Toni Braxton
- Usher
- Stevie Wonder
- Beyoncé

Pop

Pop music, along with country music, has one of the largest listening audiences in America. It's written to appeal to the majority, and, as such, is necessarily direct and simple in its musical form and structure. Successful pop singers are charismatic performers with high energy, often incorporating dance movement with their vocal performance. The genre is characterized by extensive mass-marketing and high production levels of recording. Often repetitive drum tracks are used to establish a strong dance beat.

These are a few of the major pop stars from different decades. Some are also excellent songwriters and known primarily for their own material.

- Justin Timberlake
- Christina Aguilera
- Billy Joel
- Bette Midler
- Gwen Stefani
- Laura Nyro
- Carole King
- ABBA
- Madonna
- Elton John
- Michael Jackson

Popular Singing Technique

Popular music is designed to appeal to a wide audience. These singers should seem approachable enough that listeners want to know them or be like them. It's the most imitated group of musicians and singers of all categories. Because the marketing is directed at the singers' contemporaries or younger, the music must also be accessible and not too formal or off-putting. Popular vocalists usually have lighter voices than classical or theater vocalists and are often untrained. If they were to use a full voice with training, the audience might feel too intimidated to sing along. These genres all use amplification, so there's no need to fill a theater without a microphone.

Look at this list of general characteristics of the popular voice. Not every point applies to each category of popular singing, and certainly not to every singer of popular music:

- Lighter than classical voices
- Uses amplification
- Sings in middle and low range to sound more like speech
- Less trained sound
- Uses vocal embellishments, such as the scoop, slide, or melisma

- Uses dynamics of speech
- Emphasizes text over music
- Personal charisma, stage presence, and vocal styling are more important than vocal quality
- Advertising and promotion are key elements of success

The greatest success of pop singing is also its greatest danger to the newcomer. What you hear on the radio or CD is so highly produced that there's no way someone can sound the same in an acoustic setting. Singers, as all musicians do, learn by imitation in the beginning of their study or career. If you try to imitate a sound that's impossible to re-create outside of the studio, you run the risk of harming your voice by trying to push it to the level you think you might need. The singers you're imitating have been electronically enhanced in the studio and don't necessarily sound the same without this extra boost. That's not to say they don't have wonderfully appealing voices, but rather to warn you not to force your voice to emulate a sound that only studio engineering can produce.

ALERT!

Always remember to use the proper vocal technique you've been learning. This will save your voice and enable you to use it more fully and for a longer time. You can seriously harm your voice if you push with the high energy needed for pop singing. Constantly remind yourself that you don't need to push your voice out. The audience will hear you through that microphone!

Many contemporary vocalists use too much chest voice in their overall sound to remain healthy. Overuse of chest voice without a blend of head voice mixture will eventually harm you. There are plenty of great vocalists listed in all categories who have been able to maintain healthy voices for a lifetime career. Listen carefully to their phrasing and vocal quality. It's never constant throughout the entire song, but has high points and low points, allowing the voice to rest periodically.

You should try to listen to artists in each of these categories. Listening to other singers is a great way to learn what to do and what not to do. There's so much crossover between styles in contemporary music that you might find the same singer in several of these genres. See if you can hear the unique quality of each voice, and what makes it identifiable no matter which genre they choose.

The most exciting and intelligent performers find a way to balance their energy and passion for music in a guided way. Great artists aren't out of control, but rather find a way to use their years of hard work and study to enhance expression and communication. Hopefully you'll be one of those artists who enjoys the journey by using good vocal technique. That's the only way to maintain a strong, healthy voice and a long career.

APPENDIX A:

International Phonetic Alphabet

APPENDIX B:

Music Repertoire and Study Materials

APPENDIX A

International Phonetic Alphabet

The International Phonetic Alphabet, commonly called the IPA, is a list of symbols used to determine correct pronunciation. It includes one phonetic symbol for each separate sound of most languages and is now considered to be the best standard guide for singers. You'll find IPA pronunciation in many dictionaries and vocal reference materials. This is a list of the traditional sounds of the English language.

	IPA Symbol	Sound	As In
Forward Vowels	[i]	ee	meet
	[ɪ]	ih	mitt
	[e]	a(y)	day (leave off "y")
	[ɛ]	eh	met
	[æ]	a	mat
	[a]	(bright) ah	why (with southern accent)
Back Vowels	[u]	oo	too
	[ʊ]	oo	took
	[o]	o	go
	[ɔ]	aw	saw
	[ɑ]	ah	father
Central Vowels	[ʌ]	uh (stressed)	under
	[ə]	uh (unstressed)	above
	[ɜ]	e(r)	her
	[ɚ]	er	summer
	[ɝ]	ur	girl
Diphthongs	[eɪ]	ai or ay	day
	[oʊ]	o	owe
	[aɪ]	I	night
	[aʊ]	ou or ow	out
	[ɔɪ]	oi or oy	boy
	[ju]	ew	use

	IPA Symbol	Sound	As In
Consonants	[p]	p	pit
	[b]	b	big
	[t]	t	ton
	[d]	d	dog
	[k]	k	kitten
	[g]	g	get
	[m]	m	move
	[n]	n	not
	[ŋ]	ng	sing
	[f]	f	foot
	[v]	v	very
	[θ]	th (unvoiced)	thought
	[ð]	th (voiced)	there
	[s]	s	sat
	[z]	z	zipper
	[ʃ]	sh (unvoiced)	shadow
	[ʒ]	zh (voiced)	pleasure
	[h]	h	hot
	[l]	l	land
	[r]	r	ready
	[j]	y	you
	[hw]	w (unvoiced)	where
	[w]	w (voiced)	way
	[tʃ]	ch (unvoiced)	choose
	[dʒ]	j (voiced)	edge

Music Repertoire and Study Materials

Here are some suggestions of music to sing and to study. Don't be afraid to choose some of the classical books to start with. The song choices are edited for beginning and intermediate singers. The fake books are a great source of material. They include hundreds of songs with melody, lyrics, and chord changes.

Books for Study and Practice

Concone, Joseph. *Fifty Lessons* (New York: Schirmer, 1986).

Concone, Joseph, and B. Lutgen. *School of Sight-Singing: Voice Technique* (New York: Schirmer, 1986).

Marchesi, Mathilde. *Vocal Method, Opus 31* (New York: Schirmer, 1986).

Twenty-Four Italian Songs and Arias (New York: Schirmer, 1992).
This is a standard collection for singers and also has a CD available with piano accompaniment.

Vaccai, Nicola; J. Paton, ed. *Practical Method of Italian Singing* (New York: Schirmer, 1986).
This is a great collection of short study songs. It's available in high voice and low voice editions and there is a CD available with piano accompaniment.

Books of Repertoire

Fake Books. These books sometimes have up to 1,000 songs, making them a great choice to explore new material. You'll get melody, lyrics, and chord changes, but not piano accompaniment. They tend to be divided by genre, such as pop, rock, jazz, Broadway, Latin, gospel, and classical. There are many different titles and publishers of fake books.

The First Book of Soprano Solos, compiled by Joan Frey Boytim (New York: Schirmer, 2000).
This is only one of a very large group of books full of excellent song choices for singers of every level. The books indicate the level in the title and have accompanying CDs.

Walters, Richard, ed. *Singer's Musical Theatre Anthology* (Milwaukee: Hal Leonard Publishing, 2008).
This is a wonderful series of books containing songs from musical theater. They are divided by voice type and include CDs with piano accompaniment.

Where to Find Music Online

✍ *www.sheetmusicplus.com*

This is a huge collection of almost any music you could want.

✍ *www.musicnotes.com*

This is also a large collection of music, but it has the added advantage of offering digital downloads of individual songs. Most of them can be transposed into any key you need.

Index

Abuse or damage
    alcohol, drugs and, 137–38
    career/lifestyle habits and,
        131–32
    pain indicating, 139
    signs of, 139–40
    singing incorrectly and, 132
    without pain, 139–40
Accelerando, 173
Accent mark, 152
Accidentals, 163–64
Acoustics principles, 12–15
Acting songs, 211–14
Adagio, 173
Alcohol, 137
Alignment exercises, 21–22
Allegretto and *allegro*, 173
Allergies, 135, 138, 139, 141, 248
Altos, 102–3
Amplitude, of sound, 12–13
Anatomy, of vocal instrument, 16–
    18. *See also* Breathing; Larynx;
    Posture; Resonance
Andante, 173
Appoggio, 34–35
Articulation. *See* Diction
Articulators, 90–91
The attack, 43–45

Auditions, for musical theater,
    257–60

Bands, 236–37
Baritones, 105–7
Bar lines, 184
Bass (*F*) clef, 157, 158, 160–61
Basses, 107–8
Beats per note, 167–68
Bernoulli Effect, 42–43
Blending registers, 75–77
Breathing, 25–38. *See also*
    Exhalation; Inhalation
    appoggio and, 34–35
    basic anatomy of, 26–28
    common problems, 38
    diaphragm and, 27–28, 32
    exercises, 30–31, 32–34,
        35–38, 58
    lungs and, 27
    respiration and, 26, 29
    ribs and, 28–29, 30, 31, 113
Bronchi, 26–27

Careers. *See* Performance and
    career opportunities

Caring for voice, 129–42. *See also*
    Abuse or damage; Diet and
    nutrition
    basic health concerns,
        133–35
    daily exercise and, 134
    emotional well-being and,
        134–35
    environmental hazards,
        135–36
    hormonal changes and, 134
    hydrating body and, 133
    protecting yourself, 140–41
    restorative exercises, 141–
        42
    sleep and, 134, 140
    tending to discomforts,
        130–31
    thinking like athlete, 130–31
Character analysis, 212–14
Chest voice, 68–69, 74
Choral singing, 241–52
    defined, 242
    exercises, 248–50
    performance and career
        opportunities, 232
    score in four parts, 250–52

Software License Agreement

YOU SHOULD CAREFULLY READ THE FOLLOWING TERMS AND CONDITIONS BEFORE USING THIS SOFTWARE PRODUCT. INSTALLING AND USING THIS PRODUCT INDICATES YOUR ACCEPTANCE OF THESE CONDITIONS. IF YOU DO NOT AGREE WITH THESE TERMS AND CONDITIONS, DO NOT INSTALL THE SOFTWARE AND RETURN THIS PACKAGE PROMPTLY FOR A FULL REFUND.

1. Grant of License

This software package is protected under United States copyright law and international treaty. You are hereby entitled to one copy of the enclosed software and are allowed by law to make one backup copy or to copy the contents of the disks onto a single hard disk and keep the originals as your backup or archival copy. United States copyright law prohibits you from making a copy of this software for use on any computer other than your own computer. United States copyright law also prohibits you from copying any written material included in this software package without first obtaining the permission of F+W Publications, Inc.

2. Restrictions

You, the end-user, are hereby prohibited from the following:
You may not rent or lease the Software or make copies to rent or lease for profit or for any other purpose.
You may not disassemble or reverse compile for the purposes of reverse engineering the Software.
You may not modify or adapt the Software or documentation in whole or in part, including, but not limited to, translating or creating derivative works.

3. Transfer

You may transfer the Software to another person, provided that (a) you transfer all of the Software and documentation to the same transferee; (b) you do not retain any copies; and (c) the transferee is informed of and agrees to the terms and conditions of this Agreement.

4. Termination

This Agreement and your license to use the Software can be terminated without notice if you fail to comply with any of the provisions set forth in this Agreement. Upon termination of this Agreement, you promise to destroy all copies of the software including backup or archival copies as well as any documentation associated with the Software. All disclaimers of warranties and limitation of liability set forth in this Agreement shall survive any termination of this Agreement.

5. Limited Warranty

F+W Publications, Inc. warrants that the Software will perform according to the manual and other written materials accompanying the Software for a period of 30 days from the date of receipt. F+W Publications, Inc. does not accept responsibility for any malfunctioning computer hardware or any incompatibilities with existing or new computer hardware technology.

6. Customer Remedies

F+W Publications, Inc.'s entire liability and your exclusive remedy shall be, at the option of F+W Publications, Inc., either refund of your purchase price or repair and/or replacement of Software that does not meet this Limited Warranty. Proof of purchase shall be required. This Limited Warranty will be voided if Software failure was caused by abuse, neglect, accident or misapplication. All replacement Software will be warranted based on the remainder of the warranty or the full 30 days, whichever is shorter and will be subject to the terms of the Agreement.

7. No Other Warranties

F+W PUBLICATIONS, INC., TO THE FULLEST EXTENT OF THE LAW, DISCLAIMS ALL OTHER WARRANTIES, OTHER THAN THE LIMITED WARRANTY IN PARAGRAPH 5, EITHER EXPRESS OR IMPLIED, ASSOCIATED WITH ITS SOFTWARE, INCLUDING BUT NOT LIMITED TO IMPLIED WARRANTIES OF MERCHANTABILITY AND FITNESS FOR A PARTICULAR PURPOSE, WITH REGARD TO THE SOFTWARE AND ITS ACCOMPANYING WRITTEN MATERIALS. THIS LIMITED WARRANTY GIVES YOU SPECIFIC LEGAL RIGHTS. DEPENDING UPON WHERE THIS SOFTWARE WAS PURCHASED, YOU MAY HAVE OTHER RIGHTS.

8. Limitations on Remedies

TO THE MAXIMUM EXTENT PERMITTED BY LAW, F+W PUBLICATIONS, INC. SHALL NOT BE HELD LIABLE FOR ANY DAMAGES WHATSOEVER, INCLUDING WITHOUT LIMITATION, ANY LOSS FROM PERSONAL INJURY, LOSS OF BUSINESS PROFITS, BUSINESS INTERRUPTION, BUSINESS INFORMATION OR ANY OTHER PECUNIARY LOSS ARISING OUT OF THE USE OF THIS SOFTWARE.
This applies even if F+W Publications, Inc. has been advised of the possibility of such damages. F+W Publications, Inc.'s entire liability under any provision of this agreement shall be limited to the amount actually paid by you for the Software. Because some states may not allow for this type of limitation of liability, the above limitation may not apply to you.
THE WARRANTY AND REMEDIES SET FORTH ABOVE ARE EXCLUSIVE AND IN LIEU OF ALL OTHERS, ORAL OR WRITTEN, EXPRESS OR IMPLIED. No F+W Publications, Inc. dealer, distributor, agent, or employee is authorized to make any modification or addition to the warranty.

9. General

This Agreement shall be governed by the laws of the United States of America and the Commonwealth of Massachusetts. If you have any questions concerning this Agreement, contact F+W Publications, Inc., via Adams Media at 508-427-7100. Or write to us at: Adams Media, an F+W Publications Company, 57 Littlefield Street, Avon, MA 02322.

The EVERYTHING Series!

BUSINESS & PERSONAL FINANCE

Everything® Accounting Book
Everything® Budgeting Book, 2nd Ed.
Everything® Business Planning Book
Everything® Coaching and Mentoring Book, 2nd Ed.
Everything® Fundraising Book
Everything® Get Out of Debt Book
Everything® Grant Writing Book, 2nd Ed.
Everything® Guide to Buying Foreclosures
Everything® Guide to Fundraising, $15.95
Everything® Guide to Mortgages
Everything® Guide to Personal Finance for Single Mothers
Everything® Home-Based Business Book, 2nd Ed.
Everything® Homebuying Book, 3rd Ed., $15.95
Everything® Homeselling Book, 2nd Ed.
Everything® Human Resource Management Book
Everything® Improve Your Credit Book
Everything® Investing Book, 2nd Ed.
Everything® Landlording Book
Everything® Leadership Book, 2nd Ed.
Everything® Managing People Book, 2nd Ed.
Everything® Negotiating Book
Everything® Online Auctions Book
Everything® Online Business Book
Everything® Personal Finance Book
Everything® Personal Finance in Your 20s & 30s Book, 2nd Ed.
Everything® Personal Finance in Your 40s & 50s Book, $15.95
Everything® Project Management Book, 2nd Ed.
Everything® Real Estate Investing Book
Everything® Retirement Planning Book
Everything® Robert's Rules Book, $7.95
Everything® Selling Book
Everything® Start Your Own Business Book, 2nd Ed.
Everything® Wills & Estate Planning Book

COOKING

Everything® Barbecue Cookbook
Everything® Bartender's Book, 2nd Ed., $9.95
Everything® Calorie Counting Cookbook
Everything® Cheese Book
Everything® Chinese Cookbook
Everything® Classic Recipes Book
Everything® Cocktail Parties & Drinks Book
Everything® College Cookbook
Everything® Cooking for Baby and Toddler Book
Everything® Diabetes Cookbook
Everything® Easy Gourmet Cookbook
Everything® Fondue Cookbook
Everything® Food Allergy Cookbook, $15.95
Everything® Fondue Party Book
Everything® Gluten-Free Cookbook
Everything® Glycemic Index Cookbook
Everything® Grilling Cookbook
Everything® Healthy Cooking for Parties Book, $15.95
Everything® Holiday Cookbook
Everything® Indian Cookbook
Everything® Lactose-Free Cookbook
Everything® Low-Cholesterol Cookbook

Everything® Low-Fat High-Flavor Cookbook, 2nd Ed., $15.95
Everything® Low-Salt Cookbook
Everything® Meals for a Month Cookbook
Everything® Meals on a Budget Cookbook
Everything® Mediterranean Cookbook
Everything® Mexican Cookbook
Everything® No Trans Fat Cookbook
Everything® One-Pot Cookbook, 2nd Ed., $15.95
Everything® Organic Cooking for Baby & Toddler Book, $15.95
Everything® Pizza Cookbook
Everything® Quick Meals Cookbook, 2nd Ed., $15.95
Everything® Slow Cooker Cookbook
Everything® Slow Cooking for a Crowd Cookbook
Everything® Soup Cookbook
Everything® Stir-Fry Cookbook
Everything® Sugar-Free Cookbook
Everything® Tapas and Small Plates Cookbook
Everything® Tex-Mex Cookbook
Everything® Thai Cookbook
Everything® Vegetarian Cookbook
Everything® Whole-Grain, High-Fiber Cookbook
Everything® Wild Game Cookbook
Everything® Wine Book, 2nd Ed.

GAMES

Everything® 15-Minute Sudoku Book, $9.95
Everything® 30-Minute Sudoku Book, $9.95
Everything® Bible Crosswords Book, $9.95
Everything® Blackjack Strategy Book
Everything® Brain Strain Book, $9.95
Everything® Bridge Book
Everything® Card Games Book
Everything® Card Tricks Book, $9.95
Everything® Casino Gambling Book, 2nd Ed.
Everything® Chess Basics Book
Everything® Christmas Crosswords Book, $9.95
Everything® Craps Strategy Book
Everything® Crossword and Puzzle Book
Everything® Crosswords and Puzzles for Quote Lovers Book, $9.95
Everything® Crossword Challenge Book
Everything® Crosswords for the Beach Book, $9.95
Everything® Cryptic Crosswords Book, $9.95
Everything® Cryptograms Book, $9.95
Everything® Easy Crosswords Book
Everything® Easy Kakuro Book, $9.95
Everything® Easy Large-Print Crosswords Book
Everything® Games Book, 2nd Ed.
Everything® Giant Book of Crosswords
Everything® Giant Sudoku Book, $9.95
Everything® Giant Word Search Book
Everything® Kakuro Challenge Book, $9.95
Everything® Large-Print Crossword Challenge Book
Everything® Large-Print Crosswords Book
Everything® Large-Print Travel Crosswords Book
Everything® Lateral Thinking Puzzles Book, $9.95
Everything® Literary Crosswords Book, $9.95
Everything® Mazes Book
Everything® Memory Booster Puzzles Book, $9.95

Everything® Movie Crosswords Book, $9.95
Everything® Music Crosswords Book, $9.95
Everything® Online Poker Book
Everything® Pencil Puzzles Book, $9.95
Everything® Poker Strategy Book
Everything® Pool & Billiards Book
Everything® Puzzles for Commuters Book, $9.95
Everything® Puzzles for Dog Lovers Book, $9.95
Everything® Sports Crosswords Book, $9.95
Everything® Test Your IQ Book, $9.95
Everything® Texas Hold 'Em Book, $9.95
Everything® Travel Crosswords Book, $9.95
Everything® Travel Mazes Book, $9.95
Everything® Travel Word Search Book, $9.95
Everything® TV Crosswords Book, $9.95
Everything® Word Games Challenge Book
Everything® Word Scramble Book
Everything® Word Search Book

HEALTH

Everything® Alzheimer's Book
Everything® Diabetes Book
Everything® First Aid Book, $9.95
Everything® Green Living Book
Everything® Health Guide to Addiction and Recovery
Everything® Health Guide to Adult Bipolar Disorder
Everything® Health Guide to Arthritis
Everything® Health Guide to Controlling Anxiety
Everything® Health Guide to Depression
Everything® Health Guide to Diabetes, 2nd Ed.
Everything® Health Guide to Fibromyalgia
Everything® Health Guide to Menopause, 2nd Ed.
Everything® Health Guide to Migraines
Everything® Health Guide to Multiple Sclerosis
Everything® Health Guide to OCD
Everything® Health Guide to PMS
Everything® Health Guide to Postpartum Care
Everything® Health Guide to Thyroid Disease
Everything® Hypnosis Book
Everything® Low Cholesterol Book
Everything® Menopause Book
Everything® Nutrition Book
Everything® Reflexology Book
Everything® Stress Management Book
Everything® Superfoods Book, $15.95

HISTORY

Everything® American Government Book
Everything® American History Book, 2nd Ed.
Everything® American Revolution Book, $15.95
Everything® Civil War Book
Everything® Freemasons Book
Everything® Irish History & Heritage Book
Everything® World War II Book, 2nd Ed.

HOBBIES

Everything® Candlemaking Book
Everything® Cartooning Book
Everything® Coin Collecting Book
Everything® Digital Photography Book, 2nd Ed.

Everything® Drawing Book
Everything® Family Tree Book, 2nd Ed.
Everything® Guide to Online Genealogy, $15.95
Everything® Knitting Book
Everything® Knots Book
Everything® Photography Book
Everything® Quilting Book
Everything® Sewing Book
Everything® Soapmaking Book, 2nd Ed.
Everything® Woodworking Book

HOME IMPROVEMENT

Everything® Feng Shui Book
Everything® Feng Shui Decluttering Book, $9.95
Everything® Fix-It Book
Everything® Green Living Book
Everything® Home Decorating Book
Everything® Home Storage Solutions Book
Everything® Homebuilding Book
Everything® Organize Your Home Book, 2nd Ed.

KIDS' BOOKS

All titles are $7.95
Everything® Fairy Tales Book, $14.95
Everything® Kids' Animal Puzzle & Activity Book
Everything® Kids' Astronomy Book
Everything® Kids' Baseball Book, 5th Ed.
Everything® Kids' Bible Trivia Book
Everything® Kids' Bugs Book
Everything® Kids' Cars and Trucks Puzzle and Activity Book
Everything® Kids' Christmas Puzzle & Activity Book
Everything® Kids' Connect the Dots
    Puzzle and Activity Book
Everything® Kids' Cookbook, 2nd Ed.
Everything® Kids' Crazy Puzzles Book
Everything® Kids' Dinosaurs Book
Everything® Kids' Dragons Puzzle and Activity Book
Everything® Kids' Environment Book $7.95
Everything® Kids' Fairies Puzzle and Activity Book
Everything® Kids' First Spanish Puzzle and Activity Book
Everything® Kids' Football Book
Everything® Kids' Geography Book
Everything® Kids' Gross Cookbook
Everything® Kids' Gross Hidden Pictures Book
Everything® Kids' Gross Jokes Book
Everything® Kids' Gross Mazes Book
Everything® Kids' Gross Puzzle & Activity Book
Everything® Kids' Halloween Puzzle & Activity Book
Everything® Kids' Hanukkah Puzzle and Activity Book
Everything® Kids' Hidden Pictures Book
Everything® Kids' Horses Book
Everything® Kids' Joke Book
Everything® Kids' Knock Knock Book
Everything® Kids' Learning French Book
Everything® Kids' Learning Spanish Book
Everything® Kids' Magical Science Experiments Book
Everything® Kids' Math Puzzles Book
Everything® Kids' Mazes Book
Everything® Kids' Money Book, 2nd Ed.
Everything® Kids' Mummies, Pharaoh's, and Pyramids
    Puzzle and Activity Book
Everything® Kids' Nature Book
Everything® Kids' Pirates Puzzle and Activity Book
Everything® Kids' Presidents Book
Everything® Kids' Princess Puzzle and Activity Book
Everything® Kids' Puzzle Book

Everything® Kids' Racecars Puzzle and Activity Book
Everything® Kids' Riddles & Brain Teasers Book
Everything® Kids' Science Experiments Book
Everything® Kids' Sharks Book
Everything® Kids' Soccer Book
Everything® Kids' Spelling Book
Everything® Kids' Spies Puzzle and Activity Book
Everything® Kids' States Book
Everything® Kids' Travel Activity Book
Everything® Kids' Word Search Puzzle and Activity Book

LANGUAGE

Everything® Conversational Japanese Book with CD, $19.95
Everything® French Grammar Book
Everything® French Phrase Book, $9.95
Everything® French Verb Book, $9.95
Everything® German Phrase Book, $9.95
Everything® German Practice Book with CD, $19.95
Everything® Inglés Book
Everything® Intermediate Spanish Book with CD, $19.95
Everything® Italian Phrase Book, $9.95
Everything® Italian Practice Book with CD, $19.95
Everything® Learning Brazilian Portuguese Book with CD, $19.95
Everything® Learning French Book with CD, 2nd Ed., $19.95
Everything® Learning German Book
Everything® Learning Italian Book
Everything® Learning Latin Book
Everything® Learning Russian Book with CD, $19.95
Everything® Learning Spanish Book
Everything® Learning Spanish Book with CD, 2nd Ed., $19.95
Everything® Russian Practice Book with CD, $19.95
Everything® Sign Language Book, $15.95
Everything® Spanish Grammar Book
Everything® Spanish Phrase Book, $9.95
Everything® Spanish Practice Book with CD, $19.95
Everything® Spanish Verb Book, $9.95
Everything® Speaking Mandarin Chinese Book with CD, $19.95

MUSIC

Everything® Bass Guitar Book with CD, $19.95
Everything® Drums Book with CD, $19.95
Everything® Guitar Book with CD, 2nd Ed., $19.95
Everything® Guitar Chords Book with CD, $19.95
Everything® Guitar Scales Book with CD, $19.95
Everything® Harmonica Book with CD, $15.95
Everything® Home Recording Book
Everything® Music Theory Book with CD, $19.95
Everything® Reading Music Book with CD, $19.95
Everything® Rock & Blues Guitar Book with CD, $19.95
Everything® Rock & Blues Piano Book with CD, $19.95
Everything® Rock Drums Book with CD, $19.95
Everything® Singing Book with CD, $19.95
Everything® Songwriting Book

NEW AGE

Everything® Astrology Book, 2nd Ed.
Everything® Birthday Personology Book
Everything® Celtic Wisdom Book, $15.95
Everything® Dreams Book, 2nd Ed.
Everything® Law of Attraction Book, $15.95
Everything® Love Signs Book, $9.95
Everything® Love Spells Book, $9.95
Everything® Palmistry Book
Everything® Psychic Book
Everything® Reiki Book

Everything® Sex Signs Book, $9.95
Everything® Spells & Charms Book, 2nd Ed.
Everything® Tarot Book, 2nd Ed.
Everything® Toltec Wisdom Book
Everything® Wicca & Witchcraft Book, 2nd Ed.

PARENTING

Everything® Baby Names Book, 2nd Ed.
Everything® Baby Shower Book, 2nd Ed.
Everything® Baby Sign Language Book with DVD
Everything® Baby's First Year Book
Everything® Birthing Book
Everything® Breastfeeding Book
Everything® Father-to-Be Book
Everything® Father's First Year Book
Everything® Get Ready for Baby Book, 2nd Ed.
Everything® Get Your Baby to Sleep Book, $9.95
Everything® Getting Pregnant Book
Everything® Guide to Pregnancy Over 35
Everything® Guide to Raising a One-Year-Old
Everything® Guide to Raising a Two-Year-Old
Everything® Guide to Raising Adolescent Boys
Everything® Guide to Raising Adolescent Girls
Everything® Mother's First Year Book
Everything® Parent's Guide to Childhood Illnesses
Everything® Parent's Guide to Children and Divorce
Everything® Parent's Guide to Children with ADD/ADHD
Everything® Parent's Guide to Children with Asperger's
    Syndrome
Everything® Parent's Guide to Children with Anxiety
Everything® Parent's Guide to Children with Asthma
Everything® Parent's Guide to Children with Autism
Everything® Parent's Guide to Children with Bipolar Disorder
Everything® Parent's Guide to Children with Depression
Everything® Parent's Guide to Children with Dyslexia
Everything® Parent's Guide to Children with Juvenile Diabetes
Everything® Parent's Guide to Children with OCD
Everything® Parent's Guide to Positive Discipline
Everything® Parent's Guide to Raising Boys
Everything® Parent's Guide to Raising Girls
Everything® Parent's Guide to Raising Siblings
Everything® Parent's Guide to Raising Your
    Adopted Child
Everything® Parent's Guide to Sensory Integration Disorder
Everything® Parent's Guide to Tantrums
Everything® Parent's Guide to the Strong-Willed Child
Everything® Parenting a Teenager Book
Everything® Potty Training Book, $9.95
Everything® Pregnancy Book, 3rd Ed.
Everything® Pregnancy Fitness Book
Everything® Pregnancy Nutrition Book
Everything® Pregnancy Organizer, 2nd Ed., $16.95
Everything® Toddler Activities Book
Everything® Toddler Book
Everything® Tween Book
Everything® Twins, Triplets, and More Book

PETS

Everything® Aquarium Book
Everything® Boxer Book
Everything® Cat Book, 2nd Ed.
Everything® Chihuahua Book
Everything® Cooking for Dogs Book
Everything® Dachshund Book
Everything® Dog Book, 2nd Ed.
Everything® Dog Grooming Book

Everything® Dog Obedience Book
Everything® Dog Owner's Organizer, $16.95
Everything® Dog Training and Tricks Book
Everything® German Shepherd Book
Everything® Golden Retriever Book
Everything® Horse Book, 2nd Ed., $15.95
Everything® Horse Care Book
Everything® Horseback Riding Book
Everything® Labrador Retriever Book
Everything® Poodle Book
Everything® Pug Book
Everything® Puppy Book
Everything® Small Dogs Book
Everything® Tropical Fish Book
Everything® Yorkshire Terrier Book

REFERENCE

Everything® American Presidents Book
Everything® Blogging Book
Everything® Build Your Vocabulary Book, $9.95
Everything® Car Care Book
Everything® Classical Mythology Book
Everything® Da Vinci Book
Everything® Einstein Book
Everything® Enneagram Book
Everything® Etiquette Book, 2nd Ed.
Everything® Family Christmas Book, $15.95
Everything® Guide to C. S. Lewis & Narnia
Everything® Guide to Divorce, 2nd Ed., $15.95
Everything® Guide to Edgar Allan Poe
Everything® Guide to Understanding Philosophy
Everything® Inventions and Patents Book
Everything® Jacqueline Kennedy Onassis Book
Everything® John F. Kennedy Book
Everything® Mafia Book
Everything® Martin Luther King Jr. Book
Everything® Pirates Book
Everything® Private Investigation Book
Everything® Psychology Book
Everything® Public Speaking Book, $9.95
Everything® Shakespeare Book, 2nd Ed.

RELIGION

Everything® Angels Book
Everything® Bible Book
Everything® Bible Study Book with CD, $19.95
Everything® Buddhism Book
Everything® Catholicism Book
Everything® Christianity Book
Everything® Gnostic Gospels Book
Everything® Hinduism Book, $15.95
Everything® History of the Bible Book
Everything® Jesus Book
Everything® Jewish History & Heritage Book
Everything® Judaism Book
Everything® Kabbalah Book
Everything® Koran Book
Everything® Mary Book
Everything® Mary Magdalene Book
Everything® Prayer Book

Everything® Saints Book, 2nd Ed.
Everything® Torah Book
Everything® Understanding Islam Book
Everything® Women of the Bible Book
Everything® World's Religions Book

SCHOOL & CAREERS

Everything® Career Tests Book
Everything® College Major Test Book
Everything® College Survival Book, 2nd Ed.
Everything® Cover Letter Book, 2nd Ed.
Everything® Filmmaking Book
Everything® Get-a-Job Book, 2nd Ed.
Everything® Guide to Being a Paralegal
Everything® Guide to Being a Personal Trainer
Everything® Guide to Being a Real Estate Agent
Everything® Guide to Being a Sales Rep
Everything® Guide to Being an Event Planner
Everything® Guide to Careers in Health Care
Everything® Guide to Careers in Law Enforcement
Everything® Guide to Government Jobs
Everything® Guide to Starting and Running a Catering Business
Everything® Guide to Starting and Running a Restaurant
Everything® Guide to Starting and Running a Retail Store
Everything® Job Interview Book, 2nd Ed.
Everything® New Nurse Book
Everything® New Teacher Book
Everything® Paying for College Book
Everything® Practice Interview Book
Everything® Resume Book, 3rd Ed.
Everything® Study Book

SELF-HELP

Everything® Body Language Book
Everything® Dating Book, 2nd Ed.
Everything® Great Sex Book
Everything® Guide to Caring for Aging Parents, $15.95
Everything® Self-Esteem Book
Everything® Self-Hypnosis Book, $9.95
Everything® Tantric Sex Book

SPORTS & FITNESS

Everything® Easy Fitness Book
Everything® Fishing Book
Everything® Guide to Weight Training, $15.95
Everything® Krav Maga for Fitness Book
Everything® Running Book, 2nd Ed.
Everything® Triathlon Training Book, $15.95

TRAVEL

Everything® Family Guide to Coastal Florida
Everything® Family Guide to Cruise Vacations
Everything® Family Guide to Hawaii
Everything® Family Guide to Las Vegas, 2nd Ed.
Everything® Family Guide to Mexico
Everything® Family Guide to New England, 2nd Ed.

Everything® Family Guide to New York City, 3rd Ed.
Everything® Family Guide to Northern California and Lake Tahoe
Everything® Family Guide to RV Travel & Campgrounds
Everything® Family Guide to the Caribbean
Everything® Family Guide to the Disneyland® Resort, California Adventure®, Universal Studios®, and the Anaheim Area, 2nd Ed.
Everything® Family Guide to the Walt Disney World Resort®, Universal Studios®, and Greater Orlando, 5th Ed.
Everything® Family Guide to Timeshares
Everything® Family Guide to Washington D.C., 2nd Ed.

WEDDINGS

Everything® Bachelorette Party Book, $9.95
Everything® Bridesmaid Book, $9.95
Everything® Destination Wedding Book
Everything® Father of the Bride Book, $9.95
Everything® Green Wedding Book, $15.95
Everything® Groom Book, $9.95
Everything® Jewish Wedding Book, 2nd Ed., $15.95
Everything® Mother of the Bride Book, $9.95
Everything® Outdoor Wedding Book
Everything® Wedding Book, 3rd Ed.
Everything® Wedding Checklist, $9.95
Everything® Wedding Etiquette Book, $9.95
Everything® Wedding Organizer, 2nd Ed., $16.95
Everything® Wedding Shower Book, $9.95
Everything® Wedding Vows Book, 3rd Ed., $9.95
Everything® Wedding Workout Book
Everything® Weddings on a Budget Book, 2nd Ed., $9.95

WRITING

Everything® Creative Writing Book
Everything® Get Published Book, 2nd Ed.
Everything® Grammar and Style Book, 2nd Ed.
Everything® Guide to Magazine Writing
Everything® Guide to Writing a Book Proposal
Everything® Guide to Writing a Novel
Everything® Guide to Writing Children's Books
Everything® Guide to Writing Copy
Everything® Guide to Writing Graphic Novels
Everything® Guide to Writing Research Papers
Everything® Guide to Writing a Romance Novel, $15.95
Everything® Improve Your Writing Book, 2nd Ed.
Everything® Writing Poetry Book